Menus for Entertaining

HALLIE DONNELLY
JANET KESSEL FLETCHER
Writers

SANDRA GARY
Editor

VICTOR BUDNIK
Photographer

SANDRA COOK
Food Stylist

AMY GLENN
Photographic Stylist

Hallie Donnelly (left), a native San Franciscan, has been a chef-caterer for twelve years. She holds a degree in music from the University of California, Berkeley, and attended the California Culinary Academy. In France, she studied cooking with Michel Guérard, Roger Vergé, and André Daguin. The author of a book on sushi and sashimi, she has had her own cooking school and television show. She is presently a consultant for hotels and restaurants. **Janet Kessel Fletcher** (right) is a free-lance food and wine writer and editor. She holds a degree in economics from Stanford University and attended the Culinary Institute of America in Hyde Park, N.Y. She has cooked in the highly acclaimed Chez Panisse restaurant, in Berkeley, California, and now writes a restaurant column for the Oakland, Calif., *Tribune*. In addition, she produces literature for clients in the food and wine industry. Donnelly and Fletcher are the co-authors of the California Culinary Academy books *Italian Cooking* and *Appetizers & Hors d'Oeuvres*.

The California Culinary Academy In the forefront of American institutions leading the culinary renaissance in this country, the California Culinary Academy in San Francisco has gained a reputation as one of the most outstanding professional chef training schools in the world. With a teaching staff recruited from the best restaurants of Western Europe, the Academy educates students from around the world in the preparation of classical cuisine. The recipes in this book were created in consultation with the chefs of the Academy. For information about the Academy, write the Office of the Dean, California Culinary Academy, 625 Polk Street, San Francisco, CA 94102.

Front Cover: A glittering cocktail gathering is one of many ways to entertain with personal flair. The menu can include such delicious fare as crisp vegetables with a watercress dip (see page 56), rare roast beef with tapénade (see page 54), baked Burgundy Cheese Puffs (see page 13), refreshing Minted Scallops served in clam shells (see page 91), and savory Mushroom and Pecan Tartlets (see page 13). **Title Page:** A hand-lettered invitation sets the tone for entertaining with memorable style.

Back Cover: Upper Left: Flutes of Champagne, luxurious blossoms, a savory Vegetable Tian (at left) and an abundant platter of Salade Niçoise (at right) are all part of the splendid Provençal Garden Wedding starting on page 31. **Upper Right:** Rosettes of whipped cream are piped onto a cake with a pastry bag and an open-star tip. **Lower Left:** Four Cornish hens are arranged artfully on a platter with baby carrots and green beans. Among the lessons to be learned from professional chefs is that the way food is presented is as important as how it tastes. **Lower Right:** Setting the stage for the Graduation Tea (see page 27), a silver tea service stands alongside sweet and savory nibbles (from top): Sand Cookies With Caramelized Cinnamon Sugar, Smoked Chicken in Lettuce Cups, Home-Cured Halibut With Dilled Brioche, and Sweet Pine-Nut Tarts.

Special Thanks To: Denise Cannon, Photographer's Assistant; Helen Casartelli, Food Stylist's Assistant; Claire's Antique Linens & Gifts; Xanadu/Folk Art International; J. Goldsmith Antiques; Santa Fe; Eileen West At Home; George V Collection; Dishes del Mar; Fillamento; Virginia Breier; Jeffrey Brodkin; Jerome White; Garrison Key; Upstairs Downstairs; Telaoi; Dianne McKenzie; Sherry Phelan Wright; Penelope Fried; Roberto Varriale.

Contributors

Calligraphers
Keith Carlson, Chuck Wertman

Consultant
Katie Millhiser

Additional Photographers
Laurie Black, at the Academy, page 93
Alan Copeland, at the Academy, pages 16, 43, 49, 84, 88, and 120
Marshall Gordon, page 62
Kit Morris, authors and chefs, at left
Richard Tauber, pages 75 and 83

Additional Stylists
Stephanie Greenleigh, pages 75 and 83
Doug Warne, page 62

Copy Chief
Melinda E. Levine

Editorial Coordinator
Cass Dempsey

Copyeditor
Sue Arnold

Layout & pagination by
Linda M. Bouchard

Editorial Assistants
Andrea Y. Connolly
Karen K. Johnson
Tamara Mallory

Proofreader
Judith Dunham

Indexer
Frances Bowles

Series format designed by
Linda Hinrichs and Carole Kramer

Production by
Studio 165

Separations by
Palace Press, Singapore

Lithographed in the U.S.A by
Webcrafters, Inc.

The California Culinary Academy series is produced by the staff of Ortho Information Services.

Publisher
Robert J. Dolezal

Editorial Director
Christine Robertson

Production Director
Ernie S. Tasaki

Series Managing Editor
Sally W. Smith

System Manager
Katherine L. Parker

Address all inquiries to
Ortho Information Services
Box 5047
San Ramon, CA 94583

Chevron Chemical Company
6001 Bollinger Canyon Road
San Ramon, CA 94583

C O N T E N T S

Menus for Entertaining

Preface

Entertaining, simply put, is the art of bringing people together for a good time. Like other artists, party givers learn by doing. The more you entertain, the easier it becomes as you develop a style and learn what works for you.

Anyone can cook up a party, but the most successful events need three ingredients: imagination, a dash of planning, and an honest desire to please. These make the difference between a mere gathering and a memorable day.

Imagination gives your entertaining personal flair. Planning makes the parts fit together and run smoothly. And being eager to please is the key to making guests feel special and at ease. Whether you've invited 3 friends for coffee or 50 for a backyard wedding, you'll find that the same rules for successful entertaining apply.

Appetizing food and pleasant surroundings are important to the success of a party, but a relaxed and self-assured host is even more important. This book gives you the tools to be a confident party giver, beginning with 32 theme-inspired menus for entertaining.

You'll find almost every type of party here—reception, dinner, birthday, and open house. You'll find menus for holidays major and minor: a Chinese New Year's supper, a Fourth of July barbecue, and a children's Halloween party. You'll find parties to celebrate life's major events: graduations, weddings, and births.

You'll find parties in a variety of formats, from breakfast in bed and picnic lunches to sit-down dinners. You'll find menus for a variety of settings, indoors and out: a fireside supper, lunch on the boat, a Mexican patio party. You'll find menus for breakfasts, brunches, lunches, and dinners—and some meals in between.

Menus are organized by season and take full advantage of seasonal produce. In fact, the first spring salmon can be an excuse in itself for a party.

Each menu is accompanied by a timetable to help you organize your schedule. The menus and timetables are designed to keep last-minute cooking to a minimum, so that you can enjoy the guests and party.

Each menu is accompanied by advice on presentation to help you give your party a memorable style. You can also study the photographs for creative ideas for table settings and food presentations.

Entertaining is one of life's great pleasures. The menus and planning tips in this book should allow you to relax and enjoy your parties and should inspire you to entertain often.

A Spring Afternoon Tea
April 14
3:00 o'clock

A plump artichoke and a
fragrant lilac are symbols of
spring and a reminder of the
lovely foods and flowers that can
grace springtime tables.

Spring Menus

Spring's new beginnings offer plenty of reasons for entertaining. For a June bride and groom, a magnificent Provençal Garden Wedding (see page 31) provides memories to cherish. A Graduation Tea (see page 27) can appropriately launch a student's new life. Tips on Brewing the Perfect Pot of Tea are on page 30. If you have friends who are parents-to-be, an old-fashioned Baby Shower (see page 11) is sure to delight them. A new home or even a round of redecorating can set the stage for a Housewarming (see page 14). On page 20 the Special Feature on Putting the Party Together takes you step-by-step through planning procedures for any kind of party.

SPRING ENTERTAINING

The rituals of spring mark it as a season for fresh starts. The soil is turned and readied for a new round of seeds and plants; the house is cleaned and aired from top to bottom. Why not give your entertaining some fresh thought, too, with new recipes for traditional parties and with new party ideas to celebrate the season?

The family's traditional Easter lunch takes a welcome new turn when a cool lamb salad replaces the usual roast leg of lamb (see page 17). The typical graduation tea gains new-found flair when the menu includes such delights as home-smoked chicken and sweet pine-nut tarts (see page 27).

Spring menus can take advantage of the last of the winter shellfish and citrus as well as the year's first strawberries and cherries. Early peas and zucchini provide a taste of summer bounty still to come, while asparagus, artichokes, and turnips are in full swing.

Spring weather is unpredictable but party menus can conform. The sunny days may be warm enough for a cold lunch of soup and salad (see page 21), but a blustery March evening calls for a hearty paella (see page 24).

Consider moving a spring dinner party from the dining room to a porch or patio if the weather cooperates. You may also want to set a rain date or have a backup bad-weather arrangement if you've planned an outdoor party.

To reflect the gentle warmth of the season, think of giving your spring parties a pastel palette. Lavender, lime green, aquamarine, salmon or coral, pale yellow, pink, peach, and baby blue are all colors that set a springtime mood.

Let spring flowers dominate the table settings—rely on tulips, irises, daffodils, narcissus, cherry blossoms, and lilies. A crystal bowl of gleaming cherries or a basket of perfect artichokes can also make a simple but eye-catching centerpiece.

SPRING SALMON DINNER
For 4

Chilled Soup of Mixed Peas

Roasted Salmon With Garlic Cream

Potato, Turnip, and Chard Sauté

Pecan Baba With Berries

California Sauvignon Blanc or White French Côtes-du-Rhône

The appearance of the first spring salmon is a fine excuse for a party. To make it a full-fledged salute to the season, the menu weaves in a wealth of spring bounty, from sweet peas and new potatoes to ripe strawberries.

Timetable

2 days ahead: If using Crème Fraîche, prepare 2 recipes.

8 to 12 hours ahead: Make and chill soup. Prepare salmon for roasting. Prepare and bake babas.

Up to 6 hours ahead: Prepare vegetables for sautéing.

Up to 4 hours ahead: Marinate strawberries.

At serving time: Roast salmon. Sauté vegetables.

Planning

This elegant menu requires the freshest possible ingredients. English peas quickly convert their sugar to starch after harvest; if possible, buy them from a farmers' market or from a market that specializes in farm-fresh produce. The salmon, too, should be the freshest available. It should smell sweet, not fishy, and should have a firm texture.

The dinner is an easy one on the host. Only the vegetable sauté needs last-minute attention. The salmon should be slipped into the oven after the soup course is cleared and the vegetables sautéed shortly thereafter.

A fragrant white wine, such as a California Sauvignon Blanc or a white French Côtes-du-Rhône, would be a suitable choice.

Presentation

Soft pastel colors set the mood for this simple but formal spring meal. Create a serene table setting with graceful glassware and flowers loosely arranged in a clear vase. Crystal soup mugs or bowls and dinner plates with little or no pattern will show off the meal's vivid spring colors to best advantage.

To avoid crowding the table, serve the salmon and sautéed vegetables directly on warm dinner plates.

Photograph, page 9: A table graced with pale pink tulip bulbs and dressed in soft pastels lures guests to a light spring dinner. A light blue color scheme carries through tablecloth, wineglass and china pattern. The first-course chilled soup is made with two kinds of peas—English peas and crunchy sugar snap peas. The fillet of delicate spring salmon is roasted with a smooth garlic cream and accompanied by sautéed seasonal vegetables—new potatoes, turnips, and chard. A chilled dry Sauvignon Blanc complements both courses.

CHILLED SOUP OF MIXED PEAS

This 10-minute soup is made with fresh English peas, then garnished with finely shredded sugar snap peas. The sugar snaps are entirely edible, including the pod, but they require stringing. When purchasing English peas, open a pod or two and sample; the peas inside should be small, firm, and sweet.

- ¼ pound sugar snap peas, strings removed
- ¼ cup butter
- 2 shallots, minced
- 2 pounds English peas, shelled
- 2 cups chicken stock
- 2 cups half-and-half
- ½ cup Crème Fraîche (see page 38) or sour cream
  Lemon juice, to taste
  Salt and freshly ground pepper, to taste
- ¼ cup fresh basil leaves

1. Blanch sugar snap peas 30 seconds in lightly salted boiling water; drain and plunge into ice water to stop the cooking. Julienne the peas and set aside for garnish.

2. In a medium saucepan melt butter over moderately low heat. Add shallots and sauté 1 minute. Add English peas, reduce heat to low, and cook until peas are slightly softened (about 5 minutes). Raise heat to high, add chicken stock, and bring to a simmer. Reduce heat to maintain a simmer and cook 2 minutes. Transfer soup to a blender or food processor and blend until smooth. Chill thoroughly.

3. Whisk together half-and-half and Crème Fraîche. Whisk into chilled soup. Season with lemon juice, salt, and pepper. Just before serving, shred basil finely with a knife. Ladle soup into chilled bowls. Garnish the top of each serving with julienned sugar snap peas and finely shredded basil.

Serves 4.

ROASTED SALMON WITH GARLIC CREAM

Whole garlic cloves turn soft and mild when simmered or roasted slowly. Purée the soft cloves with butter and cream, spread it on the salmon, and bake until done to your liking. The dish couldn't be simpler or more aromatic. Note that the salmon should marinate for at least 30 minutes.

- 4 whole bulbs garlic
- 3 tablespoons butter
- 1 cup Crème Fraîche (see page 38) or sour cream
- 1 teaspoon stone-ground mustard
- 2 pounds fresh salmon fillets

1. Remove papery outer shell from garlic, but leave bulbs intact and cloves unpeeled. Place bulbs in a saucepan just large enough to hold them. Add water to barely cover and bring to a simmer over high heat. Reduce heat to maintain a simmer and cook 40 minutes, adding more water as necessary to keep heads barely covered. Remove from heat, cool, and peel. Cloves will be very soft and easy to peel. Place cloves in a food processor with butter and purée. Add Crème Fraîche and mustard and process until blended. Transfer to a bowl and set aside.

2. Cut salmon into 8-ounce fillets. Spread top surface of each fillet with some of the garlic purée. Cover with plastic wrap and refrigerate for at least 30 minutes or up to 1 day.

3. Preheat oven to 350° F. Place fillets on a lightly buttered baking sheet or in a buttered baking dish and roast until done to your liking (7 to 10 minutes). Serve immediately.

Serves 4.

POTATO, TURNIP, AND CHARD SAUTÉ

For best flavor, choose small new potatoes, young turnips, and tender chard leaves with narrow ribs.

- 1 pound red new potatoes
- 1 pound turnips, peeled
- 1 pound chard
- 4 tablespoons butter
- 2 tablespoons minced shallots
- 1 teaspoon minced garlic
- 2 tablespoons olive oil
- 1 tablespoon stone-ground mustard
- 2 tablespoons Crème Fraîche (see page 38) or sour cream
- 2 tablespoons lemon juice
  Salt and freshly ground pepper, to taste

1. Boil potatoes in lightly salted water until tender when pierced with a knife. Drain and set aside. Cut large potatoes in halves or quarters; leave small ones whole.

2. Boil turnips in lightly salted water until tender when pierced with a knife. Drain and set aside. Cut large turnips in halves or quarters; leave small ones whole.

3. Cut chard ribs away from leaves. Blanch leaves and ribs separately in lightly salted water, cooking just until tender (3 to 5 minutes). Drain and plunge into ice water to stop the cooking. Drain again. Chop leaves coarsely; dice ribs.

4. In a small skillet over moderately low heat, melt 2 tablespoons butter. Add shallots and garlic and sauté until fragrant (2 to 3 minutes). Set mixture aside.

5. At serving time, in a large skillet warm remaining butter and olive oil over moderately high heat. Add softened shallot-garlic mixture and chard ribs and sauté quickly to heat through. Add potatoes and turnips and sauté quickly to heat through. Add chard leaves and cook 20 seconds. Stir in mustard and Crème Fraîche. Add lemon juice and season with salt and pepper.

Serves 4.

PECAN BABA WITH BERRIES

Lacking traditional baba molds, use custard cups or muffin tins.

- ⅓ cup milk (about 105° F)
- 1 package active dry yeast
- 2 tablespoons sugar, plus sugar for dusting molds
- 1¼ cups flour
- 1 teaspoon salt
- ½ cup toasted ground pecans
- 2 eggs
- ½ cup butter, softened
   Oil, for greasing molds
- 1 cup sweet white wine
- 2 tablespoons nut liqueur
- ½ cup strawberry jelly
- 2 pints strawberries, cored and halved
   Lightly whipped cream (optional)

1. Whisk well milk, yeast, and sugar. Let stand 10 minutes. Stir in ¼ cup of the flour, let rest 30 minutes.

2. In a bowl combine remaining flour, salt, and pecans. Add half the flour mixture and 1 egg to sponge. Beat well. Add remaining flour mixture and second egg. Beat well, then beat in butter. Divide batter among four greased and sugared 3-inch baba molds. Cover and let rise until they reach the top of the molds (about 40 minutes). Preheat oven to 350° F.

3. Bake babas until golden brown (20 to 30 minutes). Remove from oven and let cool in molds on rack.

4. Combine wine and liqueur. When babas have cooled slightly, set rack over a cookie sheet and unmold babas onto rack. Use a small sharp knife to make slits in tops and sides of babas. Brush with wine-liqueur mixture. Let cakes cool completely.

5. Over low heat melt strawberry jelly. Using a pastry brush, glaze each baba lightly with strawberry jelly. Add remaining jelly to strawberries; mix well. Let stand up to 4 hours in the refrigerator. Remove 30 minutes before serving.

6. Place one baba on each serving plate. Surround with berries, add whipped cream, if desired.

Makes four 3-inch babas.

---

menu

BABY SHOWER
For 16

Mushroom and Pecan Tartlets

Burgundy Cheese Puffs

Margarita Mousse

Blueberry Madeleines

Wines, Soda, Coffee, and Tea

Parents-to-be will be tickled pink (or blue?) at the idea of a baby shower. Invite a group of good friends to share the joy with a round of toasts and a selection of dainty dishes.

Timetable

Up to 2 days ahead: Prepare Basic Tart Dough for tartlets. Prepare tartlet filling.

Up to 12 hours ahead: Bake tartlet shells. Make mousse. Make madeleines.

Up to 6 hours ahead: Make mousse.

Up to 1½ hours ahead: Prepare and bake cheese puffs.

At serving time: Reheat tartlet filling and finish tartlets.

Planning

This menu offers two sweet and two savory dishes, in the small proportions suitable for a midafternoon party. To make the meal into a luncheon or light supper, add a large tossed green salad.

Offer a variety of beverages: chilled sodas, red and white wines, coffee, and tea. All dishes can be prepared ahead, although the tartlets must be filled shortly before serving.

Presentation

Turn your buffet table into a fantasyland with a collection of miniature figurines. Toy soldiers, if it's a boy, storybook dolls, if it's a girl, or miniature stuffed bears can be grouped in the center of the table and surrounded with a "hedge" of greenery tucked into small liqueur glasses. For a nighttime party, substitute votive candles for the hedge.

Pastel yellow, blue, pink, and white give the table a delicate tone. You can set out all the food at once, buffet-style, if you like. Or you can begin with wine and the two savory dishes passed on trays (they are finger food). Then during or after the gift opening, you can bring out coffee, plates, silverware, and the two desserts.

Photograph, page 12: Spring quince blossoms and a table set in pastel yellow and baby blue provide an inviting backdrop for this Baby Shower. A light menu of dainty foods includes (from top): Margarita Mousse in sugar-frosted glasses, Burgundy Cheese Puffs, and creamy Mushroom and Pecan Tartlets. For a whimsical centerpiece, round up a collection of miniature dolls such as these antique treasures; satin ribbons, loosely draped, add a soft touch of color and a festive look.

MUSHROOM AND PECAN TARTLETS

A foursome of mixed fresh herbs enlivens these savory mushroom tarts, with toasted pecans adding extra texture and flavor. The warm filling, bound with sour cream, is spooned into small tart shells.

  1 recipe Basic Tart Dough (see page 69)
 ⅓ cup olive oil
  2 tablespoons minced garlic
 ½ cup finely minced shallots
  4 cups finely chopped mushrooms
 ½ cup toasted and coarsely ground pecans
 ¼ cup minced fresh chives
 ¼ cup minced fresh basil
  1 tablespoon minced fresh mint
  1 cup plus 2 tablespoons minced parsley
 ⅓ cup sour cream
     Salt and freshly ground pepper, to taste
  1 teaspoon grated lemon rind
  2 tablespoons freshly grated Parmesan cheese

1. Prepare Basic Tart Dough and bake according to directions on page 69.

2. In a large skillet over moderate heat, warm olive oil. Add garlic and shallots and sauté 1 minute. Add mushrooms and pecans and cook until mushrooms are slightly softened (about 2 minutes). Stir in chives, basil, mint, and 1 cup of the parsley. Remove from heat and fold in sour cream. Season with salt and pepper. Filling may be made up to this point 2 days ahead, covered, and refrigerated. To serve, reheat slowly in a saucepan over low heat.

3. Spoon warm mushroom mixture into tart shells. Combine remaining parsley, lemon rind, and Parmesan and sprinkle atop filling. Serve immediately.

Makes 2 dozen 1½- to 2-inch tarts.

BURGUNDY CHEESE PUFFS

The baked cheese puff, called *gougère,* is a specialty of the Burgundy region of France, where it often accompanies red wine. The puffs depend on good cheese for their flavor; choose an imported Gruyère or Emmenthaler.

 ¾ cup plus 1 tablespoon milk
 ¾ cup water
 ½ cup butter
1⅓ cups flour
 ¼ teaspoon cayenne pepper
 ½ teaspoon white pepper
  1 teaspoon salt
     Pinch nutmeg
  6 eggs
1½ cups grated Gruyère cheese
  1 tablespoon Dijon mustard
  1 egg yolk
  2 tablespoons grated Parmesan or Gruyère cheese

1. Preheat oven to 400° F. In a medium saucepan combine the ¾ cup milk, the water, and butter. Bring to a boil over moderate heat, adjusting heat so that butter is melted when mixture boils. Remove from heat and add flour, cayenne, white pepper, salt, and nutmeg. Stir until smooth, then return to moderate heat and cook 1 minute, stirring constantly, to evaporate excess moisture.

2. Remove pan from heat and stir in eggs one at a time, beating well after each addition. Stir in grated Gruyère and mustard. Drop mixture by scant tablespoons onto a greased baking sheet; you should have enough to form 36 small puffs. For more uniform puffs, use a pastry bag.

3. Whisk together the remaining 1 tablespoon milk and egg yolk. Brush tops of puffs with egg glaze. Dot tops with grated Parmesan. Bake 15 minutes without opening oven door. Check for doneness; puffs should be firm and well browned. Bake an additional few minutes if necessary. Cool on racks. Serve warm or at room temperature.

Makes 3 dozen small puffs.

MARGARITA MOUSSE

All the ingredients of a margarita are combined in this fluffy mousse, but the glass is rimmed with sugar instead of salt. The mousse should be made with top-quality liquor and should be eaten the day it is made. This recipe doubles well to accommodate a large crowd. It was inspired by chef Laurie Vacha, of Scottsdale, Arizona.

1¾ cup (14 oz) sweetened condensed milk
 ½ cup plus 1 tablespoon tequila
 ½ cup orange liqueur
 ½ cup lime juice
  1 teaspoon finely minced lime rind
  1 quart whipping cream
11 egg whites
 ½ cup granulated sugar
     Superfine sugar, for garnish
     Mint leaves, for garnish
     Additional lime juice, for garnish

1. In a large bowl combine milk, tequila, liqueur, the ½ cup lime juice, and minced lime rind. Whisk to blend.

2. Whip cream to firm peaks. Gradually whisk milk mixture into cream. In a separate bowl beat egg whites to soft peaks; add granulated sugar gradually, beating until whites are stiff but not dry. Fold whites into cream mixture.

3. Dip the rims of Champagne flutes or parfait glasses in lime juice, then in superfine sugar. Spoon mousse into glasses or pipe it in with a pastry bag. Chill at least 1 hour. Garnish with mint leaves.

Serves 16.

BLUEBERRY MADELEINES

The batter for these delicate cakelike cookies needs to be refrigerated overnight. For best flavor, serve the cookies the day they are baked.

  4 eggs
  1½ cups granulated sugar
  2 teaspoons grated lemon rind
  1 teaspoon vanilla extract
  1 cup fresh blueberries, coarsely chopped if large
  1⅓ cups flour
  Pinch salt
  Pinch ground cloves
  2 teaspoons cinnamon
  10 tablespoons melted clarified butter (see Note)
  Confectioners' sugar, for dusting (optional)

1. With an electric mixer whisk together eggs and granulated sugar until thick and pale. Stir in lemon rind, vanilla, and blueberries by hand. Sift together flour, salt, cloves, and cinnamon. Resift directly over egg mixture; fold in gently by hand. Fold in 6 tablespoons of the butter. Cover mixture and refrigerate overnight.

2. Preheat oven to 425° F. Using 1 tablespoon of the butter, grease a 12-cookie, 3-inch madeleine pan. Place mold in freezer for 10 minutes. Repeat with another tablespoon of the butter and freeze again for 10 minutes. Using half the batter, divide it among molds, making sure to get a few blueberries in each one.

3. Bake 5 minutes, then reduce oven temperature to 350° F. Continue baking until cookies are light brown (about 10 more minutes). Turn madeleines out onto a rack to cool.

4. Wash and dry mold; repeat steps 2 and 3 with remaining batter. Sift confectioners' sugar over cooled cookies, if desired.

Makes 2 dozen 3-inch madeleines.

Note To make clarified butter, melt 1 cup butter in a small heavy pan over low heat. Skim off froth and carefully pour clear butter from pan, leaving the milky residue behind. Discard residue.

A CASUAL HOUSEWARMING
For 12

Chutney-Glazed Ham

Baked Beans With Creamy Onions

Vegetable Slaw

Rye Salt Logs

Baskets of Cherries

*Brown Sugar Cats' Tongues
(see page 46)*

Sand Cookies With Caramelized Cinnamon Sugar (see page 28)

Fruit Punch, Coffee, Tea, and Sparkling Cider or White Wine

A buffet of hearty, home-style dishes welcomes old friends to a new home. A whole ham shimmers under a chutney glaze, while creamy baked beans send forth an aroma of molasses and bacon. A crunchy slaw, homemade rye bread, and baskets of glistening spring cherries round out this groaning board.

Timetable

Up to 3 days ahead: Soak beans.
Up to 2 days ahead: Make cookies.
Up to 12 hours ahead: Make slaw. Make rye logs.
Up to 4 hours ahead: Glaze and bake ham.
Up to 30 minutes ahead: Slice ham.

Planning

For an open house buffet, you'll want food that stays fresh and attractive for several hours as guests come and go. This menu does just that and can be made entirely in advance. It's also designed to appeal to youngsters, for an open house is often a family occasion.

  Offer sparkling cider or white wine in addition to fruit punch, coffee, and tea.

Presentation

Baskets, wood platters, and pewter give this buffet table a warm and welcoming look. To add color and height to the table, arrange daffodils in pewter mugs and stand Rye Salt Logs in a beaker or basket.

  A big basket at the head of the table can hold plates, cutlery, and napkins. If possible, choose a handsome baking dish for the beans, so they can go from oven to table.

  Photograph, page 15: A rosy Chutney-Glazed Ham stars in this buffet, partnered with a crunchy Vegetable Slaw, home-baked Rye Salt Logs, and baskets of cherries.

RYE SALT LOGS

Buttermilk and ricotta give a subtle tang to these chewy rye logs, the perfect partners for baked beans and ham. They are bigger than a bread stick, yet smaller than a loaf—just the right size for a miniature ham sandwich.

  3 cups buttermilk
  2 tablespoons caraway seed, plus caraway seed for garnish
  2 tablespoons olive oil
  4 packages active dry yeast
  2 tablespoons butter
  3 tablespoons minced shallots
  1 cup ricotta cheese
  2 tablespoons salt
  9 cups (approximately) unbleached flour
  2 cups rye flour
  Cornmeal, for dusting
  1 egg yolk
  1 teaspoon water
  Coarse salt, for garnish

1. In a medium saucepan combine buttermilk, caraway seed, and olive oil. Heat over low heat until barely warm (about 105° F). Remove from heat, sprinkle in yeast. Whisk to blend, then let stand 5 minutes.

2. In a small skillet over low heat, melt butter. Add shallots and cook until softened (about 2 minutes). Add to buttermilk mixture along with ricotta, salt, and 5 cups of the un-bleached flour. Beat well. Stir in rye flour and beat well. Turn dough out onto a lightly floured surface and knead, adding up to 4 cups of the

unbleached flour as necessary to make a smooth, firm dough. Knead until dough is smooth and elastic (8 to 10 minutes). Place in oiled bowl, turn to coat all sides with oil, and cover with plastic wrap and a hot, wet towel. Let rise in a warm place until doubled (about 75 minutes).

3. Punch dough down and divide into 8 portions. Roll each into a log about 1¼ inches in diameter and 8 to 10 inches long. Transfer to heavy baking sheets that have been greased and lightly dusted with cornmeal. Cover loosely with a towel and let rise until doubled (about 45 minutes).

4. Preheat oven to 350° F. Mix egg yolk with the water; brush logs with mixture. Using a sharp knife or a razor blade, make small slashes in the top of each log about ¼ inch deep. Sprinkle logs with caraway seed and salt for garnish. Bake until loaves are well browned and sound hollow when tapped on the bottom (18 to 20 minutes). Cool completely on racks. To serve, slice on the diagonal.

Makes 8 logs, 16 servings.

15

CHUTNEY-GLAZED HAM

Customize a storebought cooked ham with a distinctive chutney glaze to dress it up for your party buffet.

> 1 *ham (10 to 12 lb) fully cooked, ready-to-eat Whole cloves*
> 12 *ounces tomato, mango, or Mixed Fruit Chutney (see page 99)*
> ½ *cup firmly packed brown sugar*

Seasoned Bread Crumbs

> 1 *cup soft bread crumbs*
> 1 *teaspoon salt*
> 2 *teaspoons freshly ground pepper*
> 1 *teaspoon minced garlic*
> 1 *teaspoon dried oregano*
> 1 *teaspoon dried basil*

Preheat oven to 375° F. Score fat side of ham with a small, sharp knife. Stud with cloves. Combine chutney and sugar and spread on top. Top with Seasoned Bread Crumbs. Bake until ham glaze melts and bubbles (35 to 45 minutes). Cool to room temperature before slicing.

Serves 12.

Seasoned Bread Crumbs Combine all ingredients in a small bowl.

Makes 1 heaping cup.

Baked Ham With Hot Pepper Glaze Substitute hot pepper jelly for the chutney.

Baked Ham With Peach Jam Glaze Substitute peach jam for the chutney.

BAKED BEANS WITH CREAMY ONIONS

Baked beans are a terrific party dish because they're best when made ahead. This distinctive version gets its flavor from bacon, slow-cooked onions, and marmalade. Note that the beans need to soak overnight.

> 1 *pound pinto beans*
> ½ *pound thick-sliced bacon, diced*
> ¼ *cup tomato sauce*
> 2 *cups chicken stock*
> 1 *sprig fresh thyme*
> 1 *bay leaf*
>   *Salt and freshly ground pepper, to taste*
> 3 *tablespoons butter*
> 3 *cups thinly sliced white onions*
> ¾ *cup orange marmalade*
> 3 *tablespoons Dijon mustard*
> ½ *pound bacon, cooked crisp and crumbled, for garnish*
> 2 *minced green onions, for garnish*

1. Soak beans in water to cover overnight. Drain and place beans in a large, heavy, ovenproof pot with diced bacon, tomato sauce, chicken stock, thyme, and bay leaf. Add water just to cover.

2. Preheat oven to 325° F. Bring beans to a boil on top of the stove, then cover and place in oven. Bake until tender (about 1½ hours). Check beans occasionally as they cook and add more water if they appear too dry. When done, remove from oven and discard thyme sprig and bay leaf. Season with salt and pepper. Beans can be baked up to 2 days in advance and refrigerated.

3. In a large skillet melt butter over low heat. Add onions and cook, stirring occasionally, until they are very soft (about 30 minutes). Stir in marmalade and mustard. Cook 5 minutes. Stir onion mixture into beans. Beans may be prepared to this point up to 1 day ahead and refrigerated.

4. To serve, reheat dish on top of stove or in a 325° F oven until beans are hot throughout. Stir in half the crumbled bacon; top with remaining crumbled bacon and green onions.

Serves 12.

VEGETABLE SLAW

A veritable garden in a bowl is the word on this colorful slaw, which gets its zip from a minced green chile. Make it at least two hours ahead to allow the flavors to marry; it can be made and refrigerated as much as 12 hours ahead.

> 1 *pound green cabbage, shredded*
> 1 *pound red cabbage, shredded*
> 1 *cup minced green bell pepper*
> 1 *cup minced red or mixed red and yellow bell pepper*
> ½ *cup grated carrot*
> 1 *cucumber, preferably English*
> 1 *jalapeño or serrano chile, seeded and finely minced*
> 2 *leeks, thinly sliced*
> ½ *cup sour cream*
> 3 *tablespoons rice vinegar*
> ¼ *cup minced parsley*
> ¼ *cup minced basil*
>   *Salt and freshly ground pepper, to taste*
>   *Thinly sliced red onion, for garnish*
>   *Imported black olives, preferably Niçoise, for garnish*

1. In a large bowl combine cabbages, bell peppers, and carrot. If using English cucumber, halve, seed, and dice; other varieties should be peeled first. Add diced cucumber to bowl along with chile and leeks.

2. In a small bowl combine sour cream, vinegar, parsley, basil, salt, and pepper. Add to vegetables, toss to coat well, and transfer to a serving bowl. Garnish with red onion and black olives.

Serves 12.

EASTER LUNCH
For 8

Oyster, Leek, and Tomato Tart

Lamb and White Bean Salad

Minted Zucchini

*Orange and Berry Compote
With Matching Fruit Ices*

Beaujolais or California Gamay

---

*The traditional Easter lamb
served in nontraditional
fashion gives this meal its
special flair. In place of the
usual roast, the lamb is
served as a cool lunch salad.
Completing the spring feast
in a splash of color are a
creamy oyster tart, a
sprightly salad of zucchini
and mint, and an orange
and strawberry compote
with matching fruit ices.*

Timetable

Up to 3 days ahead: Soak beans
    overnight.

Up to 2 days ahead: Prepare zuc-
    chini salad. Roast lamb and
    chill. Boil beans.

1 day ahead: Slice lamb and mari-
    nate. Finish beans.

4 to 12 hours ahead: Make fruit
    ices.

2 to 12 hours ahead: Make
    compote.

1 hour ahead: Prepare tart dough.

30 minutes ahead: Bake tart dough
    and prepare filling.

At serving time: Marinate onions.

Planning

The oyster tart must be assembled and baked shortly before serving, but all other dishes can be made ahead. You can prepare the fruit ices either the night before or in the morning; the fruit compote should be made in the morning. To save time, set the table the night before.

A glass of sparkling wine would be lovely with the fresh-from-the-oven tart; serve a lightly chilled Beaujolais or a California Gamay with the lamb.

Presentation

Set a lively spring table with bright pink, green, and yellow linens and flowers. Daffodils, primroses and tulips are pretty Easter possibilities for dressing up table and dining room.

This meal is suited to family-style service. The warm tart can be presented on an earthenware platter or wooden board, followed by the salad on a large lettuce-lined platter and the zucchini in a shallow bowl.

Photograph, page 19: Easter lunch begins with wedges of warm Oyster, Leek, and Tomato Tart (at bottom), followed by spears of Minted Zucchini (at bottom) and a cool Lamb and White Bean Salad (at top).

OYSTER, LEEK, AND TOMATO TART

A cheesy cream puff dough forms the base of this savory tart. The filling heats through in five minutes.

   3 tablespoons butter
   1 tablespoon olive oil
   *½ pounds fresh spinach, washed
    and stemmed*
   1 tablespoon lemon juice
   1 teaspoon minced garlic
   *2 small leeks, white parts only,
    thinly sliced*
   *½ cup bread crumbs
    Salt and freshly ground
    pepper, to taste*
 16 freshly shucked oysters
   *½ cup peeled, seeded, and diced
    tomato*
   *2 tablespoons minced parsley,
    for garnish*
   *2 tablespoons grated Parmesan
    cheese, for garnish*

Cream Puff Dough

   1 cup milk
   ¼ cup butter
   1 cup sifted flour
   4 eggs
   *½ cup freshly grated Parmesan
    cheese*
   *½ cup grated Gruyère or
    Emmenthaler cheese*
 *1½ teaspoons Dijon mustard
    Salt and freshly ground
    pepper, to taste*

1. While Cream Puff Dough is baking, make filling. In a medium skillet heat 1 tablespoon of the butter and olive oil over moderate heat. Add spinach and lemon juice and cook 2 minutes. Transfer to a strainer and press to extract excess liquid.

2. Return skillet to moderate heat and add remaining 2 tablespoons butter. Add garlic and leeks and sauté until leeks are softened but not browned (about 10 minutes). Stir in bread crumbs; add salt and pepper.

3. Arrange cooked spinach around sides and bottom of Cream Puff Dough. Place oysters on spinach. Top with leek mixture. Scatter tomatoes over the top. Return to oven until tart is browned and topping is hot (about 5 minutes). Let rest 3 to 5 minutes before unmolding. Garnish with parsley and Parmesan before serving.

Makes one 9-inch tart.

Cream Puff Dough

1. Preheat oven to 400° F. In a medium saucepan combine milk and butter. Bring to a simmer, adjusting heat so butter is melted when mixture simmers. Add flour all at once and stir until mixture comes away from the sides of the pan.

2. Remove from heat and add eggs one at a time, beating well after each addition. Beat in cheeses and mustard. Season with salt and pepper.

3. Pour dough into a greased 9-inch springform pan. Make a well in the center and push dough up the sides of the pan. Fill with aluminum foil to keep dough sides from sliding down. Bake 25 minutes; remove foil.

Makes dough for one 9-inch tart.

LAMB AND WHITE BEAN SALAD

Lamb and white beans are a classic spring combination, as good in a cold salad as in a stew. Make the beans at least a day ahead to allow them to develop flavor.

1½ pounds cooked leg of lamb, slivered
1½ cups dried cannellini beans or Great Northern beans
2 ounces minced prosciutto
¼ cup olive oil
2 tablespoons minced garlic
2 tablespoons minced fresh sage
3 cups peeled, seeded and diced tomato
  Salt and pepper, to taste
1 mild white onion, sliced paper-thin
1 cup mixed young lettuces, washed and dried

Thyme Vinaigrette

⅓ cup red wine vinegar
1 shallot, minced
1 tablespoon minced fresh thyme
1 cup olive oil
  Salt and freshly ground pepper, to taste

1. Put sliced lamb in a bowl and add ½ cup Thyme Vinaigrette. Toss well to coat, cover, and refrigerate overnight.

2. Soak beans in water to cover for 2 to 12 hours. Drain and cover with fresh cold water. Add prosciutto, bring to a boil over high heat, reduce heat to maintain a simmer, and cook until beans are tender but not mushy (about 1½ hours). Drain and cool. Beans may be cooked up to 2 days in advance, covered, and refrigerated.

3. In a large pot over burner set to low, heat olive oil. Add garlic and sage and cook until fragrant. Add beans and tomatoes. Bring to a simmer and cook 15 minutes. Season with salt and pepper. If desired, beans may be cooled and refrigerated overnight.

4. Marinate onion slices 10 minutes in just enough Thyme Vinaigrette to coat them. Bring lamb and beans to room temperature. If beans appear somewhat dry, moisten with Thyme Vinaigrette. Taste and reseason if necessary.

5. To serve, line a large serving platter with lettuces. Arrange beans and lamb atop lettuces. Garnish with marinated onion slices.

Serves 8.

Thyme Vinaigrette In a medium bowl whisk together vinegar, shallot, and thyme. Add olive oil in a slow, steady stream, whisking constantly. Season with salt and pepper. Set aside ¼ cup Thyme Vinaigrette for the Minted Zucchini (see below).

Makes 1 cup.

MINTED ZUCCHINI

This simple salad should be made at least a day in advance; it will retain a pleasing texture and flavor for up to two days.

8 small zucchini
  Olive oil, for frying
3 whole garlic cloves, peeled
¼ cup minced fresh mint
¼ cup Thyme Vinaigrette (see above)
  Salt and freshly ground pepper, to taste

1. Trim ends of zucchini. Slice in half lengthwise, then into long strips. Set a large skillet over moderately low heat and add just enough oil to coat the bottom. Add garlic cloves and fry until golden brown but not burnt; remove and discard cloves. Raise heat to medium-high. Fry zucchini strips in batches until golden (about 5 minutes), adding more olive oil as necessary. Transfer to paper towels to drain.

2. In a small bowl combine mint and Thyme Vinaigrette.

3. Transfer fried zucchini to a bowl while still warm; add minted Thyme Vinaigrette and toss to coat. Season with salt and pepper. Cool completely, then refrigerate. Remove from refrigerator 1 hour before serving.

Serves 8.

ORANGE AND BERRY COMPOTE WITH MATCHING FRUIT ICES

Spiced fresh fruits bathed in sparkling apple cider make an elegant dessert when paired with matching fruit ices. The fruit should marinate at least 2 hours, with some of the cider added at the last minute for its lively sparkle. The ices require no special equipment, just ice cube trays without dividers.

6 navel oranges
2 pints strawberries
3 cloves
2 whole allspice berries
½ cup sparkling apple cider
1 cinnamon stick
¼ teaspoon freshly grated nutmeg
  Vanilla Sugar, to taste (see Note, page 19)

Strawberry Ice

1 cup strawberry purée, made from blended and strained strawberries
3 cups sparkling apple cider
  Sugar, to taste

Orange Ice

1 cup fresh orange juice
1 teaspoon grated orange rind
3 cups sparkling apple cider
1 tablespoon orange liqueur
  Sugar, to taste

1. Peel oranges, removing all white pith. Section oranges over a bowl to catch the juices. Trim strawberries, halve if large, and add to bowl with oranges.

2. Tie cloves and allspice together in a cheesecloth bag or place in a tea ball. Add to bowl along with ¼ cup of the cider, cinnamon stick, and

nutmeg. Season with Vanilla Sugar. Cover and refrigerate for at least 2 hours or up to 12 hours. Just before serving, stir remaining ¼ cup cider into compote and remove cloves and allspice.

3. To serve, divide fruit among eight chilled plates. Arrange a scoop of each fruit ice on each plate. Serve immediately.

Serves 8.

Strawberry Ice Combine strawberry purée and cider. Sweeten to taste with sugar. Pour into two ice cube trays, set trays in freezer, and stir every 10 minutes. When mixture is icy, put in a food processor or blender and blend until smooth. Return to trays and refreeze.

Orange Ice Combine orange juice, orange rind, cider, and liqueur. Sweeten to taste with sugar. Follow freezing instructions for Strawberry Ice (at left).

Note To make Vanilla Sugar, place a vanilla bean in a canister of sugar. Within 1 week, the sugar will be highly perfumed with vanilla. Replace sugar as you use it. Replace vanilla bean every 6 months.

PUTTING THE PARTY TOGETHER

Organization is the key to giving a party that runs smoothly, whether you're planning dinner for 4 or 40. The hosts who relax at their own parties are the ones who know how to take care of the details long before guests arrive.

Here is a step-by-step guide to the planning you'll need to do for almost any entertaining. The decisions won't necessarily be made in the order given—sometimes you decide on your guest list before you decide on a format, for example. However, since the decisions are inextricably linked, remember to run through all the consequences when you change your mind about any aspect of your party. If you add four more guests, will you have to rent wineglasses? If you substitute soup for the salad, will you have enough soup bowls? Careful list making will keep you from overlooking those minor details that often don't come up until the very day of the party.

Type of Party What type of party suits your reason for entertaining? A cocktail party for dozens? A small dinner for neighbors? A buffet brunch for the post–New Year's crowd? Decide early on whether you're serving breakfast, lunch, dinner, tea, hearty cocktail fare, or something in between, since this decision affects most of the others.

Location Will you have the party at home or in a rented hall? Do you want to confine the action to one room, or can you spread the party throughout the house? Can you have the party outdoors—on your own lawn or patio, or in a park? For an outdoor location, you'll need a Plan B: a tent, a rain date, or a backup indoor site.

Guest List and Invitations Be realistic about how many people you

can fit in your chosen setting. If your home is too small to entertain as many people as you would like, consider having two parties on consecutive days. There are economies to such a scheme: Twice as much food is usually not twice as much work; the centerpieces and other decorative items can be reused; and most rentals are much less expensive the second day than the first.

Be sure to issue invitations on a schedule in keeping with the formality of the event. Generally, the more formal the occasion, the earlier you want to extend the invitations. For a wedding party, six weeks in advance is appropriate. For formal dinners and cocktail parties, three weeks' notice is advisable, more if the party is at a busy time of year. Informal brunches, lunches, and dinners can be scheduled 10 to 14 days in advance, although these events are often almost impromptu.

Whether to issue your invitation by phone or in writing is also determined by the formality and size of the event. Phoning, which gives you the advantage of an immediate response, is usually preferred when the party is small and informal. However, written invitations allow you to be creative and to introduce your theme on paper. Small mailing tubes can hold confetti, streamers, and a rolled invitation to a New Year's eve party. For a Children's Halloween Party (see page 73), you might cut jack-o'-lanterns out of construction paper and encourage your child to color the front, adding party details on the flip side of the paper.

Menu After you've decided on the party format and the number of guests, plan your menu. For further guidance on devising a workable menu, see page 99.

Physical Layout Mentally plan the physical layout of the party. Where will you put the buffet table or the dinner tables? For a large cocktail party, can you rearrange the furniture to create more areas for conversation? Where will you put coats? Where

will you set food? Where will you put the bar? For a sit-down meal, you'll want to make guests feel comfortable and uncrowded. For a stand-up party, you'll want to create reasons and room to circulate.

Rentals Make a list of the cooking equipment and tableware you'll need: serving pieces, dishes, flatware, glassware. Then investigate the options for borrowing or renting what you don't have (see page 102). Make sure you have not only enough pots and pans to cook in, but also enough storage equipment and enough storage space. A neighbor might be willing to lend refrigerator or freezer space, especially if you volunteer to return the favor when needed.

Help Will you need serving or clean-up help? Line up bartenders, waiters, or other assistance at least two weeks before the party.

Table Settings Plan the table setting two weeks before the party in order to give you time to execute your ideas. Wash linens and polish silver if necessary. Buy paper goods and candles. In your mind, design a look for the tables. If planning three tables of four or two tables of eight, remember that the settings do not have to match; an eclectic look, with a different setting for each table, can add interest to a room. It's all right to put paper napkins and a cloth table covering on the same table.

Your centerpiece can be as simple as a handful of flowers in an antique jar (see Presentation, page 49) or as elaborate as the "winter wonderland" described on page 114. Remember that centerpieces for sit-down dinners should not impede a diner's view across the table, although buffet centerpieces should give height to the table. Seasonal flowers are always appropriate and can be ordered from a florist; you can even take in your own vases or containers and have the florist do the arranging. However, flowers are not the only suitable items for centerpieces. Consider miniature figurines (see Presentation, page 11), a fruit or vegetable still life, or an array of candles.

SOUP AND SALAD LUNCHEON
For 8

Cold Beet and Buttermilk Borscht

Green-Onion Bread Sticks

*Artichoke, Asparagus,
And Turkey Salad*

*Marinated Fruits
With Creamy Cheeses*

*Gewürztraminer or
White Zinfandel*

---

*The spring harvest sets the
theme for this colorful lunch.
A tangy chilled beet borscht
and a turkey salad with
artichoke hearts and slender
asparagus spears give "soup
and salad" a new and
elegant meaning.*

Timetable

Up to 2 days ahead: Prepare salad
dressing. Make bread sticks.

Up to 1 day ahead: Poach and
shred turkey breast. Cook
artichoke hearts.

Up to 12 hours ahead: Make
borscht.

Up to 6 hours ahead: Marinate
fruits.

Up to 4 hours ahead: Blanch
asparagus.

Up to 3 hours ahead: Wash, dry,
and finely shred greens.

At serving time: Arrange salad
and dress.

Planning

A commiittee meeting, a bridge club
break, or an informal wedding luncheon would be well-served by this
inviting meal.

A chilled Gewürztraminer or a
White Zinfandel could accompany
both soup and salad.

Presentation

Set up two tables for four. Lilac or iris
in loose arrangements give the tables
a warm look; if possible, choose
flowers that complement the napkins
and place mats. A few bread sticks
can be tied in a napkin beside each
place, with soup bowls or mugs filled
before guests are seated.

Photograph, page 23: A wicker
place mat and mixed pastel earthenware give an informal air to this
colorful lunch of chilled borscht with
bread sticks, turkey salad with Herb
Mayonnaise, and a fresh fruit salad.

COLD BEET AND
BUTTERMILK BORSCHT

You can garnish each portion before
serving, or offer bowls of sieved egg,
minced dill, and sour cream.

> 1 *pound fresh beets, tops
> removed*
> 1 *tablespoon salt*
> 1 *cucumber, peeled, seeded, and
> minced*
> ½ *cup minced green onion*
> 1 *tablespoon honey*
> 1 *tablespoon red wine vinegar*
> 3 *tablespoons minced fresh dill*
> 2 *cups buttermilk*
> 1 *cup cooked, peeled, and diced
> potatoes*
> ½ *cup sour cream, for garnish*
> 2 *hard-cooked eggs, chopped,
> for garnish*

1. Preheat oven to 350° F. Peel beets.
Place in a roasting pan with salt and
add water to come halfway up the
sides. Cover and bake until tender
(45 minutes to 1¼ hours depending
on size). Remove from oven; when
cool enough to handle, grate beets
into their cooking water. Add cucumber, green onion, honey, vinegar, and
1 tablespoon dill. Cover; chill.

2. Just before serving, stir in buttermilk and potatoes. Garnish each serving with a dollop of sour cream,
some chopped egg, and some of the
remaining minced dill.

Serves 8.

GREEN-ONION BREAD STICKS

For a cocktail nibble, wrap the bread
sticks with thin slices of Emmenthaler
or caraway-flavored Danbo cheese.
They freeze well; reheat in a 325° F
oven directly from the freezer.

> 2 *packages active dry yeast*
> 1 *tablespoon sugar*
> ¾ *cup warm water*
> 1 *teaspoon paprika*
> 2 *tablespoons olive oil, plus
> olive oil for greasing pan*
> ⅓ *cup minced green onion*
> 2½ *cups (approximately) flour*
> ½ *cup cornmeal*
> 2 *teaspoons kosher salt*

1. In a small bowl sprinkle yeast and
sugar over the warm water. Whisk to
blend; let stand 10 minutes. Stir in
paprika, olive oil, and green onion.

2. Stir together 2½ cups of the flour,
cornmeal, and salt. Gradually add
it to the yeast mixture, stirring with
a wooden spoon until mixture is too
stiff to stir. Transfer to a lightly
floured board and knead until
smooth and elastic (6 to 8 minutes),
adding additional flour as necessary.
Put dough in a lightly oiled bowl,
turn to coat all sides with oil, cover,
and let rise in a warm place until
doubled (about 45 minutes).

3. Punch dough down. On a lightly
floured surface, roll dough into a thin
rectangle about 11 by 13 inches.
Transfer to well-oiled baking sheet.
Brush top with oil, cover, and let
rise again until doubled (about
45 minutes).

4. Preheat oven to 375° F. Using a
razor blade, cut rectangle into 24
strips that are 10 inches long. Transfer strips to another oiled baking
sheet. Bake until strips are well
browned (12 to 15 minutes). Cool
slightly before serving.

Makes 2 dozen 10-inch bread sticks.

ARTICHOKE, ASPARAGUS, AND TURKEY SALAD

Celebrate spring with a turkey salad that shows off the finest seasonal produce: pencil-thin asparagus, baby artichokes, and fresh herbs. All parts of the salad, including the Herb Mayonnaise dressing, can be prepared well in advance, then arranged and dressed just before serving.

> 1 boneless turkey breast
>   (about 2 lb)
>   Salt and freshly ground
>   pepper, to taste
> ½ cup white wine
> ½ cup water
> 8 small artichokes
>   (about 2 in. diameter)
> ½ lemon
>   Olive oil, for coating
>   artichokes
> 2 pounds thin asparagus
> 4 cups mixed greens: spinach,
>   radicchio, butter lettuce,
>   romaine

Herb Mayonnaise

> 2 egg yolks
> 2 teaspoons Dijon mustard
> 2 teaspoons lemon juice
> 1 cup olive oil
> ½ cup corn oil
> 2 tablespoons balsamic vinegar
> 2 tablespoons minced parsley
> 1 tablespoon minced fresh basil
> 1 tablespoon minced fresh chives
>   Salt and freshly ground
>   pepper, to taste

1. Preheat oven to 350° F. Salt and pepper the turkey under the skin. Place in roasting pan. Add wine and the water; cover with oiled parchment paper or aluminum foil and oven-poach until firm to the touch (about 45 minutes). Be careful not to overcook. Remove from oven; when cool enough to handle, remove and discard skin. Shred turkey coarsely by hand. Turkey may be prepared 1 day in advance; cover and refrigerate, but bring to room temperature to use.

2. Peel away and discard tough outer leaves of artichokes to reveal the pale green hearts. Trim stems and cut ¼ inch off the tips. Rub all cut surfaces with lemon to prevent browning. Bring a large pot of salted water to a boil, add the juice of the lemon, and cook artichokes until tender when pierced with a knife (about 5 minutes). Drain and cool. Halve and remove fuzzy choke, if any. Coat artichoke halves lightly with olive oil; set aside. Artichokes may be prepared 1 day in advance; cover and refrigerate, but bring to room temperature before using.

3. Peel asparagus spears if desired (thin ones will not require peeling). Boil in lightly salted water until crisp-tender, then drain and immediately plunge into ice water to stop the cooking. Drain again, pat thoroughly dry, and coat lightly with olive oil. Asparagus may be prepared and left at room temperature covered with plastic wrap for up to 4 hours.

4. Wash greens and dry thoroughly. Roll a few leaves at a time into small bundles and cut into fine shreds with a knife. Wrap in paper towels, overwrap with plastic, and refrigerate up to 3 hours.

5. To serve, line a large serving platter with the shredded greens. Arrange turkey, artichokes, and asparagus attractively on and around the greens. Drizzle lightly with Herb Mayonnaise. Offer extra Herb Mayonnaise on the side.

Serves 8.

Herb Mayonnaise In a medium bowl whisk together egg yolks, mustard, and lemon juice. Add olive oil and corn oil drop by drop, whisking to form a mayonnaise. Whisk in vinegar, parsley, basil, and chives. Season with salt and pepper, adding more lemon juice if necessary. Herb Mayonnaise may be prepared 2 days in advance and refrigerated. Bring to room temperature before using.

Makes approximately 2 cups.

MARINATED FRUITS WITH CREAMY CHEESES

Soft, creamy cheeses are a luscious counterpoint to ripe spring fruit. First marinate the fruit with honey, lemon, and aromatic lavender seed, then serve it with two or three mild and spreadable cheeses. Lavender seed is available in most health-food stores.

> 1 cantaloupe melon
> 1 honeydew melon
> 1 pound red seedless grapes
> 2 pints strawberries
> 1 tablespoon honey
> 1 tablespoon lemon pulp
> 1 tablespoon lavender seed
>   (optional)
> 2 tablespoons minced
>   candied ginger
> 1 cinnamon stick
> 2 or 3 soft, creamy cheeses
>   such as Monterey jack, teleme,
>   cream cheese, whole-milk
>   ricotta, Bel Paese, St. André,
>   mascarpone, or fresh goat
>   cheese

1. Peel and seed cantaloupe and honeydew melons; slice into wedges. Divide grapes into small clusters. Trim strawberries and halve, if large. Combine the fruits in a large bowl.

2. Combine honey, lemon, and lavender seed, if used. Let stand 20 minutes, then strain and discard lavender seed. Stir in ginger. (If not using lavender seed, add honey, lemon, and ginger directly to fruits.) Spoon mixture over fruit and toss to coat. Add cinnamon stick. Cover and refrigerate for at least 30 minutes or up to 6 hours. Remove from refrigerator 30 minutes before serving.

3. To serve, arrange fruit on individual serving plates with a small dab of each of 2 or 3 cheeses. Or, serve the fruit in a large serving bowl and offer the cheeses on individual platters for self-service.

Serves 8.

PAELLA VALENCIANA
For 10

Grilled Vegetables Romesco

*Beet, Orange, and
Sweet Red Onion Salad*

Paella Valenciana

Minted Flan

*Dry Sherry and
Red Wine or Sangria*

---

*A casual evening with a
Spanish accent brings guests
around a centerpiece of
fragrant paella, the famous
Valencia rice dish. The
cooking of sunny Valencia
centers on olive oil, garlic,
oranges, mint—all the
flavors underscoring this
lively meal.*

Timetable

Up to 12 hours ahead: Prepare
Romesco Sauce. Prepare
flan.
Up to 6 hours ahead: Marinate
beets and onions. Prepare
paella through step 4.
Up to 2 hours ahead: Grill
vegetables.
At serving time: Finish paella
preparation. Arrange beet
salad.

Planning

Everything but the paella can be
made before guests arrive. Even the
paella can be partially cooked, requiring only a few minutes of your
attention during the meal.

A dry Spanish sherry or a crisp
white wine would flatter the first two
courses, with a light-bodied Spanish
red wine for the main course. In
warm weather, you could replace the
red wine with a chilled Sangria (see
page 53). You can make the Sangria
base several hours ahead and chill it,
but soda and ice should be added at
the last minute.

Presentation

In Spain, paella is often cooked over
an outdoor fire for family picnics.
Even when cooked indoors, however,
it is a rustic dish well suited to
informal service. For best effect,
paella should be presented family
style, either in the cooking vessel or
on a warm platter. Earthenware
plates, big tea towels for napkins, and
bright red, potted geraniums give the
table a countrified look. Your local
library can probably supply you with
records or tapes of flamenco guitar
music to transport your guests
straight to Spain.

Because the paella deserves the
diners' undivided attention, the beet
and onion salad should precede it
as a separate course.

Photograph, page 25: A hearty
paella packed with shrimp, mussels,
clams, sausage, and chicken in a
fancy serving platter can be a show-
stopping party dish. Grilled skewered
vegetables with a peppery Romesco
Sauce (at top) make a light appetizer.

GRILLED VEGETABLES ROMESCO

In Spain, peppery *romesco* sauce
appears on the table most often with
fish and shellfish, but it's also a
delicious companion for skewered,
grilled vegetables. The skewers serve
equally well as stand-up appetizers or
as a first course at the table. You will
need twenty 8-inch wooden skewers
soaked in water for 20 minutes. Dry
sherry is the traditional Spanish
accompaniment, but a rosé would
also be a fine choice.

½ cup olive oil
1 tablespoon finely minced
garlic
1 eggplant (about 1 lb)
2 tablespoons salt
20 boiling onions
(about 2 in. diameter)
20 large white mushrooms
3 medium zucchini
20 cherry tomatoes
2 large red bell peppers
Minced parsley, for garnish

Romesco Sauce

¾ cup olive oil
2 tablespoons minced garlic
⅓ teaspoon hot red-pepper flakes
1½ cups peeled, seeded, and
diced tomato
½ cup soft bread crumbs
1½ teaspoons chili powder
2 teaspoons anchovy paste
1½ teaspoons tomato paste
2 teaspoons sherry vinegar
Salt and freshly ground
pepper, to taste

1. Combine olive oil and garlic in
a jar. Cover and set aside for at least
30 minutes or up to one week.

2. Peel eggplant and cut into 1½-
inch cubes. Place in a colander, toss
with salt, and let drain 30 minutes to
draw out bitter juices. Rinse quickly
and pat dry. Trim root ends of
onions, peel off papery outer skin,
and parboil until just tender (about
10 minutes). Trim stem ends of
mushrooms. Cut zucchini into 1-inch
cubes. Cut tomatoes into eighths. Core
peppers and cut into 1-inch squares.

3. Preheat broiler or prepare a medium-hot charcoal fire. Thread all vegetables alternately on wooden skewers. Baste with olive oil–garlic mixture and broil or grill, basting 2 or 3 times, until eggplant is cooked through (5 to 10 minutes). Cooking time will vary (7 to 14 minutes), depending on heat of grill or broiler. Remove from heat, baste again, and allow to cool to room temperature.

4. To serve, arrange 2 skewers on each of 10 small plates along with a spoonful of Romesco Sauce. Garnish vegetables with a dusting of parsley.

Makes 20 small skewers.

Romesco Sauce

1. In a medium skillet heat 2 tablespoons of the olive oil over moderate heat. Add garlic, pepper flakes, tomato, and bread crumbs. Sauté 3 minutes. Add chili powder and sauté an additional 2 minutes.

2. Transfer mixture to food processor or blender. Add anchovy paste, tomato paste, and sherry vinegar. Blend until smooth. With motor running, add remaining olive oil slowly as for a mayonnaise, blending to make a thick and rosy sauce. Taste and add salt and pepper if desired. If sauce is too thick for your taste, gradually whisk in cold water to thin.

Makes approximately 3 cups.

BEET, ORANGE, AND SWEET RED ONION SALAD

This piquant salad is the perfect prelude to a hearty paella. The beets and oranges are marinated separately to keep their colors distinct, then combined on lettuce leaves just before serving. Note that beets and oranges must marinate at least 1 hour.

2½ pounds medium beets
6 navel oranges
1½ red onions, sliced paper-thin
¼ cup orange juice
3 tablespoons lemon juice
⅔ cup olive oil
Salt and freshly ground pepper, to taste
1 head butter lettuce

1. Preheat oven to 350°F. Trim away any beet tops (reserve for another use). Scrub beets but do not peel. Place beets in roasting pan. Add water to come halfway up the sides. Cover and bake until beets are tender when pierced with a knife (45 minutes to 1¼ hours, depending on size). When cool enough to handle, peel and cut into ½-inch dice. Transfer to a mixing bowl.

2. Grate the rind of one orange. Halve and squeeze orange to yield ¼ cup juice. Peel remaining 5 oranges removing all white pith, then section. Combine onion and orange segments in a bowl and set aside.

3. Whisk together grated orange rind, orange juice, lemon juice, and olive oil. Season with salt and pepper. Spoon some of this vinaigrette over beets and over onion-orange mixture. Toss to coat and let marinate 1 hour at room temperature or up to 6 hours in the refrigerator. Bring to room temperature before serving.

4. Line a platter or individual salad plates with tender hearts of butter lettuce. Arrange beets atop lettuce leaves. Top with onion-orange mixture. Spoon any remaining vinaigrette over the top; serve.

Serves 10.

PAELLA VALENCIANA

Traditionally, paella is made in a wide, slope-sided pan without a lid and cooked outdoors over an open fire. In the enclosed heat of a home oven, however, a lidded pot gives the best results. Stubby short-grain rice, available in ethnic and specialty markets, is required for an authentic paella, but long-grain rice will work.

½ cup olive oil
2 small fryer chickens (3 lb each), cut into 8 pieces each
12 ounces sweet Italian sausage, sliced ½ inch thick
2 pounds jumbo shrimp (8 to 10 per lb)
1½ pounds sea scallops
1 pound squid, cleaned and sliced into rings
1½ cups thinly sliced onion
2 tablespoons finely minced garlic
4 cups chopped tomatoes, fresh or canned
1½ teaspoons hot red-pepper flakes
Salt and freshly ground pepper, to taste
1 pound cubed roasted duck meat (optional)
1 cup coarsely chopped green bell pepper
1½ teaspoons saffron threads
2 quarts hot chicken or veal stock
4 cups short-grain rice
1 pound mussels, scrubbed and debearded
1½ pounds clams, scrubbed
3 tablespoons lemon juice
1 pound spinach, blanched, squeezed dry, and chopped
1 cup diced red bell pepper
1 cup cooked peas (optional)
3 tablespoons parsley

1. Preheat oven to 350° F. In a very large skillet over moderately high heat, warm ¼ cup olive oil. Wipe chicken completely dry and brown on all sides (10 to 12 minutes). Transfer pieces as they brown to several thicknesses of paper towel to drain.

2. When all chicken has been browned, add sausage slices to skillet and brown on both sides. Transfer to paper towels to drain. Reduce heat to medium and add shrimp. Sauté 2 minutes and drain on paper towels. Shrimp will not be completely cooked. Trim away the tough muscle from the side of each scallop, then add scallops and brown 30 seconds; drain on paper towels.

3. Add 2 tablespoons of the remaining olive oil to skillet and raise heat to high. Add squid rings and cook 30 seconds. Transfer with a slotted spoon to paper towels.

4. Add remaining 2 tablespoons olive oil to skillet and reduce heat to moderately low. Add onions and garlic and cook until onions are soft (7 to 10 minutes). Stir in tomatoes, pepper flakes, and salt and pepper. Cook 10 minutes, stirring occasionally. Mixture should thicken slightly. Add chicken pieces, sausage, squid, duck (if used), and green pepper. Simmer uncovered 10 minutes.

5. Dissolve saffron in ¼ cup of the hot stock. Mix with remaining stock and add to skillet. Stir in rice. Raise heat to high and bring to a boil. Cover and transfer skillet to oven. Bake 15 minutes. Uncover and tuck shrimp and scallops into mixture. Place mussels and clams on top. Cover and bake until rice is just tender and mussels and clams open (about 10 minutes). Uncover and discard any unopened mussels or clams. Sprinkle casserole with lemon juice. Stir in spinach, red bell pepper, and peas, if used. Let stand, covered, 5 to 10 minutes. Taste for seasoning and sprinkle with parsley just before serving.

Serves 10.

MINTED FLAN

A light and creamy custard with a cool mint flavor is enticing after a spicy paella. Make it in a single 6-cup mold, as described here, or in 10 individual custard cups.

  2 cups chopped fresh mint leaves
  2 cups water
  2 cups sugar
  4 cups milk
  4 eggs
  8 egg yolks
  Fresh whole mint leaves, for garnish (optional)

1. Preheat oven to 325° F. In a saucepan combine 1 cup of the mint leaves and the water. Bring to a boil over high heat, cover, and set aside. Steep 20 minutes. Strain and discard the leaves.

2. Return ¾ cup mint-flavored water to saucepan with 1 cup of the sugar (discard remaining water). Bring to a boil over moderate heat, swirling pan until sugar dissolves, then boil until mixture caramelizes, turning a rich golden brown. Immediately pour caramel into a 6-cup mold. Swirl mold to coat bottom evenly with caramel. Set aside.

3. Combine remaining 1 cup mint leaves, milk, and ½ cup of the remaining sugar in a medium saucepan. Bring to a simmer over moderate heat, stirring occasionally. Remove from heat.

4. In a large bowl whisk together eggs, egg yolks, and remaining ½ cup sugar. Whisk a little hot milk mixture into eggs to warm them, then pour eggs into hot milk, whisking constantly. Strain mixture through a sieve into prepared mold.

5. Set mold in a large pan and add water to pan to come halfway up the sides of mold. Bake until a knife inserted in center comes out clean (25 to 30 minutes). Transfer mold to a rack to cool, then chill thoroughly. To serve, unmold on a platter. Garnish with mint leaves, if desired.

Serves 10.

---

menu

GRADUATION TEA
For 20

Smoked Chicken in Lettuce Cups

Home-Cured Halibut With Dilled Brioche

Sand Cookies With Caramelized Cinnamon Sugar

Sweet Pine-Nut Tarts

Tea and Lemonade or Sparkling Wine

Sturdy and aromatic brews alongside sweet and savory nibbles set the stage for an afternoon tea. Whether in a garden, on a covered porch, or in a sunny drawing room, a tea is a fine way to toast the beginning of a student's new life.

Timetable

Up to 5 days ahead: Make sand cookies.

Up to 2 days ahead: Marinate chicken. Marinate halibut.

Up to 1 day ahead: Smoke chicken and shred. Prepare brioche. Make tart dough.

Up to 12 hours ahead: Prepare and bake tarts.

Up to 1 hour ahead: Arrange chicken in lettuce cups. Slice halibut and make brioche triangles.

At serving time: Arrange halibut on brioche.

Planning

Set out three china teapots, each filled with a different type of tea—perhaps an herb tea, a fragrant Earl Grey and a Darjeeling. A kitchen helper can keep the pots filled with hot water and replace tea bags or tea leaves when necessary. It's also nice to offer an alternative to tea, such as lemonade for a young crowd or sparkling wine for an older one. If the weather turns exceptionally warm, set out a pitcher of iced tea as well.

The recipes can be readily doubled for a bigger crowd. All the dishes can be made in advance. The food for this menu is also well suited to a shower or a wedding reception.

Presentation

A round table draped in a floor-length pink cloth makes a pleasing backdrop for the food and beverages. Continue the color scheme with delicate pink and white nosegays in dainty vials and repeat the round shape in crystal and silver serving platters. Footed salvers, if you have them, will give height to the table. A teaspoon collection can be shown to full advantage on embroidered white linen tea napkins. If possible, dress up your table with a gleaming silver tea service or a collection of antique teaspoons, and serve a selection of teas in dainty china cups.

Photograph, page 29: This Graduation Tea is an occasion for both sweet and savory nibbles, including (from top): Sand Cookies With Caramelized Cinnamon Sugar, Smoked Chicken in Lettuce Cups with a dab of honey mustard, Home-Cured Halibut With Dilled Brioche, and Sweet Pine-Nut Tarts.

SMOKED CHICKEN IN LETTUCE CUPS

Marinate chicken overnight in a garlicky yogurt paste, and then grill over hickory or apple-wood chips. The result is fragrant smoked chicken to nestle in lettuce cups, each with a dab of mustard sauce. You'll need approximately 1 pound of hickory or apple-wood chips, soaked for 30 minutes in cold water.

- 3 small chickens (about 2½ lb each)
- 1 cup minced fresh basil
- ½ cup minced fresh chives
- ¼ cup minced fresh oregano
- ¼ cup minced garlic
- 2 tablespoons freshly ground pepper
- 2 tablespoons plain yogurt
- 2 tablespoons lemon juice
- 1 tablespoon prepared mustard
- 2 tablespoons honey
- ½ cup minced herbs (a mixture of chives, parsley, basil, and thyme, to taste)
- 3 large heads butter lettuce Minced chives, for garnish (optional)

1. Have butcher butterfly chickens, or do it yourself: Using a large, heavy knife, cut away backbone of chicken; spread chicken out flat and press down lightly to crack the breast-bones. In a blender combine basil, chives, oregano, garlic, pepper, yogurt, and lemon juice. Blend until smooth. Rub chickens all over with yogurt mixture. Cover and refrigerate overnight.

2. Prepare a large, medium-hot charcoal fire. Preheat oven to 350° F. When coals are gray, drain hickory chips and sprinkle over coals. Arrange grill rack over coals; set chickens on rack breast side down, cover, and smoke 1 hour, turning chickens over halfway through. Transfer chickens to a rack in a roasting pan; place in oven and continue roasting until done (another 15 to 30 minutes). Cool to room temperature.

3. Remove chicken meat from bones. Shred dark meat by hand. Cut white meat into 1-inch cubes.

4. In a small bowl stir together mustard, honey, and mixed herbs. Wash and dry lettuce, setting aside the tender inner leaves. Arrange inner leaves on a large serving platter. Put a small dab of mustard mixture on the bottom of each lettuce cup. Divide shredded and cubed chicken among the cups. Garnish each with minced chives, if desired.

Serves 20.

HOME-CURED HALIBUT WITH DILLED BRIOCHE

A peppery sweet-and-sour glaze based on brown sugar, lemon, and vodka penetrates halibut during the course of a two-day cure. Serve the fish, sliced thin, on rounds of Dilled Brioche spread with seasoned Homemade Mayonnaise.

- 2 tablespoons lemon juice
- 2 tablespoons balsamic vinegar
- 1 teaspoon soy sauce
- 2 tablespoons freshly ground pepper
- 1 teaspoon ground cloves
- ½ cup granulated sugar
- 1 tablespoon firmly packed brown sugar
- ¼ cup vodka
- 2 tablespoons grated lemon rind
- 3 pounds halibut fillets Homemade Mayonnaise (see page 88)
- 1 loaf Dilled Brioche (see page 120) Sprigs of fresh dill, for garnish

1. In a small saucepan combine lemon juice, vinegar, soy sauce, pepper, cloves, granulated sugar, brown sugar, vodka, and lemon rind. Bring to a simmer over moderate heat and simmer 5 minutes. Cool.

2. Cover a baking sheet with plastic wrap. Brush with half the lemon syrup, arrange fish fillets on sheet, and brush with remaining syrup. Cover with plastic wrap and a second baking sheet. Place a 5-pound weight on the top baking sheet. Refrigerate for 2 days.

3. Remove weight. Pour off excess juices and add to mayonnaise.

4. To serve, trim crusts from 10 slices of Dilled Brioche and cut diagonally to make 20 triangles. Spread a little of the mayonnaise on each triangle. Slice fish paper-thin on the diagonal. Put a piece of fish atop each triangle and arrange triangles on a platter. Garnish with sprigs of dill.

Serves 20.

SAND COOKIES WITH CARAMELIZED CINNAMON SUGAR

These buttery cookies keep for up to one week in an airtight container or up to two weeks in the freezer.

- ¾ cup butter, softened
- 1 cup superfine sugar
- ¼ cup firmly packed brown sugar
- 1 egg
- 2 egg yolks
- 1½ teaspoons vanilla extract
- 1 tablespoon grated lemon rind
- 3 cups flour Pinch salt
- 2 egg whites, lightly beaten
- ½ cup granulated sugar
- 2 tablespoons ground cinnamon
- ⅓ cup ground almonds

1. With electric mixer, cream butter. Add superfine sugar and brown sugar gradually and beat until light and fluffy. Add egg, egg yolks, vanilla, and lemon rind and beat well. Sift together flour and salt. Resift over creamed mixture and beat at low speed just until blended. Pat into a large square, wrap in plastic, and refrigerate overnight.

2. Preheat oven to 400° F. On a lightly floured surface, roll dough ¼ inch thick. Cut dough into shapes with floured cookie cutters. Transfer to lightly greased baking sheets. Gently brush cookies with egg white.

3. Combine granulated sugar, cinnamon, and almonds, and sprinkle over surface of each cookie. Bake until sandy colored (6 to 9 minutes). Transfer to racks to cool.

Makes about 5 dozen 2-inch cookies.

BREWING THE PERFECT POT OF TEA

Brewing tea is a simple process, but many people sidestep the few procedures necessary to brewing a superior cup. Loose tea leaves are preferred, since they are generally of higher quality than the broken leaves packed in tea bags. What's more, the water can circulate better through loose leaves, improving flavor extraction.

To brew a pot of tea, select a teapot that retains heat well, such as one made of china or glazed earthenware. To prevent the tea from cooling too quickly, warm the teapot: Fill it with boiling water, let stand for a minute or two, then pour off the water. Meanwhile, fill the teakettle with fresh cold water from the tap. Bring water to a full, rolling boil. Put 1 teaspoon of tea leaves per 6-ounce cup in the teakettle. Add the appropriate amount of boiling water. Cover and let steep 3 to 6 minutes for black tea, 8 to 12 minutes for herb tea. Stir once, then pour into warm cups through a strainer. Lengthy steeping brings out the full flavor of the tea.

To brew a single cup of tea, use a teaspoon of leaves in a tea ball or perforated infusing spoon; infuse 3 to 6 minutes for black tea, 8 to 12 for herb tea. Stir once with infuser, then remove infuser and serve.

To brew iced tea, make an extrastrong pot of hot tea and allow it to cool completely. Then strain tea into an ice-filled glass. To prevent cloudiness (which does not affect flavor), make a cold-water infusion: Measure 3 tablespoons tea leaves per quart of cold water, combine in a pitcher, cover, and refrigerate for several hours. Then strain over ice.

Tea can be seasoned with lemon or sugar after brewing. Many English tea drinkers add milk to soften the tannin in the tea. In India, tea leaves are often combined with spices such as cinnamon and cardamom.

For best flavor, tea leaves should be discarded after one use.

SWEET PINE-NUT TARTS

Imagine a tart filling based on a rum- and almond-flavored pastry cream with toasted pine nuts, currants, and golden raisins. That's the story behind these delectably creamy, chewy tarts—sweet mouthfuls to pair with coffee or tea.

- ¼ cup golden raisins
- 2 tablespoons currants
- 3 tablespoons orange liqueur
- ½ cup milk
- 2 egg yolks
- 1 teaspoon grated lemon rind
- 3 tablespoons sugar
- 1 tablespoon flour
- ½ teaspoon vanilla extract
- 6 ounces almond paste
- 2 tablespoons rum
- 1 cup toasted pine nuts
  Lightly sweetened whipped cream, for garnish

Rich Pastry Dough

- 4 cups flour
- 2 cups sifted confectioners' sugar
- 1 cup plus 2 tablespoons unsalted butter, chilled and cut into small pieces
- 2 eggs
- 1 tablespoon vanilla extract
- 2 tablespoons ice water

1. In a small bowl combine golden raisins, currants, and liqueur; set aside 30 minutes. In a small saucepan, bring milk to a simmer. In another small bowl, whisk together eggs yolks, lemon rind, sugar, and flour. Whisk in hot milk and blend well, making a pastry cream. Return mixture to saucepan and bring to a boil; boil 30 seconds. Remove from heat, cool slightly, and stir in vanilla.

2. In a blender or food processor, combine almond paste, pastry cream, and rum. Pulse just to blend. Transfer to a bowl and stir in raisin-currant mixture. Add ½ cup of the toasted pine nuts.

3. Preheat oven to 400° F. On a lightly floured surface, roll Rich Pastry Dough ⅛ inch thick. With a lightly floured cutter, cut out rounds slightly larger than 2-inch tart shells. Press rounds firmly into shells. Put about 1½ tablespoons filling in each shell. Top each with a few of the remaining pine nuts.

4. Bake until lightly browned and slightly puffed (12 to 15 minutes). Cool on a rack.

5. Serve at room temperature garnished with a dab of lightly sweetened whipped cream.

Makes 3 dozen 2-inch tarts.

Rich Pastry Dough

1. *To prepare in a food processor:* Combine flour and sugar in work bowl. Pulse two or three times to blend. Add butter, and pulse until mixture resembles coarse crumbs. In a small bowl whisk together eggs, vanilla, and the water. With motor running, add liquid ingredients and process just until dough comes together (about 8 seconds), adding another tablespoon water only if mixture appears too dry. *To prepare by hand:* Stir together flour and sugar. Cut in butter until mixture resembles coarse crumbs. In a small bowl combine eggs, vanilla, and the water.

2. Add coarse crumbs to dry ingredients all at once and stir just until mixture comes together, adding another tablespoon water only if mixture appears too dry.

3. Wrap dough in plastic and refrigerate 2 hours.

Makes enough dough for 3 dozen 2-inch tarts.

PROVENÇAL GARDEN WEDDING
For 50

Cold Rare Beef With Tapénade
(see page 54)

Whole Salted Almonds

Radishes With Basil Butter

Vegetable Tian

Salade Niçoise With Fresh Tuna

Fresh Cherries and Apricots

Rosewater and Mint Ice Cream

Wedding Cake

Champagne, Sauvignon Blanc

A summer garden ablaze with color is a fairy-tale setting for a wedding feast. This sunny menu can be served family style, at long tables draped in white and dressed with flowers.

Timetable

Up to 4 days ahead: Make Candied Rose Petals.

At least 3 days ahead: Make 2 recipes of *tapénade*.

3 days ahead: Steep mint.

Up to 2 days ahead: Assemble and bake *tian*. Make dressing for Niçoise, basil butter, and custard for ice cream.

Up to 1 day ahead: Bake tuna. Prepare beans, potatoes, beets, and eggs for Niçoise. Roast beef. Trim radishes. Freeze ice cream.

Up to 4 hours ahead: Prepare almonds. Slice tian.

Up to 1 hour ahead: Assemble beef sandwiches. Butter radishes.

Planning

Greet guests upon arrival with a flute of chilled sparkling wine and enjoy an hour of prelunch mingling. To keep appetites at bay while kitchen helpers put finishing touches on lunch, two servers can pass salted almonds and trays of Radishes With Basil Butter (see page 76).

As guests locate their names on place cards, they find tables set with baskets of bread and platters of Vegetable Tian. When the first course *tians* are cleared, long platters of Salade Niçoise replace them. Bowls of cherries and apricots are brought out just before the wedding cake is cut.

A Sauvignon Blanc or a blush wine would pair nicely with the luncheon. With the wedding cake and fruit, offer more Champagne. Two cases each of a still wine and a sparkling wine should be enough. Be sure to include a nonalcoholic alternative.

The cooking can be spread out over four days and requires no last-minute preparation. Still, no ambitious bridal couple should attempt the menu without plenty of help. Wedding cake can be ordered from a bakery. Three or four pairs of hands will be needed the day before the party. On the day of the luncheon, three people will be needed in the kitchen to do the finishing touches. A bartender and two waiters can handle wines, hors d'oeuvres, table service, and cleanup.

Presentation

White tablecloths, china, and napkins provide a pure backdrop for the visual delights of the garden. To bring color to the table, wrap the cutlery in white napkins and tie each with red, white, and blue ribbons; tuck a flower into each. Arrange flowers loosely in glass vials or vases and set them randomly along the length of the table.

Photograph, page 32: A savory Vegetable Tian (at left) is the first course of this wedding feast, followed by platters of Salade Niçoise made with fresh tuna and a bouquet of vegetables (at right).

VEGETABLE TIAN

The Provençale *tian* is named after the earthenware dish it is made in.

2 cups (approximately) olive oil
3 cups diced onion
¼ cup minced garlic
12 red bell peppers
12 yellow bell peppers
25 large tomatoes, sliced about ¼ inch thick
½ cup tarragon vinegar
  Salt, to taste
3 cups chopped fresh basil
10 yellow zucchini or summer squash, washed and sliced ½ inch thick
10 green zucchini, washed and sliced ½ inch thick
1½ cups soft bread crumbs
2 cups freshly grated Parmesan
¾ cup minced parsley
2 teaspoons minced fresh rosemary

1. Preheat oven to 375° F. In a large skillet heat ¾ cup of the olive oil over moderate heat. Add onion and garlic and sauté until softened but not browned (about 5 minutes).

2. Roast red and yellow peppers according to directions for Roasting Bell Peppers and Chiles (see page 62). Quarter the peppers.

3. Lightly oil 6 oven-to-table baking dishes, approximately 11 by 13 inches. Line bottom of each dish with sliced tomatoes. Divide onion mixture among dishes and spread over tomatoes. Drizzle with olive oil and vinegar and sprinkle with salt and basil. Add layers of red peppers, yellow zucchini, green zucchini, and yellow peppers, drizzling between each layer with olive oil and vinegar and sprinkling with salt and basil. Combine bread crumbs, Parmesan, parsley, and rosemary; sprinkle over top and drizzle with olive oil.

4. Bake 25 minutes. Cool to room temperature and serve. Dish may be baked up to 2 days ahead, covered with plastic wrap, and refrigerated. To serve individual portions in neat squares, slice when cold, then allow to come to room temperature.

Serves 50.

SALADE NIÇOISE WITH FRESH TUNA

Even in Nice, the town of its origin, the *salade niçoise* is typically made with canned tuna. It is good that way, but fresh tuna makes it great.

- 12 *pounds fresh tuna fillet, skinned, and cut into chunks about 1½ inches thick and 4 to 5 inches long*
- 2 *cups white wine vinegar or cider vinegar*
- ½ *cup olive oil*
- 1½ *cups minced celery*
- 2 *cups minced onion*
- ½ *cup minced shallots*
- 1 *cup minced carrot*
- ⅓ *cup coarsely chopped garlic*
- 4 *cups coarsely chopped tomatoes*
- 5 *bay leaves*
- 3 *oranges, thickly sliced*
- 3 *cups dry white or rosé wine*
- 6 *pounds young tender beans, blanched and stemmed*
- 35 *small new potatoes, boiled, and halved if large*
- 5 *pounds fresh beets, boiled, peeled, and quartered or halved*
- 3 *dozen hard-cooked eggs, peeled and halved*
- 3 *pounds Niçoise olives*
- 2 *pounds small red radishes*
- 6 *ounces anchovies, packed in salt or olive oil*
- 2 *pounds cornichons (tiny French pickles)*
- 3 *cups sliced red onion*

Tomato and Tarragon Vinaigrette

- 4 *pounds tomatoes, seeded and chopped*
- 4 *cucumbers, peeled, seeded, and chopped*
- 4 *red bell peppers, seeded and minced*
- 1½ *cups minced onion*
- 1 *cup capers*
- ¼ *cup minced fresh tarragon*
- ½ *cup strong mustard*
- ¾ *cup cider vinegar*
- 4 *cups olive oil*
  Salt and freshly ground pepper, to taste
- 1½ *cups minced parsley*

1. Place tuna in one or several large shallow pans. Combine vinegar and olive oil; pour over fish, cover, and refrigerate for at least 1 hour or up to 4 hours.

2. Preheat oven to 350° F. In a large bowl, combine celery, onion, shallots, carrot, garlic, tomatoes, bay leaves, and oranges. Mix well. Divide mixture among enough large roasting pans to hold all the tuna in one layer. Place tuna over the vegetable mixture. Pour wine around fish. Cover loosely with lid or aluminum foil and bake 25 minutes, or until fish is just barely done. Add more wine if mixture appears to be drying out. Remove from oven and let cool in the vegetable mixture. Cover and refrigerate for up to 1 day.

3. To serve, divide tuna among several long oval platters, placing it in the center. Top with Tomato and Tarragon Vinaigrette. Surround with neat mounds of beans, potatoes, beets, and eggs. Garnish platter with olives, radishes, anchovy fillets, and *cornichons*. Scatter red onion rings over all.

Serves 50.

Tomato and Tarragon Vinaigrette In a large bowl combine tomatoes, cucumbers, peppers, onion, and capers. In a separate bowl whisk together tarragon, mustard, and vinegar. Add olive oil gradually, whisking constantly. Pour herb and olive oil mixture over vegetables and toss to blend. Season with salt and pepper. Cover and store at least 24 hours or up to 2 days at room temperature. Just before serving, stir in parsley and adjust seasoning.

Makes about 18 cups.

ROSEWATER AND MINT ICE CREAM

Serve this exotic ice cream in small scoops with wedding cake, garnishing each plate with a candied rose petal.

- 6 *cups half-and-half*
- 6 *cups milk*
- 3 *cups fresh mint leaves*
- 30 *egg yolks, beaten*
- 1½ *cups sugar*
- ½ *cup rosewater*
- 3 *tablespoons vanilla extract*

Candied Rose Petals

- 50 *unblemished red rose petals from unsprayed roses*
- 1 *egg white*
  Sugar, for coating

1. In a large pot over moderate heat bring half-and-half and milk to a simmer. Add mint leaves and remove from heat; cover and steep overnight.

2. Strain and discard mint. Return milk to a clean saucepan and return to a simmer over moderate heat.

3. In a large bowl whisk together yolks and sugar. Add hot milk gradually, whisking constantly. Return mixture to saucepan and cook, stirring constantly with a wooden spoon, until mixture reaches 180° F. Mixture will thicken visibly and coat the back of the spoon. Do not allow mixture to boil. Strain into a bowl set over ice; stir until cool. Stir in rosewater and vanilla. Cover and chill for at least 1 hour or up to 1 day. Transfer to ice cream freezer and freeze according to manufacturer's directions. Serve with a candied rose petal.

Makes 1 gallon.

Candied Rose Petals Use only unsprayed roses. Dip each petal in unbeaten egg white. Let excess egg white drip off, then dip in a large bowl of sugar, sprinkling with sugar to coat the entire petal. Place on rack to dry. Store petals in an airtight container, stacking them if desired, for up to 4 days.

Makes 50 candied rose petals.

COME FOR COCKTAILS
June 25
6:00 P.M.
Holly and Raymond Bass
18 Country Club Drive

Icy blue and white set a cool color scheme for summer. For foods to counteract the heat, look to the refreshing flavors of ripe summer fruit.

Summer Menus

Summer's relaxed schedules permit more frequent entertaining, and the pleasant weather is an excuse to abandon the dining room. A Mexican Patio Party (see page 60), a Southern Fish Fry (see page 49) served on the porch, or a backyard barbecue for the Fourth (see page 36) takes you outdoors but keeps you close to the kitchen. Summer sporting enthusiasts can enjoy a Hikers' Picnic (see page 42) or a Lunch on the Boat (see page 57). In this chapter, you'll find useful tips for whenever you entertain, such as how to handle lights and music (see page 63). A Special Feature on page 52 provides recipes for party drinks.

SUMMER ENTERTAINING

Entertaining is never easier than it is in summer. Markets abound with full-flavored fruits and vegetables that need little preparation. The possibility of entertaining outdoors opens up dozens of settings: on a patio, on the beach, or beside a mountain trail.

Summer appetites respond to simple grilled foods and to cool or cold dishes. An outdoor barbecue grill is the summer cook's best friend (see Tips on Grilling, page 38). Salads can be the mainstay of a menu (see page 40). A cocktail party built entirely of cold foods (see page 54) can be especially appealing at the end of a scorching day. For the ultimate in warm-weather refreshment, try an ice cream social (see page 46).

The season's best menus highlight the summer market bounty. Red ripe tomatoes, fat purple eggplants, shiny bell peppers in vivid summer colors, crisp cucumbers, firm zucchini, and tender green beans beckon vegetable shoppers. Fragrant summer fruits make simple and wonderful desserts: Consider aromatic cantaloupe, casaba, and honeydew melons; raspberries, blackberries, and blueberries; plump honeyed figs, both black and green; peaches and nectarines.

Summer parties offer the chance to become acquainted with the many excellent domestic and imported beers on the market. With grilled spareribs, fried fish, or a dinner laced with hot chiles, chilled beer is the perfect companion. For large parties, you may want to present an international assortment to compare a variety of styles. Wines for summer meals should be light bodied, fruity, and fresh. Chenin Blanc and Sauvignon Blanc, blush wines, and lightweight red wines such as Beaujolais, Chianti, or California Gamay Beaujolais provide pleasant summer beverages.

Summer tables should reflect the informal mood and the brilliant colors of the season. Fire-engine red, white, bright blue, yellow, orange, emerald green, and hot pink are among the hues that give a summer flavor to a table setting.

menu

**BBQ ON THE FOURTH
For 12**

Grilled Shrimp With Chiles and Lime

Spareribs With Mustard and Whiskey

Grilled Summer Vegetables

Yankee Lemon-Maple Tart

Beer and Lemonade

Spicy shrimp in the shell, heaping platters of spareribs, and grilled peak-of-the-season vegetables tempt Fourth of July guests and provide a stylish change from the usual hamburgers and franks.

Timetable

2 days ahead: Make Crème Fraîche and Maple Praline for tart.

Up to 2 days ahead: Make sparerib marinade, but do not marinate spareribs yet.

Up to 1 day ahead: Prepare shrimp marinade, but do not marinate shrimp yet.

1 day ahead: Marinate spareribs.

12 hours ahead: Prepare lemon filling and prepare prebaked shell for tart.

Up to 6 hours ahead: Bake vegetables; set aside. Fill and bake tart.

Up to 4 hours ahead: Roast spareribs; set aside.

Up to 2 hours ahead: Shred greens for shrimp, wrap, and chill.

30 minutes ahead: Marinate shrimp.

Planning

Unless you have a large grill, you'll need to stagger the cooking of shrimp, spareribs, and vegetables. One solution is to prebake the ribs and vegetables, then grill them just long enough to give them a smoky flavor. Even if your grill is large enough to hold everything at once, you'll want to prebake the spareribs to tenderize them.

The shrimp go on the grill first, to be served as the opening course. When appetites are ready, the spareribs take their turn. When the spareribs come off, the vegetables go on while a helper carves the pork slabs into separate ribs.

Ice down plenty of American beer for this country-style menu, with pitchers of lemonade for the youngsters. Given the messiness of shrimp and ribs, festive bibs are a fine idea.

Presentation

Red, white, and blue are the colors, of course, for this festive Fourth of July. Gather friends and family at long picnic tables for a meal served family style on bountiful platters.

Paper cloths and plenty of sturdy paper napkins are essential for a meal that's as messy as this one. If you're eating in your own backyard, you can use real plates and stainless cutlery and finger bowls.

Serve the shrimp platters first, to seated guests. Follow with platters of ribs and grilled vegetables spaced the length of the table. Dessert and coffee can be offered later, following the fireworks.

Photograph, page 39: No one will miss the hamburgers when your Independence Day backyard barbecue includes platters of Grilled Shrimp With Chiles and Lime (at left), followed by smoky Spareribs With Mustard and Whiskey and Grilled Summer Vegetables sprinkled with Parmesan cheese (at right). Pitchers of iced lemonade provide cool refreshment.

GRILLED SUMMER VEGETABLES

Eggplant, garlic, zucchini, and tomatoes can be prebaked at the cook's convenience, then grilled briefly.

>   6 large whole bulbs garlic
>   Olive oil, for drizzling
>   Kosher salt, for sprinkling
>   1 large eggplant, sliced ½ inch
>   thick
>   12 to 15 small zucchini, cut in
>   2-inch chunks
>   12 small whole tomatoes
>   ¼ cup finely grated Parmesan
>   cheese
>   2 teaspoons grated lemon rind
>   3 tablespoons minced parsley

1. Preheat oven to 450° F. Peel away papery outer skin from garlic, leaving bulbs intact and cloves unpeeled. Place bulbs in a baking dish just large enough to hold them in one layer. Drizzle with olive oil and sprinkle with salt. Cover tightly with aluminum foil; bake 45 minutes. Transfer garlic to a clean plate (bulbs will not be completely tender).

2. In the same baking dish, place eggplant rounds and zucchini. Baste with oil remaining in the dish, adding more as needed to coat vegetables lightly. Salt lightly. Cover pan; bake 15 minutes. Transfer vegetables to another plate. Add tomatoes to the baking dish and bake uncovered until softened (12 to 15 minutes). Prepare a hot charcoal fire.

3. Stir together Parmesan, lemon rind, and parsley. Set aside.

4. Wrap garlic bulbs together in heavy-duty aluminum foil. Bury foil package in coals. Cook until cloves are fully soft (30 to 45 minutes).

5. Grill eggplant on each side until browned and softened (about 2 minutes per side). Arrange slices around the edge of a large serving platter. Grill zucchini on all sides until browned and softened (about 4 minutes). Arrange zucchini inside the eggplant ring. Grill tomatoes quickly and carefully (about 2 minutes); grill tomatoes quickly and carefully (about 2 minutes); arrange them inside the zucchini ring. Unwrap garlic package and place bulbs in the center of the platter. Garnish vegetables with Parmesan mixture.

Serves 12.

GRILLED SHRIMP WITH CHILES AND LIME

For best flavor and texture when grilling, select shrimp in the shell.

>   1 pound red bell peppers
>   2 tablespoons butter
>   ¼ cup olive oil
>   1 serrano or jalapeño chile,
>   seeded and minced
>   2 pickled peppers, seeded
>   and minced
>   ⅔ cup fresh lime juice
>   ¼ cup firmly packed dark
>   brown sugar
>   1 teaspoon ground turmeric
>   1 teaspoon ground cumin
>   2 tablespoons tomato paste
>   1 teaspoon kosher salt
>   4 pounds large shrimp
>   (10 to 12 per lb)
>   4 cups shredded greens
>   (romaine, spinach, escarole)

1. Roast peppers as directed in Roasting Bell Peppers and Chiles (see page 62). Chop coarsely; set aside.

2. In a medium saucepan over moderate heat, melt butter. Add oil, roasted peppers, chile, pickled peppers, lime juice, brown sugar, turmeric, cumin, tomato paste, and salt. Bring to a simmer and cook 1 minute. Cool slightly; transfer contents of pan to blender or food processor and blend until smooth.

3. Make a slit on the back of each shrimp, remove black vein; leave shell on. Place deveined shrimp in a stainless steel, glass, or enamel bowl; add pepper purée, cover, and refrigerate 30 minutes. Prepare a hot fire.

4. Grill shrimp until shells turn bright pink but flesh remains moist (about 5 minutes), basting often with marinade. Transfer shrimp to a platter mounded with shredded greens.

Serves 12.

SPARERIBS WITH MUSTARD AND WHISKEY

Use a fine Tennessee whiskey to spike this marinade and to give the ribs a true-blue American flavor. To keep the spareribs moist, they are baked until tender, then grilled just long enough to impart a smoky finish.

>   12 slabs (1½ to 2 lb each)
>   spareribs

Whiskey Marinade

>   1 navel orange
>   ¾ cup soy sauce
>   1½ cups firmly packed brown
>   sugar
>   2 tablespoons Worcestershire
>   sauce
>   ½ cup minced shallots
>   ¼ cup minced green onion, plus
>   ½ cup coarsely chopped green
>   onion, for garnish
>   1½ cups strong mustard
>   ¾ cup whiskey

1. Prepare Whiskey Marinade. Place ribs in large glass or earthenware bowls and slather with 2 cups marinade; reserve remaining marinade. Marinate 2 hours at cool room temperature or, preferably, cover and refrigerate overnight.

2. Preheat oven to 350° F. Set ribs on racks in roasting or baking pans; ribs should not touch. Roast until tender (1½ to 2 hours), basting occasionally with pan drippings and with additional 1 cup marinade. Prepare a hot charcoal fire.

3. Grill ribs, turning once, until well browned (5 to 10 minutes). Baste once or twice with remaining marinade. Pile ribs high on large platters. Garnish with chopped green onions.

Serves 12.

Whiskey Marinade Peel orange, removing all white pith. Section. Chop flesh fine. Combine orange and all remaining marinade ingredients in a bowl; whisk to blend. Cover and refrigerate for up to 2 days.

Makes about 6 cups.

...ON GRILLING

Getting the best from your outdoor grill involves practice, patience, and proper equipment. To aid your results:

☐ Allow 30 to 45 minutes for coals to burn down; when ready, they should be covered with a light ash. Cooking over a direct flame only burns the outside of the food, leaving the inside raw.

☐ Your hand is the best judge of when a fire is ready. If you can hold your hand over the fire at grill level for only 2 seconds, the fire is very hot; for 3 to 4 seconds, the fire is medium-hot; for any longer, the fire is not hot enough.

☐ Try to arrange the coals so that there are areas of the grill with no heat under them. That way, finished food can keep warm while the remainder of the meal cooks.

☐ Brush the grill lightly with oil before you put it over the fire to prevent food from sticking.

☐ Always keep the grill clean.

☐ To judge how many coals you need, first imagine the cooking surface that the food requires. Spread the coals in a single layer to cover an area about 1 inch past the edges that you have imagined. Add about half again as much charcoal, and you should have enough for 1 hour of heat. Usually 30 to 40 briquettes are enough to cook food for four people.

☐ Use indirect heat when cooking foods that are in an oil-based marinade or foods that contain a lot of fat. Set an aluminum pan or some heavy-duty aluminum foil underneath the grill, beneath the items being cooked, to catch drippings that would otherwise cause flare-ups. Arrange the hot coals on either side of the pan.

☐ To make a fire for slow cooking, as required for Sugar and Spice Smoked Pork Loin (see page 67), use about 25 briquettes on each side of the drip pan. Plan on adding 8 to 10 briquettes to each side for every hour of additional cooking time. For slow cooking, it is helpful to have a second grill so you can keep a mound of hot coals ready to stoke the main fire.

☐ To maintain optimal flavor and prevent accidents, do not squirt starter fluid onto the fire or add briquettes impregnated with starter fluid to coals already cooking.

☐ Briquettes? Mesquite charcoal? Hardwoods? Wood chips? To choose the right fuel, consider the special features of each: Briquettes are inexpensive, widely available, easy to use, and burn evenly and consistently; but they do not impart the appealing flavor of hardwoods or burn as hot. Mesquite charcoal burns very hot, cooking foods quickly and sealing in juices. It also imparts a more subtle, smoky flavor to foods than do hickory, oak, or fruit woods, making mesquite preferable for fish and delicate-flavored foods. Leftover pieces can be reused, which can't be said for briquettes. Hardwoods such as oak, hickory, and apple provide a flavorful smoky complement to food; the disadvantages are scarcity, price, and—most significant—the inability to burn as hot as mesquite. Hardwoods also take a long time to burn down to coals, and then don't burn very long. To provide maximum smoke, hardwood chips or chunks can be soaked in cold water for 30 minutes.

To combine the best of all worlds, try using mesquite charcoal as your fuel source and pre-soaked hardwood chunks as your smoke source. Hardwood chips and sawdust can be used to impart a smoky flavor to foods cooked over gas or charcoal briquettes.

YANKEE LEMON-MAPLE TART

Top a tangy lemon tart with a finely ground praline made from toasted almonds and pure maple syrup. The praline can also be folded into home-made Crème Fraîche to make a luscious sauce for the tart or for other desserts.

   1 recipe Basic Tart Dough (see page 69)
   8 eggs, separated
  ¾ cup plus ⅔ cup sugar
1⅓ cups freshly squeezed lemon juice
   4 tablespoons grated lemon rind
  ½ cup butter
     Pinch cream of tartar

Maple Praline

   1 cup pure maple syrup
   1 cup chopped toasted almonds

Crème Fraîche

   1 cup whipping cream, not ultra-pasteurized
   1 tablespoon buttermilk

1. Prepare Basic Tart Dough and bake according to directions on page 69. Cut tart dough in half. Roll each half on a lightly floured surface into a round ⅛ inch thick. Transfer each round to a 10-inch tart tin and trim to fit. Prick surface of dough well with a fork. Chill 1 hour. Preheat oven to 400° F. Bake tart shells until lightly browned (about 10 minutes). Let cool on racks.

2. In a large bowl whisk together egg yolks and ¾ cup sugar until mixture becomes pale and thick (about 3 minutes). Whisk in lemon juice and lemon rind.

3. In a large saucepan over low heat, melt butter. Cool slightly, then whisk in egg mixture. Return saucepan to low heat and cook, whisking constantly, until mixture thickens (5 to 7 minutes). Immediately remove from heat, cool slightly, cover with plastic wrap, then refrigerate until cold.

4. Preheat oven to 375° F. In a large bowl beat egg whites with cream of tartar to soft peaks; add remaining ⅔ cup sugar gradually, whisking to firm peaks. Stir one third of meringue into yolk mixture, then fold in remaining meringue. Pour mixture into prebaked tart shells. Dust each with 2 tablespoons Maple Praline.

5. Bake tarts until lightly browned and well risen (about 15 minutes). Transfer to a rack to cool; filling will fall slightly as it cools. At serving time, stir remaining Maple Praline into Crème Fraîche. Serve each slice with a dollop of maple-flavored cream on the side.

Makes two 10-inch tarts.

Maple Praline Lightly oil a baking sheet. In a small saucepan bring maple syrup to a boil over high heat and continue cooking until candy thermometer registers 300° F. Immediately remove from heat and stir in nuts. Pour mixture onto oiled sheet and let cool. Break into bits by hand. In a food processor or blender, grind to a powder. Store in an airtight container.

Makes 1 cup.

Crème Fraîche Combine whipping cream and buttermilk in a clean glass jar. Cover and shake well. Let stand at room temperature until thickened (24 to 36 hours). Refrigerate and use within 5 days.

Makes 1 cup.

MEDITERRANEAN SALAD SUPPER
For 8

Mezze:
Cool Cucumber Salad
Herb Custard
Feta Cheese
Greek Olives
Warm Pita Bread

Cracked Wheat Salad With Scallops And Green Beans

Warm Figs With Gorgonzola

California Sauvignon Blanc

Olives and olive oil, mint and garlic, figs and feta are foods that give a meal a Mediterranean flavor. Here, they lend a Greek allure to a menu of cool supper dishes, suitable for late-night, warm-weather dining.

Timetable

At least 3 days ahead: Make Dill Vinegar.

Up to 12 hours ahead: Make Herb Custard. Make Cool Cucumber Salad. Prepare cracked wheat salad.

Up to 1 hour ahead: Prepare figs for baking.

30 minutes ahead: Remove salad from refrigerator.

Planning

Throughout the eastern Mediterranean, meals often begin with an assortment of small dishes. Known as *mezze* in Greece, the spread almost always includes black olives, feta cheese, spiced yogurt, vegetable salads, and warm pita bread triangles for dipping.

This menu begins with a modest mezze, followed by a cool cracked wheat salad and baked figs. The meal is a perfect one to bring guests home to—say, after an evening concert—because all but the figs can be prepared beforehand.

It is well worth searching for a Middle Eastern or Mediterranean market that carries imported French, Bulgarian, or Greek feta; Greek Kalamata olives in brine; and pita bread delivered fresh daily.

A California Sauvignon Blanc would be an excellent choice with this informal supper.

Presentation

Set a table that suggests the beach, with votive candles in a sandy centerpiece and patterns of pastel stripes. The mezze is presented first, with each item in a separate serving piece. The dishes are cleared and a giant platter of cracked wheat salad takes their place. The figs and cheese can be presented on individual plates or family style.

A shady terrace is the perfect setting for this Mediterranean meal, but a porch or breezy kitchen would do nearly as well. Serving pieces and tableware should underline the menu's informal feel.

Photograph, page 41: A cool and colorful mezze—a Middle Eastern appetizer assortment—gets a Mediterranean Salad Supper under way. All the mezze dishes are served at once (clockwise from right): shiny Greek Kalamata olives, wedges of warm pita bread, tangy feta cheese, cucumbers in yogurt sauce with fresh dill, and a smooth herb custard.

COOL CUCUMBER SALAD

Homemade Dill Vinegar, ready in only three days, adds a distinctive note to cucumbers in yogurt. For best texture and flavor, choose a premium brand of whole-milk yogurt. Cucumbers other than the thin-skinned English or hothouse varieties should be peeled first.

2 *large English cucumbers, halved, seeded, and cut into ½-inch dice*
1 *tablespoon kosher salt*
2 *tablespoons Dill Vinegar*
2 *cups plain yogurt, preferably whole milk*
½ *teaspoon sugar*
3 *tablespoons minced red onion*
1 *green onion, minced*
2 *teaspoons minced garlic*
2 *tablespoons minced fresh dill*
2 *tablespoons olive oil*
  Salt, to taste
  Freshly ground black pepper, for garnish
  Fresh dill sprigs, for garnish

Dill Vinegar
1 *cup fresh dill sprigs*
1 *quart white wine vinegar*

1. Place diced cucumbers in a large colander; sprinkle with kosher salt and 1 tablespoon of the Dill Vinegar. Toss to blend. Let drain 30 minutes, then rinse and pat dry.

2. Transfer cucumbers to a large bowl. Add remaining tablespoon Dill Vinegar, yogurt, sugar, red onion, green onion, garlic, dill, and olive oil. Toss to blend, then season with salt. Cover and refrigerate 30 minutes. To serve, garnish with black pepper and dill sprigs.

Serves 8.

Dill Vinegar Steep dill sprigs in white wine vinegar for at least 3 days. Vinegar will keep indefinitely in a cool place.

Makes 1 quart.

HERB CUSTARD

This easy custard can be readied for the oven in 15 minutes. Once baked, its silky texture and herbal fragrance are a delight.

    5 tablespoons unsalted butter
    ⅓ cup minced shallots
    ¼ cup roughly chopped fresh
       basil
    ¼ cup roughly chopped parsley
    6 eggs
    ⅛ teaspoon nutmeg

    2 cups whipping cream
       Salt and freshly ground
       pepper, to taste

1. Preheat oven to 350° F. In a small skillet over moderately low heat, melt 4 tablespoons of the butter. Add shallots and sauté until softened (3 to 5 minutes). Remove from heat.

2. In a blender or food processor, combine shallot-butter mixture, basil, parsley, eggs, nutmeg, cream, salt, and pepper. Blend until smooth (about 1 minute).

3. With remaining tablespoon butter, grease eight ½-cup custard cups. Place cups in a roasting pan big enough to hold them without touching. Pour custard into cups and set pan in oven. Pour boiling water into roasting pan to come halfway up the sides of the cups. Bake until a knife inserted in the center comes out clean (15 to 18 minutes). Remove from oven and cool cups on a rack. Serve at room temperature or chilled.

Serves 8.

CRACKED WHEAT SALAD WITH SCALLOPS AND GREEN BEANS

Cooked cracked wheat tossed with scallops and a rainbow of summer vegetables makes a light but satisfying main-course salad.

2 *pounds bay scallops or sea scallops*

1½ *pounds fresh green beans*
Salt, to taste

2 *cups cracked wheat*

2 *red bell peppers*

2 *large tomatoes, seeded and diced*

½ *cup finely diced green cabbage*

2 *medium zucchini in ¼-inch dice*

6 *green onions, minced*

2 *heads butter lettuce*

Herb Vinaigrette

1 *small hot chile pepper, seeded and minced*

1½ *cups minced Italian parsley*

1 *cup minced fresh mint*

½ *cup minced cilantro*

5 *tablespoons apple cider vinegar*

¾ *cup olive oil*
Salt and freshly ground pepper, to taste

1. If using sea scallops, trim away any tough muscle. Steam bay or sea scallops over, not in, a large pot of boiling salted water until they taste done (bay scallops take only 1 minute or less; sea scallops 3 to 5 minutes). Cut sea scallops into quarters; leave bay scallops whole. Moisten with 2 tablespoons of the Herb Vinaigrette; cover and refrigerate.

2. Trim green bean tips. Cook in a large pot of boiling salted water until crisp-tender (5 to 7 minutes). Drain and plunge into a bowl of ice water to stop the cooking. When beans are completely cool, drain again. Cut into ½-inch pieces.

3. In a medium saucepan over high heat, bring 3 cups water with salt to a boil. Add wheat, cover, and remove from heat; let stand 30 minutes.

4. Roast peppers according to directions on Roasting Bell Peppers and Chiles (see page 62). Peel and dice.

5. In a large bowl combine peppers, tomatoes, cabbage, zucchini, green onions, cracked wheat, green beans, and scallops. Add remaining Herb Vinaigrette; toss with a fork to blend. Cover and refrigerate at least 2 hours or up to 12 hours.

6. Remove salad from refrigerator 30 minutes before serving. Wash and dry hearts of butter lettuce. Arrange lettuce leaves on a large serving platter. Spoon cracked wheat mixture onto center of platter.

Serves 8.

Herb Vinaigrette In a bowl combine chile, parsley, mint, cilantro, and vinegar. Whisk to blend; let stand 5 minutes. Gradually whisk in olive oil. Add salt and pepper.

Makes about 1¾ cups.

WARM FIGS WITH GORGONZOLA

The appeal of sweet figs with salty cheese is delightful. A nonsweet walnut or dense whole wheat bread would be a delicious companion.

2 *tablespoons honey*

1 *tablespoon lemon juice*

8 *large ripe figs*

¾ *pound Gorgonzola cheese*

¼ *pound cream cheese (optional)*

1. Preheat oven to 350° F. In a small saucepan combine honey and lemon juice and cook over low heat, stirring, until honey melts. Lightly brush outside of figs with honey mixture. Cut figs in half and place cut side up on a baking sheet. Lightly brush cut surfaces with honey mixture. Bake until warmed through and slightly softened (7 to 10 minutes). Remove from oven and let stand 10 minutes.

2. To serve, place warm figs on a platter accompanied by Gorgonzola in one piece. Or, serve each guest a small plate with 2 fig halves and a small wedge of Gorgonzola. If desired, Gorgonzola can be blended with cream cheese for a milder flavor and packed into a crock.

Serves 8.

HIKERS' PICNIC
For 6

Vegetable Chowder

Handwich

Cold Stuffed Chicken Legs

Hallie's High-Energy Bars

Chilled Water and Juice or Beer

Easy to carry, easy to eat, and substantial enough to revitalize weary muscles, this portable picnic is specially designed for hikers. Chowder and chicken, Handwiches and high-energy cookies will restore your strength as you take in a mountainside view.

Timetable

Up to 2 days ahead: Make bars.
Up to 1 day ahead: Make chowder. Stuff and bake chicken legs.
Up to 6 hours ahead: Prepare Handwich ingredients, but do not assemble.
1 hour ahead: Slice and wrap chicken legs. Assemble Handwiches.

Planning

A hearty soup and a sandwich prepare tired hikers for the trek home, with high-energy bars for added insurance. The meal is designed around foods that are easy to pack and unlikely to spill or spoil. For the cook's convenience, all preparation can be done up to six hours before leaving, with only the final assembly of sandwiches at the last minute.

No hiker should set forth without a good supply of liquids. Pack chilled water and juice or beer, unless you'll be passing a store on the way to the picnic site. You'll want to take along a bottle opener and a garbage bag for packing out trash.

Presentation

If the trail is at all demanding, hikers will want to carry as little as possible on their backs. To that end, this meal requires no plates or utensils.

Use large, colorful napkins or bandannas to bundle up a lunch for each backpack: a chicken leg and a foil-wrapped sandwich, with two date bars and a sturdy paper napkin tucked into a disposable soup cup. When unwrapped, the napkins make a handy placemat. If there's room, one hiker can pack a blanket to use as a ground-cover "tablecloth."

Photograph, page 44: An unfurled bandanna serves as a ground cloth for this revitalizing fare (clockwise from top left): a shredded-vegetable Handwich, hot chowder, date-filled energy bars, and a plump stuffed chicken leg.

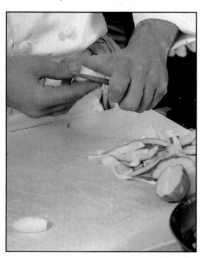

VEGETABLE CHOWDER

This chunky curried chowder is as good cold as it is hot. Pack it into a couple of widemouthed insulated containers and tuck them into two backpacks.

>   2 tablespoons butter
>   1 tablespoon olive oil
>   ½ cup chopped white onion
>   ½ cup minced green onion
>   1½ tablespoons minced garlic
>   ½ cup minced celery
>   ½ cup minced carrot
>   ½ cup peeled and minced
>   zucchini
>   2 cups peeled potatoes,
>   in ½-inch cubes
>   5 cups cauliflower florets
>   1 teaspoon curry paste or
>   powder, or more to taste
>   2 tablespoons lemon juice, or
>   more to taste
>   6 cups vegetable or chicken stock
>   ¼ cup fresh basil
>   ¼ cup minced parsley
>   Salt and freshly ground
>   pepper, to taste

1. In a large soup pot over moderately low heat, melt butter and add olive oil.

2. Add white onion, green onion, and garlic and sauté until fragrant (about 3 minutes).

3. Add celery, carrot, zucchini, potatoes, and cauliflower. Sauté 3 minutes.

4. Add curry paste, lemon juice, and stock. Cook until vegetables are tender (15 to 20 minutes).

5. Add basil, parsley, and salt and pepper. Add more lemon juice or curry, if desired. Serve hot or cold.

Serves 6.

PACKING LIKE A PRO

Packing safely and smartly is the first step to a successful picnic. Who wants to discover a broken bottle of vinaigrette in the hamper? The following tips should help you get your provisions to the site in good condition.

Keep cold foods cold. A Styrofoam container will do the job on short trips, but a good ice chest is a wise investment. Foods that spoil quickly—such as those containing fish, raw egg, or mayonnaise—should be packed tightly and surrounded with ice or an ice substitute.

If using ice to chill food, pack it in doubled plastic bags or garbage bags to reduce the chance of water seeping into the food containers. Choose large cubes over crushed ice; they melt more slowly.

Don't pack glass. Use sturdy plastic containers with tight-fitting lids, and tape the lids down securely.

Pack the items in reverse order of need. The picnic blanket, for example, should be on top; dessert can be on or near the bottom.

For convenience, it's nice to have a separate ice chest for beverages such as wine, water, and soda. Don't forget to pack a corkscrew, a bottle opener, and a can opener, if needed.

Always pack a sturdy garbage bag for trash. Extra paper towels come in handy, too.

Wrapping warm foods, such as fried chicken or muffins, in a double thickness of heavy-duty aluminum foil will help keep them warm.

Most variety stores carry a wide assortment of handsome and hardy picnic supplies. For portable meals, sturdy plastic plates and utensils and plastic tumblers for beverages are better choices than breakable items.

A good insulated container can keep soup or coffee hot for hours. Warm the inside first with boiling water, then drain.

HANDWICH

Middle Eastern pita bread makes a neat, handy pocket for layers of fresh vegetables and avocado sauce. The well-stuffed Handwiches, wrapped in aluminum foil, are easy to pack; to eat, simply peel back the foil as you go. Feel free to substitute other vegetables—mushrooms or peppers, for example—for those listed.

>   2 tablespoons lemon juice
>   1 large ripe avocado, peeled and pitted
>   1 to 2 teaspoons minced serrano chile
>   3 tablespoons olive oil
>   Salt and freshly ground pepper, to taste
>   Dash hot pepper sauce
> 1½ cups snow peas
>   6 pita breads
>   ¼ cup grated carrot
>   ¼ cup grated zucchini
>   3 ounces grated mozzarella
>   ¼ cup minced green onion
>   1 cup diced tomatoes
> 1½ cups shredded romaine lettuce

1. In a blender or food processor, combine lemon juice, avocado, 1 teaspoon minced chile, and olive oil. Blend until smooth; add salt, pepper, and hot pepper sauce, and add more chile to taste.

2. Blanch snow peas in a large pot of boiling salted water 10 seconds; drain and plunge into ice water to stop the cooking. Drain again and pat dry. Julienne snow peas and set aside.

3. In a steamer over hot water, steam pita breads until they are warm, pliable, and easy to open (about 3 to 5 minutes). Cut about 1½ inches off one side.

4. Stuff each pita with layers of snow peas, carrot, and zucchini. Top the last layer with some of the avocado sauce. Continue with layers of mozzarella, green onion, and tomato, adding a little sauce between each layer. Top with lettuce and wrap each sandwich carefully in foil.

Serves 6.

COLD STUFFED CHICKEN LEGS

Enjoy these sliced stuffed chicken legs as finger food at the picnic site, or take extra pita bread, lettuce, and mayonnaise (see Homemade Mayonnaise, page 88) for chicken sandwiches. Butchers should be willing to bone chicken legs for you; be sure to remove tough tendons before stuffing.

> 12 boned but unskinned chicken legs, tendons removed
>   Salt and freshly ground pepper, to taste
>   1 cup soft bread crumbs
>   ⅓ cup minced red onion
>   1 tablespoon minced garlic
>   6 large eggs, lightly beaten
>   1 cup roughly chopped fresh basil
>   ½ cup minced parsley
>   ¾ cup freshly grated Parmesan cheese
>   ⅓ cup coarsely chopped toasted walnuts
>   6 tablespoons melted butter
>   2 tablespoons tarragon vinegar or white wine vinegar
>   1 tablespoon paprika

1. Preheat oven to 350° F. Salt and pepper chicken legs on both sides.

2. Combine bread crumbs, onion, garlic, eggs, basil, parsley, Parmesan, walnuts, and 2 tablespoons of the melted butter. Mix well. Moisten with vinegar and toss to blend. Season with salt and pepper.

3. Lay each leg open, skin side down. Place about 2 tablespoons stuffing in the center of each leg, forming it into a log. Bring sides of legs up to enclose the stuffing and place legs seam side down in roasting pan.

4. Combine remaining melted butter and paprika and brush over rolled legs. Bake until juices run clear (20 to 25 minutes), basting occasionally with pan drippings. Let cool. Slice each leg on the diagonal about ½ inch thick. Reform slices into leg shape and wrap in plastic.

Serves 6.

HALLIE'S HIGH-ENERGY BARS

Use rolled oats, often labeled "old-fashioned oats," or quick-cooking rolled oats for this recipe. Do not use instant oatmeal.

>   1 cup flour
>   1 teaspoon cinnamon
>   ½ teaspoon mace
>   ¼ teaspoon nutmeg
>   2 teaspoons baking powder
>   1 teaspoon kosher salt
>   ½ cup sugar
>   1 cup cold butter, cut in small pieces
>   1 teaspoon vanilla extract
>   ¼ cup molasses
>   2 cups rolled oats
>   1 tablespoon grated orange rind

Date Filling

> 1½ cups pitted dates
>   ¼ cup white port
>   ½ cup water
>   1 tablespoon honey
>   ¼ cup orange marmalade

1. Sift together flour, cinnamon, mace, nutmeg, baking powder, and salt. *To prepare in a food processor:* Transfer sifted ingredients to work bowl along with sugar. Pulse briefly to blend. Add butter and vanilla and process until crumbly. Add molasses, oats, and orange rind and pulse just to blend. *To prepare by hand:* In a large bowl combine sifted ingredients and sugar; stir to blend. Cut in butter with two knives until mixture resembles coarse crumbs. Add vanilla, molasses, oats, and orange rind and stir.

2. Pat one half of crust mixture into an 8- by 11-inch pan. Spread Date Filling evenly over base. Top with remaining oat mixture. Bake until well browned (50 to 60 minutes). Cool on a rack. Cut into squares.

Makes 16 bars.

Date Filling Preheat oven to 325° F. In a medium saucepan combine dates, port, the water, and honey. Bring to a simmer: maintain simmer and cook until dates are very soft (about 10 minutes). Stir in marmalade and set aside to cool.

Makes 2½ cups.

ICE CREAM SOCIAL
For 16

Brown Sugar Cats' Tongues

Walnut Wafers

Old-fashioned Ice Cream Pie

Peaches and Cream Ice Cream

Clover Honey Ice Cream

Iced Tea or Lemonade and Coffee

This summer celebration is devoted to everyone's favorite indulgence: ice cream. All-you-can-eat in several flavors with a sea of cookies and toppings is a prospect that appeals to all ages.

Timetable

Up to 2 weeks ahead: Make Walnut Wafers.

Up to 1 week ahead: Make Chocolate Cookie Crust.

Up to 2 days ahead: Make Brown Sugar Cats' Tongues. Prepare Crème Fraîche.

1 day ahead: Make Clover Honey Ice Cream through step 2. Make Peaches and Cream Ice Cream.

Up to 1 day ahead: Make ice cream pie.

Planning

The charm of an old-fashioned Sunday afternoon social is its informality. Encourage guests to leave ties and silk shirts at home and to wear something that goes well with chocolate sauce. The casual format is a perfect one for a neighborhood block party or a birthday party for teens.

Check a store that specializes in cake-decorating supplies for ornamental candies suitable for topping ice cream. A party rental service (see page 102) can supply you with silver sundae dishes.

Set out pitchers of iced tea or lemonade and pots of hot coffee for self-service.

You can dazzle your guests with an array of sundae fixings from fruits to nuts. Here is just a glimpse of the possibilities.

Bitter chocolate sauce
Hot caramel sauce
Raspberry sauce
Marshmallow sauce
Butter-roasted pecans
Pistachios
Toasted, sliced almonds
Chopped macadamia nuts
Maple Praline (see page 38)
Grated coconut
Sliced peaches marinated in honey and lemon
Blueberries
Bananas
Strawberry or other homemade preserves
Candied lemon and orange rind
Crushed gingersnaps
Crushed peppermints
Round, flat candies, such as M&Ms
Shaved white and bittersweet chocolate
Pretzels
Chocolate-covered espresso beans
Whipped cream

Presentation

To keep guests circulating, present the party food in more than one room. The ice creams can be set in a kitchen sink or washtub and surrounded with ice. If possible, divide both ice creams into two 1-quart containers, and set up two separate ice cream stations to ease traffic flow.

Arrange the toppings on a kitchen table, with several spoons for each to keep the line moving. Add visual excitement to the table with a variety of pitchers, bowls, and candy dishes for the toppings. Hot toppings—such as caramel sauce and bitter chocolate sauce—should be in double boilers on the stove with ladles for self-service.

On a table in the dining room, arrange napkins, plates, spoons, cookies, ice cream pie, and coffee service. It helps to have a friend, or perhaps a child, serve the ice cream pie and then remove any uneaten portions before the pie starts to melt. Guests can then move onto the patio or into the living room to eat.

Yellow napkins and white plates give this menu a sunny summer feel, with yellow and white daisies carrying out the scheme. Tulip-shaped parfait glasses contribute to the soda-fountain theme, and glass bowls give guests room to work in.

Photograph, page 47: Peaches and Cream Ice Cream with crisp Brown Sugar Cats' Tongues (left) and a luscious Old-fashioned Ice Cream Pie with whipped cream topping (right) highlight a summer Ice Cream Social.

BROWN SUGAR CATS' TONGUES

Crisp "cats' tongue" cookies are the perfect foil for smooth ice cream.

½ *cup plus 2 tablespoons flour*
¼ *teaspoon ground cinnamon*
 Pinch salt
 Pinch nutmeg
¼ *cup unsalted butter, at room temperature*
¼ *cup firmly packed dark brown sugar*
¼ *cup firmly packed light brown sugar*
2 *egg whites, beaten until frothy*

1. Preheat oven to 400° F. Sift together flour, cinnamon, salt, and nutmeg. *To prepare in a food processor:* Put butter and sugars in work bowl and pulse until smooth. With machine running, add egg whites; pulse 2 seconds. Add dry ingredients and pulse just until no flour remains

on surface. *To prepare with an electric mixer:* Cream together butter and sugars until light. Add egg whites and beat to blend. On lowest speed, add dry ingredients and beat just until blended.

2. Transfer batter to a pastry bag fitted with a ¼-inch plain or star tip. Pipe 2-inch lengths onto a buttered baking sheet, about 2½ inches apart. Bake until edges are a light brown color (about 5 minutes). Cool 2 minutes on baking sheet, then transfer cookies to a rack to finish cooling. Store them in an airtight container and use within 2 days.

Makes about 6 dozen small tongues.

WALNUT WAFERS

You might want to make a double batch of these buttery shortbread wafers. They keep well and taste nice with a cup of hot tea.

    1   cup flour
    1   cup coarsely ground toasted
        walnuts
    ½   cup butter, softened
    2   tablespoons confectioners'
        sugar
    3   tablespoons superfine sugar
    2   teaspoons vanilla extract

1. Preheat oven to 325° F. In a small bowl combine flour and walnuts and stir to blend. With an electric mixer cream butter with confectioners'

sugar and 2 tablespoons of the superfine sugar until light. Beat in vanilla. On lowest speed, add flour and nut mixture, beating just until blended.

2. Press dough into a buttered 8- by 10-inch baking pan. Prick top well with a fork. Dust with remaining superfine sugar. Bake until cookies are a rich golden brown (15 to 20 minutes). Cut immediately into 36 bars. Cool completely in pan, then transfer them to serving platter. Cookies can be stored in an airtight container for 2 weeks or frozen for up to 2 months.

Makes about 3 dozen wafers.

OLD-FASHIONED ICE CREAM PIE

Turn storebought ice cream into a dream of a pie in no time flat. To gild the lily, add toasted nuts and garnish with whipped cream and chocolate cookie crumbs.

- 1½ quarts vanilla ice cream, softened slightly
- 1½ quarts chocolate ice cream, softened slightly
- 1 cup mixed chopped toasted nuts
- 2 tablespoons amaretto liqueur or fruit brandy (optional)
- 1 cup lightly sweetened whipped cream, for garnish
- 2 ounces grated white chocolate, for garnish (optional)
- 2 ounces grated bittersweet chocolate, for garnish (optional)

Chocolate Cookie Crust

- 3 cups chocolate cookie crumbs
  Pinch salt
- 1 teaspoon cinnamon
- ½ teaspoon nutmeg
- 1 teaspoon instant espresso coffee powder
- ¾ cup butter, melted
- ¼ cup ground almonds

1. In a large bowl place both vanilla and chocolate ice cream and stir together quickly to marble. Stir in nuts and liqueur, if used. Spoon into chocolate crust and return to freezer. Freeze until solid.

2. Just before serving, garnish with whipped cream, white chocolate, and bittersweet chocolate, if used.

Makes one 12-inch pie or two 8-inch pies.

Chocolate Cookie Crust In a large bowl combine all ingredients and stir to blend. Spoon into a 12-inch springform pan or into two 8-inch cake pans with removable bottoms. Pat firmly onto bottom and press ¾-inch up the sides. Chill overnight or freeze for up to 1 week.

Makes one 12-inch crust or two 8-inch crusts.

Variations Caramel or pistachio ice cream may be substituted for the vanilla or chocolate ice cream.

PEACHES AND CREAM ICE CREAM

The classic marriage of peaches and cream succeeds in an ice cream, too. Here, brown sugar and Crème Fraîche impart intriguing flavor and texture.

- 2½ pounds ripe peaches, peeled and roughly chopped
- 2 tablespoons brandy (optional)
- 1 cup whipping cream
- ½ cup milk
- ½ cup half-and-half
- 1 whole vanilla bean, split lengthwise
- 4 egg yolks
- 6 tablespoons dark brown sugar
- 6 tablespoons light brown sugar
- 1 cup Crème Fraîche (see page 38)

1. Place peaches in a large bowl and sprinkle with brandy, if used. Let marinate at least 1 hour at room temperature or cover and refrigerate overnight. In a food processor or blender, purée peaches.

2. In a large saucepan combine cream, milk, and half-and-half. Scrape vanilla seeds into the milk mixture, then add whole bean to milk. Bring to a simmer over moderate heat and remove from heat.

3. In a medium bowl whisk together egg yolks and sugars. Add hot milk to egg mixture gradually, whisking constantly. Return mixture to a clean, large saucepan. Cook over moderate heat, stirring constantly with a wooden spoon, until mixture reaches 180° F. It will visibly thicken and coat the spoon. Do not allow to boil. Immediately remove from heat; strain through a fine sieve into a bowl set over ice. Return vanilla bean to mixture. Stir until cool.

4. Stir puréed peaches into cooled custard along with Crème Fraîche. Cover and chill at least 6 hours or overnight. Transfer mixture to ice cream freezer and freeze according to manufacturer's directions. Allow ice cream to mellow in freezer at least 1 hour before serving.

Makes 2 quarts.

CLOVER HONEY ICE CREAM

For maximum flavor, use a fragrant, top-quality clover honey.

- 4 cups whipping cream
- 2 cups milk
- ½ cup sugar
- ½ cup clover honey
- ½ teaspoon salt
- 1 vanilla bean, split lengthwise
- 6 egg yolks
- 1 teaspoon vanilla extract

1. In a large saucepan combine cream, milk, sugar, honey, and salt. Scrape vanilla seeds into saucepan then add whole vanilla bean. Cook over low heat, stirring, until honey melts (about 5 minutes).

2. In a medium bowl whisk egg yolks. Add warm cream mixture to egg yolks gradually, whisking constantly. Return mixture to a clean, large saucepan. Cook over moderate heat, stirring constantly with a wooden spoon, until mixture reaches 180° F (8 to 10 minutes). Mixture will thicken visibly and will coat the back of the spoon. Do not allow to boil. Immediately strain into a bowl set over ice. Stir in vanilla extract and return vanilla bean to mixture. Stir until cool, then cover and chill 24 hours.

3. Transfer mixture to ice cream freezer and freeze according to manufacturer's directions.

Makes 2 quarts.

menu

**SOUTHERN FISH FRY
For 6**

Cornmeal-Fried Fish

Black-eyed Salad

Smothered Greens, Hocks, and Corn

*Sweet Onion and Tomato Salad
(See Planning)*

Lemon and Sour Cream Tarts

Iced Tea or Cold Beer

---

*On a balmy summer night,
guests gather on the porch
for a family-style southern
fish fry. Crisp fried fish piled
high on a platter and bowls
of steaming smothered
greens and black-eyed peas
are edible proof of just how
good home cooking can be.*

Timetable

Up to 3 days ahead: Make Tartar Sauce. Make tart dough.

Up to 2 days ahead: Soak black-eyed peas. Prepare sour cream topping for tart.

Up to 1 day ahead: Cook black-eyed peas. Make tart filling.

Up to 6 hours ahead: Dress black-eyed peas. Prepare seasoned flour for fish.

2 hours ahead: Roll tart dough.

1 hour ahead: Assemble and bake tarts.

Up to 1 hour ahead: Prepare greens through step 2.

30 minutes ahead: Remove black-eyed peas from refrigerator.

At serving time: Flour and fry fish. Finish cooking greens.

Planning

Good fried fish cannot be prepared ahead; it must be rushed from pan to table with guests at the ready. A meal centered around fried fish should be a casual one, with friends who might even be recruited for frying duty. The onions and tomatoes for the salad can be sliced about an hour before dinner and dressed with a simple vinaigrette.

All these dishes except dessert can be presented at once. The tarts can be served away from the table, if desired, with coffee. With dinner, offer pitchers of iced tea or cold beer.

Presentation

This down-home menu calls for a no-fuss setting. Place your table on the porch or in the shade of a tree, then give it a country look with rusitc tableware and muslin napkins.

Feathery flowers and herbs can make impromptu bouquets for the table, tucked into antique mason jars or Depression glass.

Photograph, page 50: A warm earthenware plate holds cornmeal-coated fillets, smothered greens and corn, and onion and tomato salad. Refills stand ready (from left): greens, black-eyed peas, and sizzling fish.

CORNMEAL-FRIED FISH

Choose a firm, lean white fish such as snapper, cod, or catfish for these cornmeal-fried fillets. If you have two large skillets, you can fry all the fish at once; otherwise, work in batches to avoid overcrowding the pan.

- ½ cup flour
- ½ cup yellow cornmeal
- 1 teaspoon cayenne pepper
- ½ teaspoon freshly ground black pepper
- ½ teaspoon powdered bay leaves
- 2 teaspoons kosher salt
- 2½ pounds fish fillets
- ½ cup (approximately) peanut or corn oil, for frying
- 3 tablespoons minced green onion, for garnish
- 1 teaspoon grated lemon rind, for garnish

Tartar Sauce

- 1 whole egg
- 2 egg yolks
- 2 tablespoons lemon juice
- 1 cup corn oil
- 2 green onions, minced
- 2 tablespoons minced sweet pickle
- 1 tablespoon minced parsley
- 1 tablespoon minced fresh dill
- 1 tablespoon capers
- Salt and cayenne pepper, to taste

1. Stir together flour, cornmeal, cayenne pepper, black pepper, bay leaves, and salt. Place dry ingredients on a plate or on a sheet of waxed paper. Dip fish fillets in flour mixture and shake off excess. Transfer floured fillets to a clean plate.

2. In a large skillet heat 3 tablespoons of the oil over moderate heat. Fry fish in batches, turning once, until golden on both sides. Add more oil to pan as necessary. Transfer fried fish to paper towels to drain briefly, then place them on a platter in a warm oven until all fish are done. Garnish with a mixture of green onion and lemon rind, and serve immediately with Tartar Sauce.

Serves 6.

Tartar Sauce In a small bowl, combine egg, egg yolks, and lemon juice and whisk well. Add oil drop by drop, whisking constantly to make a mayonnaise. Stir in green onions, pickle, parsley, dill, and capers. Season with salt and cayenne pepper.

Makes 1¾ cups.

BLACK-EYED SALAD

Most Southerners think of black-eyed peas as a hot side dish, but the peas are also pleasing as a marinated salad. Taste and adjust seasoning just before serving, as the balance of flavors can shift.

1½ cups dried black-eyed peas
 2 pounds ham hocks
 1 bay leaf
 1 onion, minced
 2 teaspoons minced garlic
 1 red bell pepper, minced
 1 green bell pepper, minced
 3 green onions, minced
 ½ cup minced celery
 1 cup seeded and diced tomato
 ¾ cup parsley, minced
 5 tablespoons white vinegar
 ¾ cup peanut or corn oil
 2 teaspoons minced orange rind
    Salt and freshly ground
    pepper, to taste

1. Soak black-eyed peas overnight in water to cover. Drain and place in a large pot; cover with cold water. Add ham hocks, bay leaf, onion, and garlic. Bring to a simmer over high heat, then reduce heat to maintain a simmer. Cover and cook until peas are tender (about 1½ hours). Drain and discard bay leaf. Remove hocks and reserve for use in Smothered Greens, Hocks, and Corn (see page 51). Cool peas completely.

2. Place cooled peas in a large bowl and add red and green peppers, green onions, celery, tomato, and parsley. In a small bowl whisk together vinegar, oil, and orange rind. Add dressing to peas and mix gently. Season with salt and pepper. Cover and chill. Remove from refrigerator 30 minutes before serving; taste and adjust seasoning if necessary.

Serves 6.

SMOTHERED GREENS, HOCKS, AND CORN

Greens and fresh corn are combined in this colorful southern side dish and braised together with bits of boiled ham hock.

> 2 pounds ham hocks, boiled until tender, reserved from Black-eyed Salad (see page 50)
> 1½ pounds chard, washed and dried
> 3 tablespoons butter
> 1 tablespoon lard or corn oil
> 1⅓ cups coarsely chopped onion
> 1 pound mustard greens or spinach, washed, trimmed, and coarsely chopped
> ¾ cup chicken or pork stock
> 2 cups fresh raw corn kernels
> ¼ cup minced parsley
> Salt and freshly ground pepper, to taste
> Lemon juice, to taste
> Cider vinegar, for accompaniment
> Hot pepper sauce, for accompaniment

1. Trim meat from hocks and chop coarsely; set aside. Separate the chard ribs from the leaves. Chop the leaves coarsely and chop the stems into ½-inch pieces.

2. In a large skillet melt butter and lard over moderately low heat. Add onion and sauté until slightly softened (about 3 minutes). Add ham, chard leaves, chard ribs, chopped greens, and stock. Bring to a simmer, cover, and reduce heat to maintain a simmer. Cook 10 minutes.

3. Uncover and add corn. Cook uncovered until corn is done and greens are tender (about 5 more minutes). Stir in parsley, salt, and pepper, and a few drops lemon juice. To serve, offer cider vinegar and hot pepper sauce on the side.

Serves 6.

LEMON AND SOUR CREAM TARTS

The fresh flavor of lemon is particularly appealing after a fried fish dinner. Here, a sweet nut crust is baked with a lemon filling, then drizzled with a sour cream sauce.

> 6 tablespoons butter, at room temperature
> ⅓ cup sugar
> 2 teaspoons cornstarch
> Pinch salt
> 2 eggs
> 2 egg yolks
> ½ cup lemon juice
> 1 tablespoon lemon rind
> 1 teaspoon vanilla extract
> Whole mint leaves, for garnish

Almond Tart Dough

> ½ cup plus 1 tablespoon flour
> ⅓ cup ground almonds
> 1 teaspoon lemon rind
> 2 tablespoons sugar
> Pinch salt
> ¼ teaspoon cinnamon
> 4 tablespoons cold butter, cut into small pieces
> 1 egg yolk
> 1 tablespoon heavy cream

Lemon Sour Cream Topping

> 1 cup sour cream
> 2 tablespoons lemon juice
> 1 tablespoon orange liqueur
> 1 tablespoon brown sugar

1. With an electric mixer cream butter; add sugar gradually and beat until light. Sift cornstarch and salt over mixture and beat. In a small bowl whisk together eggs and egg yolks; add to mixture and beat to blend. Add lemon juice, lemon rind, and vanilla and beat until blended. Use immediately or cover and refrigerate for up to 1 day.

2. Prepare Almond Tart Dough. Reduce oven heat to 350° F. Divide lemon filling among tart shells. Return to oven until filling is firm (15 to 20 minutes). Cool on rack. Just before serving, drizzle tarts with Lemon Sour Cream Topping and garnish with a mint leaf.

Makes six 2½- to 3-inch tarts or one 9-inch tart.

Almond Tart Dough

1. *To prepare in a food processor:* Place flour, almonds, lemon rind, sugar, salt, and cinnamon in work bowl. Pulse to blend. Add butter and pulse until mixture resembles coarse crumbs. In a small bowl whisk together egg yolk and cream. Add to mixture and pulse just until blended. *To prepare by hand:* Stir together flour, almonds, lemon rind, sugar, salt, and cinnamon. Cut in butter until mixture resembles coarse crumbs. In a small bowl whisk together egg yolk and cream. Add to mixture and toss with a fork until mixture begins to come together.

2. Shape dough into a flat disk and wrap in plastic. Chill at least 2 hours or up to 3 days. Dough may also be frozen for up to 1 month.

3. Preheat oven to 400° F. Lightly butter six 2½- to 3-inch tart pans or one 9-inch tart pan. On a lightly floured surface, roll Almond Tart Dough ⅛ inch thick. Cut dough rounds with a lightly floured cutter and press into prepared pans. Prick all over with the tines of a fork. Place in freezer 1 hour. Bake until barely golden (8 to 10 minutes); remove from oven and cool slightly.

Makes enough dough for six 2½- to 3-inch tarts or one 9-inch tart.

Lemon Sour Cream Topping In

a small bowl, combine sour cream, lemon juice, liqueur, and brown sugar. Cover and refrigerate for up to 2 days.

Makes 1¼ cups.

A PRACTICAL GUIDE TO THE PARTY BAR

"Be prepared" is as good a motto for the home bartender as it is for the Boy Scouts. Here's a practical guide to the party bar, with suggested equipment and supplies, a few mixing guidelines, and special drink recipes.

Spirits

Benedectine liqueur
Blended whiskey
Bourbon whiskey
Brandy or Cognac
Canadian whiskey
Cream liqueurs
Crème de cacao
Crème de menthe
Dark rum
Dry sherry
Dry vermouth
Gin
Kahlua liqueur
Light rum
Medium sherry
Pernod liqueur
Rye
Scotch whisky
Sweet vermouth
Tequila
Triple Sec or Grand Marnier liqueur
Vodka

Equipment

Bar spoons (or iced-tea spoons)
Cocktail napkins
Cocktail shaker
Combination bottle-cap
    remover/can opener
Corkscrew
Electric blender
Flat cocktail strainer
Ice bucket
Ice tongs
Jigger
Lemon juicer
Lemon peeler
Muddler
Stainless steel paring knife
Swizzle sticks
Towels

Supplies

Bitter lemon
Bitters
Carbonated water (club soda)
Cocktail onions
Cola
Eggs
Ginger ale
Grapefruit juice
Green olives (pitted, unstuffed)
Grenadine
Lemons
Limes
Maraschino cherries
Oranges
Pineapple juice
Sugar, superfine and confectioners'
Sugar syrup
Tomato juice
Tonic water

Mixing Do's and Don'ts

1. Always make one round at a time. Discard any "overpour," which would dilute the following round.

2. Always use the best ingredients—the best liquors, the best juices, the best mixers. A bad mixer can spoil even the best liquor.

3. Never reuse the ice in the shaker.

4. Shake vigorously those cocktails meant to be shaken; don't "rock."

5. Measure ingredients carefully. Measurements of alcoholic beverages are typically given in ounces, perhaps because the standard measuring device is a jigger and a jigger contains 1½ ounces. One ounce equals 2 tablespoons.

6. Use fresh lemons, limes, and oranges for juice.

7. Use superfine or confectioners' sugar where sugar is called for. It dissolves more easily than does granulated sugar.

8. Don't serve overly sweet or overly creamy drinks before dinner.

9. Use cracked ice or ice cubes for shaken drinks; shaved ice melts too fast and dilutes the drink before it chills it.

10. Make sure carbonated beverages are fresh and cold. Do not use if flat. Always add carbonated beverages and mixers last.

RED WINE COOLER

    1 bottle (750 ml) red wine
    1 stick cinnamon
    4 whole cloves
    6 tablespoons fresh lemon juice
    ¼ cup superfine sugar
    2 cups carbonated water
    6 slices lemon

1. Uncork wine bottle and put cinnamon and cloves in it; recork and set aside for 2 to 12 hours.

2. In each of 6 tall, frosty glasses, put 1 tablespoon lemon juice and 2 teaspoons sugar. Stir well, then add ½ cup of the spiced wine, being careful to strain out the spices. Add ⅓ cup sparkling water to each glass, stir again, add ice cubes, and float a lemon slice on top.

Makes 6 servings, about 7 ounces each.

WHITE WINE COOLER

    2 teaspoons fresh lime juice
    ⅓ cup dry white wine
    ⅓ cup lemon-lime soda
    2 drops grenadine (optional)
       Lime slice

In a tall, frosty glass combine lime juice, white wine, and soda. Stir to blend. Add grenadine, if used; stir and add ice. Garnish rim of glass with lime slice. (see photograph opposite, top left).

Makes 1 serving, about 6 ounces.

CHAMPAGNE WITH RASPBERRY LIQUEUR

    ½ ounce raspberry liqueur
    5 ounces chilled Champagne or
       sparkling wine

Put liqueur in a Champagne flute. Add Champagne or sparkling wine; stir and serve.

Makes 1 serving, about 5 ounces.

BELLINI

Some say this inviting drink originated at Harry's Bar in Venice.

> 1 large ripe peach, peeled and pitted
> 2 teaspoons water
> 1 teaspoon superfine sugar
> Lemon juice, to taste
> Chilled sparkling wine, to taste

In a blender or food processor, purée peach with the water and sugar. Add lemon juice to taste and blend again. Put 1½ tablespoons peach purée in each of four Champagne flutes. Fill with sparkling wine and stir (see photograph, center left).

Makes 4 servings, about 6 ounces each.

CHAMPAGNE COCKTAIL

> 1 sugar cube
> Angostura bitters
> Chilled Champagne or sparkling wine, to taste
> Lemon twist

Saturate sugar cube with a dash or two of bitters. Put cube in Champagne flute and add one ice cube. Fill with Champagne. Top with a lemon twist.

Makes 1 serving, about 5 ounces.

SUMMER MINT CUP

> ¼ cup superfine sugar, or more to taste
> 1 bottle (750 ml) white wine
> ½ cup loosely packed mint leaves
> 2 oranges
> ½ bottle (750 ml) chilled sparkling wine

1. In a punchbowl combine ¼ cup sugar and 1 cup of the white wine. Stir until sugar dissolves. Bruise mint leaves slightly with your fingers and add to bowl along with remaining white wine. Cover and let macerate in refrigerator for 2 to 3 hours.

2. To serve, remove mint with a slotted spoon. Add juice of both oranges. Taste and add more sugar if necessary. Gently stir in the sparkling wine. Serve in Champagne flutes.

Makes 8 servings, about 6 ounces each.

SANGRIA

> ⅓ cup sugar, plus more as needed
> ½ cup brandy
> 5 oranges, each cut into 12 thin wedges
> 3 lemons, sliced thin
> ½ cup orange liqueur
> 10 cups dry red wine
> 1 quart club soda

1. In a large bowl combine sugar, brandy, 36 orange wedges, and lemon slices. Let steep at room temperature for 2 hours.

2. Add liqueur and wine and taste; add more sugar, if desired. Add club soda, stir, and taste again for sweetness. Add remaining orange wedges. Stir briskly. Pour over a block of ice in a punchbowl or pitcher (see photograph, right) or divide among glasses half-filled with cracked ice.

Makes 20 servings, about 6 ounces each.

EGGNOG

> 1 dozen eggs, separated
> 2 cups superfine sugar
> 2 cups brandy
> 2 cups dark rum
> 1 cup bourbon
> 4 pints whipping cream
> Freshly grated nutmeg

1. In large bowl, either by hand or with electric mixer, beat egg yolks until light and thick. Add sugar slowly and beat until very light and fluffy. Gradually add brandy, beating well. Let mixture steep at room temperature for 2 hours.

2. Add rum and bourbon to egg yolk mixture, beating well. Beat in cream. Chill mixture several hours or overnight.

3. In large mixing bowl beat egg whites to soft peaks. Fold gently into egg-cream mixture. Taste; adjust sugar, liquor, or cream as necessary. Serve in old-fashioned (6 ounce) glasses with a dusting of nutmeg on top (see photograph, bottom).

Makes 24 servings, about 6 ounces each.

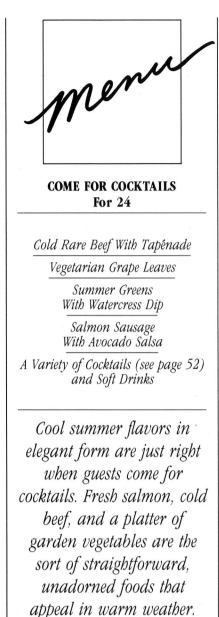

COME FOR COCKTAILS
For 24

Cold Rare Beef With Tapénade

Vegetarian Grape Leaves

*Summer Greens
With Watercress Dip*

*Salmon Sausage
With Avocado Salsa*

*A Variety of Cocktails (see page 52)
and Soft Drinks*

---

*Cool summer flavors in
elegant form are just right
when guests come for
cocktails. Fresh salmon, cold
beef, and a platter of
garden vegetables are the
sort of straightforward,
unadorned foods that
appeal in warm weather.*

Timetable

At least 3 days ahead: Make
Tapénade.

Up to 3 days ahead: Make Watercress Dip: Stuff and bake
grape leaves. Prepare Crème
Fraîche.

Up to 1 day ahead: Make Salmon
Sausage and Avocado Salsa.
Roast beef.

Up to 8 hours ahead: Prepare
vegetables for dipping.

Planning

For cooks, the typical American cocktail party is a puzzling hybrid, more
substantial than drinks-before-dinner
but less than a meal. The menu must
answer varied needs. Some guests will
go on to dinner elsewhere; others
may make an entire meal of the
cocktail nibbles. In any case, the fare
should be hearty and abundant
enough to cushion the cocktails.

Cocktail-party fare should also be
easy to make ahead, so the host can
feel free to mingle. Unless your home
can offer most guests a place to sit,
finger food is the best option. The
dishes in this menu could be arranged on trays and passed with
cocktail napkins. Or, the trays could
be stationed at strategic points
around the room, with small plates or
napkins alongside. It is a good idea
to position food around the room to
give guests a reason to circulate.

Presentation

With the exception of the greens, all
of the hors d'oeuvres in this menu
can be served from passed trays. If
you don't have serving help, you'll
want to make up two trays of each
and set the two in opposite ends of
the party area.

To keep the look cool and light,
arrange salmon sausage and beef
rounds on clear glass trays. Shells are
a pretty summer motif for garnishing
platters or using as serving pieces.
You can serve the watercress dip in a
large shell and present the greens on
a flat wicker tray, for example. You
might also use small shells around
the edge or in the center of a platter
of grape leaves.

You may want to set out small
plates so guests can help themselves
to several items at once. Even if you
have servers passing three of the hors
d'oeuvres, a stack of plates beside the
greens and dip will encourage guests
to help themselves more generously.
Forks are unnecessary.

Photograph, page 55: A summer
cocktail spread has cool appeal when
it includes (clockwise from top left):
grape leaves, salmon sausage with
avocado, cold beef with olive paste,
and crisp seasonal greens.

COLD RARE BEEF
WITH TAPÉNADE

The pungent olive paste called
tapénade is popular in southern
France, where it's used as a sandwich
spread, a pasta sauce, a cocktail
spread, or a relish. Here, it adds zest
to open-faced cocktail sandwiches of
rare roast beef.

> 36 slices French bread (2 in.
> diameter and ¼ in. thick)
> 2 pounds lean, rare roast
> beef fillet, sliced thin
> ¼ cup finely minced chives,
> for garnish

Tapénade

> 1½ pounds Kalamata olives
> 3 ounces anchovies
> 2 teaspoons minced garlic
> ⅓ cup capers
> ⅓ cup olive oil
> Freshly ground pepper, to taste
> Additional olive oil

Lightly brush bread rounds with some
of the oil that rises to the surface of
the Tapénade. Lay a slice of beef on
each round. Top with a small spoonful of Tapénade. Garnish with chives.

Makes 36 open-faced rounds.

Tapénade Remove pits from olives.
Place anchovies and garlic in food
processor and process to a paste. Add
olives, capers, and olive oil and pulse
until blended but not puréed. Season
with pepper. Tapénade should be
made 2 to 3 days in advance to allow
flavors to mellow. Place in a glass
jar, cover top with olive oil, cover
and refrigerate. It will keep for up to
1 month if undisturbed.

Makes about 4 cups.

VEGETARIAN GRAPE LEAVES

A barley-based stuffing with fresh herbs and vegetables takes these grape leaves out of the ordinary. Vegetarians will want to use water instead of chicken stock in the recipe.

- 1 large jar (about 2 lb) grape leaves, pickled in brine
- ¼ cup butter
- 2 tablespoons olive oil
- ¼ cup shallots
- 2 tablespoons minced garlic
- 1½ pounds mushrooms, finely chopped
- ¼ cup dry vermouth or white wine
  Salt and freshly ground pepper, to taste
- 3 cups chicken stock or water
- ½ cup barley
  Grated rind of 1 lemon
- ½ cup minced red bell pepper
- ½ cup minced yellow squash
- ⅓ cup minced celery
- ⅓ cup minced fresh basil
- ⅓ cup minced fresh mint
- 2 tablespoons minced parsley
- 1 large head romaine lettuce, washed and separated
- 1 cup orange juice
- 3 to 4 sprigs fresh mint
  Lemon wedges, for garnish

1. Preheat oven to 350° F. In a large pot of boiling water, blanch grape leaves for 30 seconds. Drain and plunge into ice water to stop the cooking. Drain again and pat dry. Lay flat on paper towels. You should have 40 to 50 leaves.

2. In a large skillet over low heat, melt butter and oil. Add shallots and garlic and sauté 5 minutes. Add mushrooms and vermouth. Mushrooms will exude liquid; cook until liquid evaporates (about 30 minutes). Season with salt and pepper.

3. In a small pan bring 1 cup of the chicken stock to a boil over high heat and add barley. Cover, reduce heat to low, and cook 20 minutes.

4. In a large bowl combine mushroom mixture, barley, lemon rind, red pepper, squash, celery, basil, mint, and parsley. Season with salt and pepper.

5. Place a small amount of filling on each grape leaf and wrap like an envelope, enclosing stuffing. Place outer leaves of romaine on the bottom of a roasting pan and place stuffed grape leaves on top of lettuce.

6. Combine remaining chicken stock and orange juice and pour gently into sides of pan, taking care not to pour directly on top of grape leaves. Place whole mint sprigs on top of grape leaves and cover tightly with aluminum foil. Bake 25 minutes. Cool to room temperature in liquid, then refrigerate for up to 3 days; bring to room temperature before serving. To serve, arrange on a platter and garnish with lemon wedges.

Serves 24.

SUMMER GREENS WITH WATERCRESS DIP

Cool colors and crisp textures appeal to summer appetites. If possible, visit a farmers' or produce market for slender young green beans and just-picked sugar snap peas.

- 2 pounds green beans
- 1 pound sugar snap peas
- 2 large English cucumbers
- 4 heads romaine

Watercress Dip

- 2 large bunches watercress, stems removed
- 2 tablespoons lemon juice
- 3 egg yolks
- 2 teaspoons herb mustard or honey mustard
- 1 cup safflower oil or vegetable oil
- ½ cup olive oil
- 3 tablespoons Crème Fraîche (see page 38)
- 2 green onions, minced
  Salt and freshly ground pepper, to taste
  Additional lemon juice (optional)

1. In a large pot of boiling salted water, blanch green beans until tender-crisp. Remove with a large wire-mesh strainer and plunge into ice water to stop the cooking. Drain

again and pat dry. In the same pot of water, blanch sugar snap peas 15 seconds; drain and plunge into ice water to stop the cooking. Drain again and pat dry.

2. Cut cucumbers into 3-inch spears. Wash and dry romaine; remove outer leaves, reserving only the hearts.

3. To serve, arrange green beans, cucumber spears, romaine hearts, and sugar snap peas on a platter and accompany with Watercress Dip.

Serves 24.

Watercress Dip In a large pot of boiling salted water, blanch watercress 10 seconds. Drain and plunge into ice water to stop the cooking. Drain again and squeeze dry in clean kitchen towels. Combine lemon juice, egg yolks, and mustard and whisk to blend. Add safflower oil and olive oil in a slow steady stream, whisking constantly to make a mayonnaise. Stir in Crème Fraîche and green onions. Fold in watercress; chill thoroughly. Just before serving, season with salt and pepper, adding more lemon juice, if desired.

Makes about 3 cups.

SALMON SAUSAGE WITH AVOCADO SALSA

This distinctive salmon mousse flavored with avocado was inspired by Arizona chef Ralph Peterson. For an elegant sit-down dinner, arrange sliced salmon and salsa on individual plates and omit the bread rounds.

- 3 cups dry white wine
- 1 cup water
- 1 bay leaf
- 2 sprigs fresh thyme or ½ teaspoon dried thyme
- 3 parsley stems
- 2 pounds salmon fillet, skinned and cut into 2-inch cubes
- 1½ cups whipping cream
- 2 eggs
- 1 tablespoon kosher salt
- 1½ teaspoons freshly ground white pepper
  Vegetable oil
- 36 slices French bread (2 in. diameter and ¼ in. thick)

Avocado Salsa

- 4 ripe tomatoes, peeled, seeded, and chopped
- 3 green onions, minced
- 1 serrano chile, seeded and minced, or more to taste
- 1 cucumber, peeled, seeded, and chopped
- ⅓ cup minced cilantro
- 2 avocados, slightly firm but ripe, in ¼-inch dice
- 2 tablespoons lime juice, or more to taste
  Kosher salt, to taste

1. Prepare Avocado Salsa. Then in a large roasting pan or fish poacher, combine wine, the water, bay leaf, thyme, and parsley. Bring to a simmer over high heat, then reduce heat to maintain a simmer.

2. In a food processor combine salmon, cream, eggs, salt, and pepper, in batches if necessary. Process until smooth; do not overprocess or cream will turn to butter. Stir in ½ cup Avocado Salsa by hand.

3. Oil 2 large pieces of parchment paper or plastic wrap. Divide mixture in half and spoon each half down the center of the oiled paper in a 10-inch-long line. Roll securely into a tight sausage shape and twist the ends. If using plastic wrap, overwrap with aluminum foil. Lower packages into simmering poaching liquid and poach until firm (about 20 minutes). Carefully lift out and set aside to cool. Chill thoroughly.

4. To serve, unwrap mousse and slice ¼ inch thick. Place a slice on each bread round and top with a small spoonful of Avocado Salsa. Serve immediately.

Makes 3 dozen rounds.

Avocado Salsa In a large bowl combine tomatoes, green onions, chile, cucumber, cilantro, avocado, and lime juice. Stir gently to blend. Season with salt. Mixture may be made up to 1 day ahead, covered, and chilled. If making ahead, add salt just before serving.

Makes about 4 cups.

Menu

LUNCH ON THE BOAT
For 8

Green Bean Soup in a Mug

Antipasto Sandwich

Fresh Fruit Skewers

Chocolate Rum Macaroons

Iced Tea and Beer

Fresh air and sunshine seem to wake up appetites. When all hands come on deck for lunch during a day of sailing, waterskiing, or fishing, the fare should be hearty and handy—such as soup in a mug, a well-stuffed sandwich, and mouth-watering cookies.

Timetable

Up to 4 days ahead: Bake macaroons.
Up to 3 days ahead: Make pesto.
Up to 1 day ahead: Make soup. Cook and marinate artichokes.
Up to 12 hours ahead: Prepare fruit.
Up to 2 hours ahead: Assemble sandwiches.

Planning

Because few boats have the luxury of a spacious galley, this menu requires no on-site cooking. The soup is made ahead and packed, either hot or cold, into insulated containers.

The sandwiches, well-wrapped in aluminum foil, benefit from a few hours of marinating. The fresh fruit can be skewered before leaving shore; however, if seas are calm, it's fun to let guests spear their own. For safe-keeping, pack macaroons in a sturdy, decorative cookie tin. You'll want to pack napkins and paper plates, but note that the food needs no utensils.

The most refreshing drinks for a day on the water come from an ice chest stocked with iced tea and beer.

Presentation

Pack the lunch in a large, flat basket lined with red-and-white-checked tea towels, which serve as napkins once the meal is unpacked. Plastic storage containers, mugs, plates, and utensils are best for a day on the water.

Photograph, page 58: Green bean soup and a hearty sandwich (at bottom) satisfy hungry boaters, with fresh fruit skewers and chocolate macaroons (at top) for dessert.

FRESH FRUIT SKEWERS

Thread melon balls and grapes on 6-inch wooden skewers for easy service.

- 2 cups watermelon balls
- 2 cups cantaloupe balls
- 2 cups honeydew balls
- 4 cups grapes, in assorted colors
- 3 tablespoons lemon juice
- 1½ tablespoons honey

1. In a large plastic container or in several smaller containers, combine watermelon, cantaloupe, honeydew, and grapes.

2. In a small saucepan combine lemon juice and honey. Cook over low heat, stirring, until honey melts. Cool, then drizzle over fruits and toss.

3. Skewer fruits just before serving, or offer skewers and bowls of fruit and allow guests to spear their own.

Serves 8.

GREEN BEAN SOUP IN A MUG

This quickly made soup with fresh summer basil is ready to change with the weather. On warm days, chill it well and pack it in an ice chest or insulated container. If the day is chilly, nothing feels more warming than a mug of hot soup. You can pack it hot in insulated containers, or reheat it slowly in the galley just before serving.

- 3 tablespoons olive oil
- 1 tablespoon butter
- ½ cup minced onion
- 1 shallot, minced
- 3 cups green beans, in 1-inch lengths
- 1 quart chicken or vegetable stock, preferably homemade
- 1 cup half-and-half
- 1 cup whipping cream
- Salt and freshly ground pepper, to taste

Pesto

- 1 tablespoon minced garlic
- 3 tablespoons toasted pine nuts
- ½ cup fresh basil leaves
- ½ cup chopped cooked spinach
- 1 teaspoon kosher salt
- ⅓ cup olive oil
- ⅓ cup freshly grated Parmesan

1. In a medium skillet over moderate heat, warm olive oil and butter. Add onion and shallot and sauté until softened (about 5 minutes).

2. In a large pot of boiling salted water, blanch green beans until almost tender. Cooking time will depend on maturity of beans; test often. Drain beans and plunge into a bowl of ice water to stop the cooking. When completely cool, drain again.

3. In a medium pot over high heat, bring stock to a simmer. Add onion, shallot, and beans; return to a simmer, then reduce heat to maintain a simmer and cook 5 minutes.

4. Purée mixture in a food processor or blender, in batches if necessary. Transfer to a plastic storage container and stir in half-and-half and cream. Season to taste with salt and pepper. Chill if desired.

5. *To serve hot:* Reheat soup over moderate heat; do not allow to boil. Ladle soup into 8 mugs and top each portion with a small spoonful of pesto garnish, or swirl pesto through the soup. *To serve cold:* Whisk garnish into soup, then ladle into mugs.

Serves 8.

Pesto Combine garlic, pine nuts, basil, spinach, salt, and olive oil in a food processor or blender and mix until smooth. Transfer to a plastic container; stir in cheese by hand.

Makes about 2 cups.

ANTIPASTO SANDWICH

The components of a good antipasto—artichoke hearts, tomatoes, prosciutto and cheese—are also the makings of a fine portable sandwich.

- 8 medium artichokes
- 3 tablespoons lemon juice
- ½ cup olive oil
- ⅓ cup cider vinegar
- 1 lemon, sliced thin
- 1 bay leaf
- 1 tablespoon kosher salt
- 1 tablespoon minced fresh oregano or 1 teaspoon dried oregano
- 8 fresh Italian-style sandwich rolls (about 6 in. long)
- 8 ounces sliced prosciutto or other ham
- 8 ounces sliced fontina cheese
- 4 tomatoes, sliced

1. Peel away and discard dark green artichoke leaves until you reach the pale green heart. Trim stem end; cut about 1 inch off the top with a serrated knife. Cut artichokes in half. With a small spoon, scrape away the fuzzy choke. Brush artichokes all over with lemon juice. Place in a bowl, add olive oil, and stir to coat.

2. In a large pot combine 1 quart water, cider vinegar, sliced lemon, bay leaf, salt, and oregano. Bring to a boil over high heat and cook 5 minutes. Drain artichokes, reserving oil; add artichokes to boiling liquid, reduce heat to maintain a simmer, and cook until artichokes are very tender (12 to 15 minutes). Remove artichokes from liquid with a slotted spoon and set aside. Reduce poaching liquid over high heat to 1 cup, then strain through a fine sieve. Combine artichokes, reduced poaching liquid, and reserved olive oil.

3. Cut rolls in half lengthwise and pull out about a third of the insides. Brush halves with some of the juices from the artichokes. Salt each half lightly. On bottom half, layer artichokes, prosciutto, cheese, and tomatoes. Top with upper half and wrap in aluminum foil. Serve cold or reheat.

Serves 8.

CHOCOLATE RUM MACAROONS

These nutty meringue cookies can be served direct from a decorative tin or piled high in a small basket and served alongside the fruit.

- 4 ounces ground almonds
- ¼ cup granulated sugar
- 1 tablespoon brown sugar
- 3 tablespoons grated bittersweet chocolate
- 1 tablespoon dark rum
- 2 egg whites
- Pinch salt
- ½ teaspoon almond extract
- 16 whole blanched almonds

1. Preheat oven to 350° F. In a blender combine ground almonds, 2 tablespoons of the granulated sugar, and brown sugar; blend until very fine. Transfer to a mixing bowl and stir in chocolate and rum.

2. Beat egg whites and salt to soft peaks. Add remaining granulated sugar and beat until firm. Beat in almond extract.

3. Gently fold egg whites into nut mixture. Oil a heavy baking sheet and line with parchment paper. Fit a pastry bag with a ½-inch star tip and pipe 16 mounds onto baking sheet. Or, drop mounds onto baking sheet with a spoon dipped in cold water. Stud each cookie with a whole almond and bake until peaks are golden brown (about 20 minutes). Let cool 5 minutes, then remove from sheet and finish cooling on rack. Store in an airtight container.

Makes 16 macaroons.

**MEXICAN PATIO PARTY
For 20**

Stuffed Chiles

Shrimp Burros

Grilled Vegetable Fajitas

Strawberry Tequila Sherbet

*Iced Beer and Sangria
(see page 53)*

Bright colors, lively flavors, and a stereo playing a salsa beat are good ways to lend a Latin flavor to a party. Corn, chiles, avocados, and shrimp give this patio meal its south-of-the-border flair.

Timetable

Up to 1 day ahead: Prepare sherbet.

Up to 8 hours ahead: Boil and shell shrimp.

Up to 6 hours ahead: Prepare vegetable skewers. Prepare tomato salsa.

Up to 4 hours ahead: Stuff chiles. Prepare avocado sauce for *burros.*

Up to 2 hours ahead: Shred lettuce for burros. Slice and marinate berries, if desired.

Planning

You'll want to set up three service tables on the patio or the lawn. On one table, organize a self-service bar with iced beer, water, and glasses. You might also want to hire a helper to make blended daiquiris here at the start of the party and to handle grilling chores at mealtime. As soon as guests arrive, bring out the platter of Stuffed Chiles and set it on the bar table alongside a stack of plates, forks, and napkins. Guests can help themselves to appetizers when they get their drinks.

You'll also want to set up a table on each side of the grill—one for the *burros,* the other for the *fajitas.* The shrimp burro filling goes on one table along with a stack of plates and napkins. On the other table, you'll need more plates and napkins as well as the salsa for the fajitas and a stack of skewered vegetables ready for grilling. Guests can step up to the grill when hunger strikes and take the food to a table or eat standing.

When the coals are dying down and the fireflies are warming up, bring out a tray of wineglasses filled with sherbet.

Presentation

Transport your guests to the tropics with lush hibiscus and paper flowers in torrid tropical colors. Import stores are a good source for table runners and fringed napkins in lively Latin stripes. Piñatas and earthenware platters will enhance the Mexican theme.

This casual meal is well suited to stand-up eating, although you'll want to have tables and chairs for those who prefer to sit. There's no need to set formal tables, however. Simply outfit the dining tables with bright-colored cloths to match the service tables, and add candles or a festive centerpiece. Guests can bring plates, napkins, and glasses along with them to the tables.

Photograph, page 61: (from top) A cooked tomato salsa and an avocado salsa accompany lime-marinated shrimp, Grilled Vegetable Fajitas (at right), and corn-stuffed Anaheim chiles in this Latin-American-inspired menu.

SHRIMP BURROS

When made with a large flour tortilla, the burrito becomes a *burro.*

> 5 *pounds shrimp, boiled and shelled*
> 4 *tablespoons lime juice*
> 1 *cup minced white onion*
> 4 *cups chopped tomatillos, canned or freshly cooked*
> 2 *serrano or jalapeño chiles, minced*
> ½ *cup minced cilantro*
> 1 *clove garlic, minced*
> 4 *large ripe avocados*
> 1 *teaspoon ground cumin*
> ¼ *cup minced green onion*
> *Salt, to taste*
> 6 *to 8 cups shredded iceberg or romaine lettuce*
> *Lime wedges, for garnish*
> *Fresh cilantro, for garnish*
> 24 *large (10 in.) flour tortillas*
> *Sour cream, for garnish*

1. Cut shrimp into large chunks. Place in a large bowl and add 2 tablespoons of the lime juice; toss.

2. In a food processor or blender, in batches if necessary, combine white onion, tomatillos, chiles, ¼ cup of the cilantro, garlic, and avocados. Blend briefly; mixture should still be slightly chunky. Transfer to a bowl and stir in remaining 2 tablespoons lime juice, cumin, remaining ¼ cup cilantro, green onion, and salt. Cover and chill avocado sauce.

3. Mound lettuce on a large platter. Top with shrimp. Garnish with lime and cilantro. Cover and chill up to 2 hours; remove from refrigerator 30 minutes before serving.

4. Heat tortillas briefly on a charcoal grill. To serve, place hot tortillas in a cloth-towel-lined basket next to lettuce-lined shrimp platter, a bowl of the avocado sauce, and a bowl of sour cream.

5. To make burros, guests fill tortillas to taste with shrimp and lettuce, avocado sauce, and sour cream, and add a squeeze of lime, if desired. After filling, fold tortilla like an envelope.

Serves 20.

Step·by·Step

ROASTING BELL PEPPERS AND CHILES

To remove the papery outer skin of bell peppers and chiles, first blister the skin thoroughly, then let the vegetables steam until cool in a tightly closed bag. Peeled bell peppers are delicious in salads, pasta dishes, and sandwiches; peeled whole chiles can be seeded and stuffed, minced, or puréed for use in such dishes as salsas, soups, and stews.

1. *Char peppers over an open gas flame or charcoal fire or under a broiler. Turn often until blackened on all sides. Transfer peppers to a paper or plastic bag; close and let steam until cool (15 to 20 minutes).*

2. *Peel peppers; halve; remove stem and seeds. Lay halves flat and use dull side of a small knife to scrape away any bits of black skin and stray seeds.*

GRILLED VEGETABLE FAJITAS

Traditionally, *fajitas* are made with sliced beef or chicken, grilled quickly with onions, and wrapped in corn tortillas. Here, the concept gets a twist, with skewered vegetables in place of the meat. The vegetables come off the grill and their skewers into hot, soft corn tortillas. You will need forty 8-inch bamboo skewers, soaked in water for one hour.

> 2 *large eggplants, in ¾-inch cubes*
> 1 *tablespoon salt*
> 4 *green bell peppers, halved, deribbed, seeded, and cut into 1-inch squares*
> 2 *red onions, cubed*
> 2 *pints cherry tomatoes*
> 2 *pounds zucchini, in ½-inch chunks*
> 2 *pounds small mushrooms*
> 1 *cup olive oil*
> ½ *cup vegetable oil*
> *Salt and freshly ground pepper, to taste*
> 24 *corn tortillas (6 in.)*

Cooked Tomato Salsa

> 5 *pounds ripe tomatoes*
> 1 *large yellow onion, chopped*
> 1 *tablespoon minced serrano chile, or more to taste (optional)*
> ½ *cup vegetable oil*
> 2 *tablespoons lime juice*
> ½ *cup roughly chopped cilantro, plus 2 tablespoons minced cilantro for garnish*
> *Salt, to taste*

1. Sprinkle eggplant cubes with 1 tablespoon salt; toss well to coat. Place in a colander and let drain 30 minutes. Rinse and pat dry.

2. Prepare a medium-hot charcoal fire. Thread skewers with eggplant cubes, bell pepper, red onion, cherry tomatoes, zucchini, and mushrooms. Whisk together olive oil and vegetable oil; season with salt and pepper. Drizzle seasoned oil over vegetables.

3. Grill vegetables, basting often with seasoned oil, until lightly charred and softened (5 to 7 minutes). Heat tortillas on charcoal grill. To serve, push vegetables off skewers into hot corn tortillas and top with Cooked Tomato Salsa.

Serves 20.

Cooked Tomato Salsa

1. Preheat broiler. Core tomatoes; cut an X in the bottom of each one. Place on a baking sheet. Put sheet 6 inches from heat and broil until blackened on all sides. Transfer to a plastic bag to steam. When cool enough to handle, slip off skins.

2. Place tomatoes in blender or food processor along with onion and chile. Blend briefly; salsa should still be chunky.

3. In a large skillet over medium heat, warm vegetable oil. Add tomato mixture and simmer until slightly reduced and thickened (about 12 minutes). Stir in lime juice and chopped cilantro. Season with salt and add more chile, if desired. Transfer to a serving bowl and garnish with minced cilantro.

Makes about 6 cups.

STUFFED CHILES

For a stand-up appetizer, set out a platter of mild Anaheim chiles filled with spicy corn stuffing.

> 24 *Anaheim chiles*
> 4 *cups cooked, fresh corn kernels*
> ½ *cup minced white onion*
> 2 *teaspoons minced hot green chile pepper*
> ½ *cup Homemade Mayonnaise (see page 88)*
> ¼ *cup sour cream*
> 1 *teaspoon mustard*
> 2 *tablespoons lemon juice*
> 1 *teaspoon grated lemon rind*
> ⅓ *cup minced cilantro*
> *Salt, to taste*
> ¼ *cup minced green onion, for garnish*

1. Preheat broiler. Prepare chiles as directed in Roasting Bell Peppers and Chiles (see page 62) through step one. After peeling, do not halve them. Instead, carefully slit the chiles along one side and scrape out the seeds. Set chiles aside.

2. In a large bowl combine corn kernels, onion, minced chile, mayonnaise, sour cream, mustard, lemon juice, lemon rind, cilantro, and salt. Using a teaspoon, fill chiles with corn mixture and place, seam side down, on a platter. Cover and chill. Serve each guest a whole chile, garnished with minced green onions.

Serves 20.

STRAWBERRY TEQUILA SHERBET

Give strawberry sherbet a Latin kick with a little tequila and lime, then spoon the spiked sherbet over sliced strawberries in balloon wineglasses. For best results, use only premium liquor and sweet, ripe berries.

> 2 cups sugar, or more to taste
> 2 quarts strawberries
> ¾ cup fresh lime juice
> ¾ cup tequila, or more to taste
> ½ cup orange-flavored liqueur
> 1 egg white

1. In a large saucepan combine sugar and 1 quart water. Bring to a boil over high heat, swirling pan until sugar dissolves; boil 3 minutes, then set aside.

2. Wash, dry, and remove stems from strawberries. Place half the berries in a blender or food processor with lime juice, tequila, liqueur, and egg white; blend until smooth (3 to 4 seconds). Transfer to a bowl and stir in sugar syrup to taste. Cover and chill at least 2 hours or up to 1 day. Transfer to ice cream freezer and freeze according to manufacturer's directions.

3. Slice remaining berries. If desired, sprinkle with additional tequila and sugar and let marinate 30 minutes. To serve, divide berries among 20 glasses, preferably balloon wineglasses. Top each portion with a scoop of sherbet.

Serves 20.

LIGHTS AND MUSIC

Lighting and music are two of the tools that help set the mood of a party. Creative thinking about these two elements can go a long way toward giving a party tremendous style at little expense.

Should the music be soft or loud, classical or jazz? Or should you play music at all? A cocktail party almost always benefits from some lively background music, especially as the first few guests arrive. The music eliminates awkward silences, sets a festive mood, and forces guests to speak a little louder than they otherwise might. As more people arrive and the noise level rises, the volume of the music can be gradually lowered.

Obviously, a string quartet will give a party a much more subdued mood than would jazz or rock. Choose music that corresponds to the effect you're trying to create and to the likely preferences of your guests.

You probably won't have time during the party to be bothered with changing records and deciding on the next selection. Take the time beforehand to organize your records, choosing enough music to fill the evening. You might want to appoint a youngster to be in charge of the stereo during the party. Even easier, if you have access to the equipment, is to make some long-playing tapes of selections from your favorite albums.

Theme parties provide even more opportunities for the creative disc jockey. For a Mexican Patio Party (see page 60), you can accentuate the theme with Latin music; a paella party (see page 24) calls for the strains of a flamenco guitar. A used record store can supply you with inexpensive recordings, and many libraries lend records.

If budget and space allow, consider hiring professional musicians. A string trio at a Champagne reception or a fiddler at a chili feed can lend memorable flair to a party.

Many people say that music is out of place at a formal dinner. Use your own good judgment about the desirability of music at your dinner parties. Should you choose to use it, make sure it is suited to a formal occasion and that it is kept at a low volume. Extraloud music is always distracting and inadvisable. Never play music so loud that your guests have to shout or have difficulty hearing each other.

Lighting is another element that requires sophisticated and thoughtful use for best effect. At a children's party or a high-spirited dinner, such as the Fare From the Fifties party (see page 87), bright lights set a lively mood. At other times, subdued lighting is more appropriate.

A centerpiece candelabra or a cluster of candles can give an intimate, glamorous feel to a dinner table. Before you depend entirely on the light from such an arrangement, have a practice run a night or two before. The candles may need to be supplemented by a dim overhead electric light.

Candles or hurricane lamps add drama to a buffet, but you should make sure they provide enough light for guests to see what they're choosing.

In a spacious home you can create several different environments with lighting. For a cocktail party you might light the main party area well, but leave some corner seating areas dimly lit. A roaring fire in the fireplace in an otherwise dimly lit area can offer an intimate setting away from the traffic.

Safety is also an issue when plotting your lighting scheme. Candles are rarely a good idea at a children's party, and even at an adult function, the candles should be placed where they are unlikely to be upended. Lighting should always be sufficient to allow guests to see rugs, steps, and stairs. Insufficient lighting can be dangerous if you're serving food with small bones or shells. For an evening function, make sure that guests have a well-lit path between their cars and your home.

AN·OPEN·HOUSE

Mr. Vic... ...
30 Kin... ...
San ... ... A J4103

Russet fabrics and feathers and
new-crop apples and pecans set a
harvest theme and give seasonal
flair to cool-weather party menus.

Autumn Menus

Autumn hosts can take advantage of the fall market bounty in parties for festive occasions. A local football game can prompt a Pregame Tailgate picnic (see page 84); a postgame group might convene at a Wassail Open House (see page 66). At a Halloween party for children (see page 73), young revelers can gather for such holiday treats as Pumpkin Muffins and a steaming "witch's caldron." Adults might fête an autumn birthday with retrospective Fare From the Fifties (see page 87), such as Alphabet Soup and Dagwood Sandwiches. Perennially useful tips on preparing for unexpected guests are revealed in the Special Feature on Quick Cocktail Nibbles (see page 76).

AUTUMN ENTERTAINING

A chill in the autumn air gives a boost to appetites and prompts menu makers to plan more robust fare. Roast meats, hearty stews, and rich desserts fortify guests and replace energy lost raking leaves.

Pork and beef return to the table, replacing summer's fish and chicken. Cheese-based dishes and courses have renewed appeal. Hot soup and warming drinks, such as a simmering wassail or hot cider, are welcome.

Wines with autumn meals should be relatively full-bodied and rich. Among whites, look to Chardonnay, French white Burgundy, or white Rhône wines. For red wines, consider California Zinfandel, Pinot Noir, or Cabernet Sauvignon; French Burgundy or Bordeaux; or Italian Chianti Classico, Barbera, or Barbaresco.

Cocktail parties know no season, but an autumn date has advantages. By avoiding the crush of the holiday season, you stand a better chance of getting a good turnout. To distinguish your endeavor from the usual cocktail party, consider giving the evening an Italian theme (see page 90).

Fall brings leisurely weekends and a yen for bigger morning meals, since no one is rushing off to the beach or the lake. An invitation to a bountiful brunch of French Buckwheat Crêpes (see page 70) is likely to find plenty of enthusiastic takers.

The autumn produce market offers a harvest of fresh yams, hard squashes, and pumpkins for eating and for carving; juicy apples—red, green, and gold; fresh almonds, walnuts, pecans, and filberts; fat green and purple grapes; Bosc, Anjou, and Comice pears; bright green broccoli; and firm, pale green fennel with its feathery leaves. Bell peppers and eggplant peak in early autumn, giving way to celery root and cabbage.

Nature's own colors suggest appealing color schemes for fall: Russet, brown, gold, maroon, olive green, ivory, navy blue, and rich purple are hues well suited to an autumn table. Leaves, pinecones, marigolds, and mums, and the wealth of new-crop nuts are among the inviting materials you can use to grace a fall table.

**WASSAIL OPEN HOUSE
For 24**

Wassail Bowl

Sugar and Spice Smoked Pork Loin

Dilled Celery Root Rémoulade

Pickled Relish Platter (see page 113)

Savory Stilton Tart

Chunky Applesauce (see page 115)

Baskets of Grapes and Pears

Dried Figs

Toasted Almonds

Irish Fruitcake

Sparkling Cider, White Wine, Coffee, and Tea

"Waes Hael!" ("Good Health!") is the appropriate Saxon toast when clinking glasses of spicy wassail. While the fragrant brew warms your guests, the buffet table beckons with home-smoked pork, a creamy celery root rémoulade, fruit cake doused with dark beer, and a warm Stilton and walnut tart.

Planning

Few large parties are as easy on the cook as this one, as most preparations take place before the day of the party. The Savory Stilton Tart must be filled and baked shortly before guests arrive, but both the dough and the filling are made ahead. The Wassail Bowl is the only last-minute dish.

To round out the buffet table, compose baskets of fresh grapes and pears and candy dishes of halved dried figs and whole toasted almonds.

As well as wassail, offer sparkling cider or white wine, coffee, and tea.

Presentation

To minimize traffic congestion, you can set two buffet tables. On the larger table put pork loin, celery root, pickled relish, and applesauce with dinner plates and flatware; on the smaller table put fresh and dried fruits, almonds, tart, and cake with dessert plates and forks. Wassail and wine can be on the large table; coffee and tea on the other. Surround the Wassail Bowl with a holly wreath for a festive holiday look, or use a willow as a dramatic backdrop.

Photograph, page 68: Steaming wassail complements a hearty buffet of (from top) a dense fruitcake nestled in a basket of fresh fruit, pork loin, celery root, and squares of Stilton tart.

Timetable
Up to 1 week ahead: Make fruitcake. Make pickles.
Up to 4 days ahead: If smoking pork loin 2 days ahead, marinate garlic.
Up to 2 days ahead: Smoke pork loin. Make Crème Fraîche.
Up to 1 day ahead: Make applesauce. Prepare filling for Stilton tart.
1 day ahead: Make tart dough for Stilton tart.
Up to 12 hours ahead: Make celery root.
Up to 2 hours ahead: Fill and bake Stilton tart.
30 minutes ahead: Bake apples for wassail.
At serving time: Make wassail.

WASSAIL BOWL

Sugar-roasted apples rest in the bottom of the Wassail Bowl, lending sweetness to this fragrant holiday brew. Wassail should be drunk while it's hot; depending on the pace of your party, you may prefer to have a bartender or kitchen helper make half a batch of wassail at a time.

12 green apples, quartered and cored
5 cups firmly packed brown sugar
½ cup chopped fresh ginger
5 cloves
3 cinnamon sticks
2 teaspoons ground ginger
1 teaspoon ground mace
1 tablespoon freshly grated nutmeg
2 gallons dark beer
3 bottles (750 ml each) sherry
18 eggs, separated
3 cups brandy

1. Preheat oven to 350° F. In a large baking dish or roasting pan, toss apples with 1 cup of the sugar. Bake until apples soften and sugar caramelizes (about 30 minutes).

2. Tie fresh ginger, cloves, and cinnamon sticks in a cheesecloth bag. In a large stockpot over moderate heat, place cheesecloth bag, remaining 4 cups sugar, ground ginger, mace, nutmeg, beer, and sherry. Bring to a simmer.

3. In a large bowl whisk egg yolks or beat with a handheld electric mixer until pale (5 to 7 minutes). In a separate bowl, beat whites until they are stiff but not dry. Fold yolks gently into whites.

4. Remove spice bag from beer mixture. Gradually, 1 tablespoon at a time, add 1 cup simmering beer mixture to eggs, whisking constantly. Then add remaining beer mixture somewhat faster, whisking constantly. Whisk in brandy.

5. In a warm punch bowl, place hot apples. Pour egg-beer mixture into bowl. Serve Wassail immediately in warm cups.

Serves 24.

DILLED CELERY ROOT RÉMOULADE

The knobby, gnarly celery root isn't much to look at, but its mild celery flavor is worth discovering. French cooks dress it with a mustardy rémoulade sauce; here, some minced dill adds a distinctive touch.

5 pounds celery root
¼ cup lemon juice
Salt and freshly ground pepper, to taste
Dill sprigs, for garnish
1 tablespoon minced fresh dill, for garnish

Rémoulade Sauce

3 egg yolks
2½ tablespoons Dijon mustard
¼ cup white wine vinegar
½ cup fresh lemon juice, or more to taste
2 cups olive oil
3 tablespoons minced fresh dill
1 tablespoon grated lemon rind
Salt and freshly ground pepper, to taste

1. Peel celery root. Cut into strips about 1½ inches long and ⅛ inch wide. Immediately place in a bowl of water acidulated with lemon juice.

2. Drain celery root thoroughly and pat dry. In a large bowl combine celery root and Rémoulade Sauce. Toss to blend. Cover and refrigerate at least 4 hours, or overnight.

3. To serve, taste and adjust seasoning. Mound salad in a bowl or on a platter. Surround with feathery dill sprigs and garnish top with additional minced dill.

Serves 24.

Rémoulade Sauce In a blender or food processor, place egg yolks and mustard. Blend until smooth. Add vinegar and ½ cup of the lemon juice and blend again. With motor running, add olive oil in a slow, steady stream to make a mayonnaise. Transfer to a bowl and stir in dill and rind. Season with salt and pepper and more lemon juice, if desired.

Makes 3½ cups.

SUGAR AND SPICE SMOKED PORK LOIN

Slow cooking over coals imbues these pork loins with a subtle, smoky flavor from end to end; a spice rub gives them a marvelous crust. Boned, rolled, and tied, the loins are easy to carve in neat slices. You will need a covered grill to smoke the pork.

1 cup olive oil
¼ cup butter, melted
1 tablespoon garlic, minced
½ cup kosher salt
⅓ cup firmly packed brown sugar
1 tablespoon each ground cinnamon and ground mustard
2 teaspoons ground bay leaf
1 teaspoon thyme
¾ teaspoon cayenne pepper
2 boneless pork loins (6 lb each), rolled and tied

1. In a clean jar combine olive oil, butter, and garlic. Cover and let stand at room temperature for 4 to 8 hours, or refrigerate for up to 2 days. Bring to room temperature before using.

2. In a large baking dish, stir together salt, sugar, cinnamon, mustard, bay leaf, thyme, and cayenne. Roll pork in mixture, patting it on liberally. Place pork loins in a baking dish, cover, and refrigerate 12 hours.

3. Bring pork to room temperature. Prepare a slow (about 250° F) charcoal or hardwood fire in a grill (see Grilling, page 38). Lightly brush pork with oil-butter mixture and place pork on racks above coals. Cover and cook until internal temperature of pork reaches 160° F (7 to 8 hours). Baste every 2 hours with butter-oil mixture. Add more firewood or charcoal as necessary, keeping temperature inside grill as constant as possible.

4. Remove cooked pork from smoker; cool completely before slicing. If desired, cooled pork may be wrapped in plastic and refrigerated for up to 2 days. Bring to room temperature before serving. To serve, cut pork in thin slices and arrange on a platter.

Serves 24.

SAVORY STILTON TART

Stilton cheese and walnuts are a classic pair, here joined in a creamy tart. Because tart squares are easier to maneuver than wedges, the recipe calls for using a rectangular half-sheet pan, available at restaurant supply stores (see page 115). Two 10-inch tart pans could be substituted.

  10 *eggs*
   1 *pound Stilton cheese*
  ½ *pound cream cheese*
  ½ *cup sour cream*
  1½ *cups whipping cream*
  ½ *teaspoon each nutmeg and cayenne pepper*
  1¼ *cups chopped toasted walnuts*

Basic Tart Dough

  2½ *cups flour*
  1½ *teaspoons salt*
  12 *tablespoons unsalted butter, chilled*
   2 *eggs, lightly beaten*
   2 *tablespoons ice water*

1. Prepare Basic Tart Dough and refrigerate overnight. Preheat oven to 375° F. In a food processor or blender, in batches if necessary, place eggs, Stilton, cream cheese, sour cream, cream, nutmeg, and cayenne. Process until blended but still slightly lumpy. Transfer mixture to a large bowl. (Filling may be prepared up to 1 day in advance and refrigerated, tightly covered.)

2. On a lightly floured surface, roll chilled Basic Tart Dough into a rectangle large enough to cover the bottom and sides of a 12- by 16-inch half-sheet pan. Transfer dough to pan and press in place.

3. Sprinkle walnuts evenly over surface of dough and press in place. Pour filling over walnuts. Bake until tart is firm to the touch and golden brown (25 to 30 minutes). Let rest until warm, then cut into small squares.

Makes about 4 dozen small squares.

Basic Tart Dough

1. *To prepare in a food processor:* Combine flour and salt in work bowl. Pulse to blend. Cut butter into 24 pieces and add to bowl. Pulse until mixture resembles coarse cornmeal. In a separate bowl beat eggs with the ice water. With motor running, add one half of the egg mixture and pulse to blend. Add 1 to 2 tablespoons more egg mixture, pulsing until dough begins to come together. Discard any remaining egg mixture. *To prepare by hand:* Stir together flour and salt. Cut in butter with a pastry blender or two knives until mixture resembles coarse crumbs. In a separate bowl beat eggs with the ice water. Sprinkle egg mixture over flour-butter mixture, tossing with a fork until dough can be formed into a ball. Discard any remaining egg mixture.

2. Gather the dough by hand into a ball, kneading it lightly if necessary. Flatten it slightly, wrap in plastic, and chill at least 1 hour, or overnight, or freeze for up to 1 month.

Makes enough dough for one 12- by 16-inch half-sheet or two 10-inch tarts.

Sweet Tart Dough Add 2 tablespoons sugar to flour and salt mixture before cutting in butter.

IRISH FRUITCAKE

The sizable amounts called for in this recipe are easy to handle if you have two large stainless steel bowls and a handheld mixer. A restaurant supply store (see page 115) can provide the bowls at modest cost, and you'll soon find you have dozens of uses for them. Lacking the large bowls, you may want to halve the recipe and make it twice.

   9 *cups flour, sifted*
   1 *tablespoon baking soda*
   1 *teaspoon baking powder*
   1 *tablespoon each kosher salt, cinnamon, and cardamom*
   1 *teaspoon each ground nutmeg and ground cloves*
   1 *cup each sliced toasted almonds and chopped toasted walnuts*
  ½ *cup each chopped dried apricots, golden raisins, currants, and minced dried figs*
   3 *tablespoons grated orange rind*
   2 *tablespoons grated lemon rind*
   3 *cups unsalted butter, softened*
   3 *cups firmly packed light brown sugar*
  ½ *cup molasses*
   9 *eggs*
  1½ *cups stout beer or porter, at room temperature*
   1 *cup brandy*
   2 *cups Crème Fraîche (see page 38)*

1. Preheat oven to 325° F. Grease two 9-inch springform pans. Sift together flour, baking soda, baking powder, salt, cinnamon, cardamom, nutmeg, and cloves. Transfer to a large bowl and stir in almonds, walnuts, apricots, raisins, currants, figs, and rinds.

2. In a large bowl cream butter with a handheld electric mixer. Add sugar gradually and beat until light. Add molasses and blend well. Add eggs, 2 at a time, beating well after each addition. Mixture may look somewhat curdled. On lowest speed, add dry ingredients and beat until blended. Mixture will be very dry.

3. Add stout by hand and stir to blend. Batter will be very sticky, about the consistency of chocolate chip cookie batter. Divide mixture between the prepared pans and spread evenly.

4. Bake 45 minutes, then check color. If cake appears brown on top, cover with foil. Continue baking until cake pulls away from sides of pan (about another 1¼ hours). Remove from oven and place pans on rack to cool 5 minutes.

5. Using a skewer or thin knife, pierce cakes in several places. Brush tops of cakes with brandy, a little at a time, until all the brandy has been absorbed. Remove pan sides and bottoms and cool cakes completely on a rack. Wrap cakes well in plastic wrap; store at room temperature for at least 4 days or up to 1 week before slicing.

6. To serve, cut cake into thin slices. Accompany with Crème Fraîche.

Makes two 9-inch cakes.

**BRITTANY BRUNCH
For 8**

Buckwheat Crêpes

Mixed Vegetable Crêpes

Breakfast Link Crêpes

Egg, Ham, and Cheese Crêpes

Honey-Pear–Butter Crêpes

Prune-and-Almond-Filled Crêpes

Preserve-Filled Crêpes

Apple, Raisin, and Walnut Crêpes

Sparkling Apple Cider and
Café au Lait (see Planning)

*Hot-from-the-skillet
Buckwheat Crêpes are spread
with smooth honey-pear
butter or wrapped around
sizzling breakfast links, just
two of the sweet and savory
fixings for this festive do-it-
yourself brunch. Toast the
day with sparkling apple
cider, a Breton specialty and
the classic partner to
buckwheat crêpes.*

Timetable

Up to 1 week ahead: Make prune
and almond filling.
Up to 2 days ahead: Make crêpe
batters. Make pear butter.
Up to 1 day ahead: Make vegetable
filling, ham and cheese.
Up to 2 hours ahead: Make apple,
raisin, and walnut filling.
At serving time: Make crêpes, fry
breakfast links, and reheat
vegetable filling.

Planning

Part of the fun of a crêpe party is
turning everyone into a chef. Provide
aprons for all your guests and encourage each to take a turn at the
crêpe pans. With two chefs and two
or three pans working at once, the
crêpes can be made almost as fast as
they are eaten.

The hot crêpes should go directly
from pans to guests' warm plates,
where they can be filled at will from
the offerings on the table.

All the sweet fillings—preserves;
apple, raisin, and walnut filling;
Honey-Pear Butter; prune and almond
filling—can be prepared ahead and
placed on the table before guests sit
down. While two chefs concentrate
on turning out crêpes, you can fry the
breakfast links and sauté the vegetables. A warming tray on the dining
table or sideboard can keep sausages
and vegetables hot. You might also
put a ramekin of melted butter on the
warming tray, so guests can brush the
tops of their crêpes. The fried egg
crêpes must be made to order. You
can demonstrate the first one, then
encourage guests to make their own.

In addition to chilled sparkling
cider, you might want to offer café au
lait: equal parts of extrastrong coffee
and steaming extrarich milk, poured
simultaneously into a warm cup.

Presentation

If you have room in the kitchen to set
a table for eight, this party is the time
to do it. A kitchen setting provides the
shortest distance from crêpe pan to
guest and keeps the chefs in full view
of the diners.

Set a cozy table with large tea
towels for napkins, perhaps in a blue-
and-white check, and a centerpiece
of autumn fruits and foliage. White,
yellow, and blue make a good color
scheme for this meal. Bottles of cider
can go right on the table, along with
the sweet fillings.

Photograph, page 71: Buckwheat
Crêpes make a tasty wrap for apples,
raisins, and walnuts (at left), and a
mixed vegetable sauté and the French
favorite—fried egg, ham, and cheese
(at bottom).

BUCKWHEAT CRÊPES

To serve eight guests generously,
make the recipe twice. The first time,
use all the optional ingredients to
make a sweet batter suitable for sweet
fillings. The second time, omit all the
optional ingredients to make a savory
batter suitable for savory fillings.
Leftover batter can be frozen for up
to six months. Crêpes can be frozen
for up to six months, if well wrapped.

¾ cup buckwheat flour
¾ cup plus 2 tablespoons
    unbleached flour
2 tablespoons dark brown
    sugar (optional)
½ teaspoon kosher salt
¼ teaspoon cinnamon
    (optional)
    Pinch nutmeg (optional)
3 eggs
2 cups milk
⅔ cup half-and-half
¼ cup minced golden raisins
    (optional)
    Melted clarified butter
    (see Note, page 14)

1. In a blender or food processor,
place flours, sugar (if used), salt,
cinnamon (if used), and nutmeg
(if used). Pulse to blend.

2. Add eggs and process to blend.
With machine running, add milk and
half-and-half. Add raisins (if used)
and blend. Transfer to a clean bowl,
cover, and let rest at room temperature for 30 minutes. Or, refrigerate
batter for up to 2 days; bring to room
temperature before using.

3. If necessary, add water to batter to
make it pourable. Heat a 6- to 7-inch
crêpe pan or skillet over moderately
high heat. Lightly brush pan with the
melted butter. When butter sizzles,
add 3 tablespoons batter and swirl to
coat pan. Cook until crêpe is browned
on the bottom. Turn and brown
briefly (about 5 seconds) on second
side. Transfer crêpe to a plate and
repeat with remaining batter.

*Makes about thirty 6- to 7-inch
crêpes.*

MIXED VEGETABLE CRÊPES

This quick vegetable sauté offers a welcome contrast to the sweet crêpe fillings.

  2 *tablespoons butter*
  6 *tablespoons minced shallot*
  3 *cups coarsely grated zucchini*
  ¾ *cup coarsely grated carrot*
  ½ *cup toasted pine nuts*
  ¼ *cup balsamic vinegar*

Salt and freshly ground pepper, to taste
8 *savory Buckwheat Crêpes (see page 70)*
Melted butter, for garnish

1. In a large skillet over moderate heat, melt butter. Add shallot and sauté 1 minute. Add zucchini and carrot and sauté until wilted (about 3 minutes). Add pine nuts and vinegar and cook 30 seconds. Add salt and pepper. Vegetables may be sautéed up to 1 day in advance and refrigerated; undercook vegetables slightly to allow for reheating. Reheat quickly over high heat before using.

2. To serve, spoon one eighth of filling down the center of each crêpe and roll. Brush rolled crêpes with a little melted butter, for garnish.

Makes 8 filled crêpes.

71

BREAKFAST LINK CRÊPES

You can substitute any type of link sausage for the breakfast links, but large sausages should be sliced after cooking.

> 8 breakfast link sausages (about 1 lb)
> 8 savory Buckwheat Crêpes (see page 70)
> Honey-Pear Butter (at right) or Chunky Applesauce (see page 115), optional

Prick sausages with a fork. In a lightly oiled skillet over moderate heat, brown sausages. Drain on paper towels. Spread warm crêpes with Honey-Pear Butter, if used. Wrap a hot sausage in each crêpe and serve immediately.

Makes 8 filled crêpes.

EGG, HAM, AND CHEESE CRÊPES

Almost every *crêperie* and street crêpe vendor in France sells a version of these fried-egg crêpes.

> Melted clarified butter (see Note, page 14)
> 2 cups savory Buckwheat Crêpes batter (see page 70)
> 8 eggs
> 4 ounces each *shredded Danish ham* and *shredded Monterey jack or mozzarella cheese*

1. Heat a 9- or 10-inch crêpe pan or skillet over moderately high heat. Brush generously with melted butter. When butter sizzles, add ¼ cup of Buckwheat Crêpes batter and swirl to coat pan.

2. Into center of batter gently break one egg, keeping yolk whole. Cook just until white is set; yolk should remain runny. Top with ½ ounce ham and ½ ounce cheese. Gently fold sides of crêpe in over cheese. Remove crêpe to a warm plate with a spatula. Continue with remaining crêpe batter and eggs.

Makes 8 filled crêpes.

HONEY-PEAR–BUTTER CRÊPES

The butter can be made up to two days in advance and refrigerated. If mixture separates, return to food processor and process briefly to reblend.

> 8 sweet Buckwheat Crêpes (see page 70)

Honey-Pear Butter

> 1 cup very ripe pear, peeled, cored, and cubed
> 1 cup butter, softened
> ¼ cup honey

Spread about 1½ tablespoons Honey-Pear Butter evenly over surface of hot crêpes; fold crêpes in quarters and serve immediately.

Makes 8 filled crêpes.

Honey-Pear Butter Place pear in a food processor or blender and blend until puréed. Add butter and honey and process until completely smooth.

Makes about 2¼ cups.

PRUNE-AND-ALMOND-FILLED CRÊPES

The filling can be made up to one week in advance and refrigerated in an airtight container; bring to room temperature before using.

> 1½ cups pitted prunes
> ½ cup water
> 3 tablespoons light brown sugar
> 2 tablespoons lemon juice
> ½ teaspoon cinnamon
> 2 tablespoons sliced toasted almonds
> 8 sweet Buckwheat Crêpes (see page 70)

1. In a medium saucepan place prunes and the water. Bring to a simmer over moderate heat, reduce heat to maintain a simmer, and cook until prunes are very soft (about 10 minutes). Purée prunes in a food processor or blender; mixture will be very thick.

2. Transfer prune purée to a medium bowl and stir in sugar, lemon juice, cinnamon, and almonds. Spread about 2 tablespoons filling on each warm crêpe; fold in quarters; serve.

Makes 8 filled crêpes.

PRESERVE-FILLED CRÊPES

Use homemade or best-quality storebought preserves of any variety.

> 1 cup fruit preserves or marmalade
> 8 sweet Buckwheat Crêpes (see page 70)
> Melted butter, for garnish

Spread 2 tablespoons preserves evenly over the surface of each hot crêpe. Fold in quarters, brush with butter, and serve.

Makes 8 filled crêpes.

APPLE, RAISIN, AND WALNUT CRÊPES

This filling should be made no more than two hours in advance to keep the apples crisp.

> ¼ cup raisins
> 1½ tablespoons apple brandy
> 1½ cups coarsely grated green apple
> ½ teaspoon cinnamon
> ¼ cup chopped toasted walnuts
> 1 teaspoon grated lemon rind
> 2 tablespoons honey
> 1 tablespoon lemon juice
> 8 sweet Buckwheat Crêpes (see page 70)
> Melted butter, for garnish
> Cinnamon Sugar (see Note), for garnish

1. In a small bowl combine raisins and brandy and let stand 30 minutes. In a medium bowl combine raisin mixture, apple, cinnamon, and walnuts and stir to blend. Stir in lemon rind, honey, and lemon juice.

2. To serve, spoon about ¼ cup filling down the center of each hot crêpe and roll into a cylinder. Brush with melted butter and sprinkle with Cinnamon Sugar.

Makes 8 filled crêpes.

Note To make Cinnamon Sugar, in a small bowl stir together ¼ teaspoon cinnamon and 2 tablespoons sugar.

CHILDREN'S HALLOWEEN PARTY
For 12

Handburgers

Pumpkin Muffins

Penny's Parlor Whimsies

Frozen Banana-Nut Yogurt

Fresh Apples

*Hot Apple Juice With Cinnamon
(see Planning)*

---

*Eye of newt and toe of frog
are banished from this
Halloween menu in favor of
fare guaranteed to enchant
children: open-faced
Handburgers on English
muffins; creamy frozen
yogurt served in billowing
dry ice; dentist-defying bars
of marshmallow, granola,
and popcorn; and a
steaming "witch's caldron"
of hot apple juice scented
with cinnamon sticks.*

Timetable

Up to 1 week ahead: Make
  whimsies.
Up to 1 day ahead: Freeze yogurt.
Up to 4 hours ahead: Make
  Handburger mixture and
  shape patties.
Up to 2 hours ahead: Bake pumpkin muffins.
At serving time: Heat apple juice
  and cinnamon for witch's
  caldron. Broil Handburgers.

Planning

Entertaining a dozen youngsters at a Halloween party at home can be as much fun for the adults as for the children. Costumes are a must, of course—for parents, too—and the food should be full of surprises.

Begin with snacks of toasted pumpkin seeds (see page 75) to fuel a costume contest and a round of bobbing for apples. Then the little goblins may be ready to take seats. While you bring in a tray full of sizzling Handburgers, a helper can carry in the steaming witch's caldron (4 quarts apple juice with 2 cinnamon sticks brought to a simmer). The open-faced Handburgers must be cooked to order, but the other dishes can be made well ahead. To end the meal with a dramatic flourish, present the yogurt on a platter in a cloud of dry ice.

Presentation

Create a spooky effect by placing a couple of bowls of hot water on the table and dropping a 2-inch piece of dry ice into each. The sound of bubbling amid billowing clouds is bound to draw gasps.

Each year, the major paper-goods manufacturers introduce delightful black and orange table decorations for Halloween. You'll want a paper tablecloth, sturdy paper plates and napkins, thick paper cups for the hot cider, and plastic cutlery.

Place a bowl of red and green apples in the center of the table and sprinkle popcorn liberally over the tablecloth. The Pumpkin Muffins can be fitted with place cards and set at each place; to keep the fever pitch down, seat boy next to girl, calm child next to active. Sew trick-or-treat bags from inexpensive black cloth and hang one over the back of each chair.

Photograph, page 74: Accompanied by clusters of red and green apples, jack-o'-lanterns stand guard over Frozen Banana-Nut Yogurt surrounded by billowing dry ice and personalized Pumpkin Muffins.

HANDBURGERS

It takes only one hand to manage one of these open-faced Handburgers, a variation on the favorite food of youth almost everywhere. You can shape the patties up to four hours ahead and arrange them on rimmed baking trays; then cover and refrigerate until baking time. Figure you need another couple of minutes' baking time if the patties are cold when they go in the oven.

  2 cups soft bread crumbs
  ¾ cup milk
  3 pounds lean ground beef
  1 pound fresh Italian-style
    sausage meat
  4 eggs
  1 to 2 tablespoons hot
    pepper sauce
  2 tablespoons soy sauce
  ¼ teaspoon freshly ground
    pepper, or more to taste
  1 tablespoon kosher salt, or
    more to taste
  12 whole wheat or sourdough
    English muffins, split
    Catsup
  24 slices mozzarella cheese
    Sweet pickle relish, for
    accompaniment

1. Preheat oven to 450° F. Soak bread crumbs in milk 15 minutes. In a large bowl combine soaked bread crumbs, beef, sausage meat, eggs, hot pepper sauce, soy sauce, pepper, and salt. Mix lightly but thoroughly using your hands. In a lightly oiled skillet, fry a small amount; taste and adjust seasoning.

2. Form mixture into 24 thin patties of the same diameter as the English muffins. Place patties on ungreased, rimmed baking sheets and bake until done (8 to 10 minutes).

3. Preheat broiler. Toast muffins briefly, then spread with a light layer of catsup; top with hamburger patties. Cover patties with thin slices of mozzarella; broil until cheese browns and bubbles. Serve with pickle relish.

Makes 2 dozen Handburgers.

PUMPKIN MUFFINS

These tender spice muffins are delicious on their own or with honey butter, made by whipping softened butter with honey to taste. The optional pumpkin seed garnish adds color and crunch.

- ¾ cup butter, softened
- ¼ cup corn oil
- 1½ cups firmly packed light brown sugar
- ½ cup molasses
- 1½ cups cooked canned pumpkin
- 2 eggs
- 3½ cups flour
- 1 teaspoon salt
- 2 teaspoons baking soda
- 1 tablespoon cinnamon
- ½ teaspoon each *mace* and *nutmeg*
- 48 hulled pumkin seeds, for garnish (optional)

1. Preheat oven to 400° F. In a large mixing bowl, combine butter, oil, sugar, molasses, pumpkin, and eggs. Beat well.

2. Sift together flour, salt, baking soda, cinnamon, mace, and nutmeg. Add to liquid ingredients and mix just to blend. Spoon into buttered 2½-inch muffin tins.

3. If using hulled pumpkin seeds, place 3 on each muffin. Bake until golden brown (12 to 15 minutes). Remove from tins and cool on racks.

Makes sixteen 2½-inch muffins.

PENNY'S PARLOR WHIMSIES

Chewy bars of marshmallow, popcorn, and granola are a variation on a famous treat from Penny's Parlor in Phoenix, Arizona. The recipe is flexible. To vary the mix, substitute 1 cup raisins, chopped dried apricots, or toasted nuts for 1 cup of granola.

- ½ cup butter
- 2 bags (10 oz each) marshmallows
- 5 cups granola
- 5 cups freshly popped popcorn, unbuttered and unsalted

1. In a large pot over low heat, melt butter. Add marshmallows and melt, stirring constantly with a wooden spoon. Add granola and popcorn and stir until well blended.

2. Pat mixture into a buttered 9- by 13-inch baking pan. Chill until firm (at least 4 hours, or up to 1 week).

3. To serve, cut mixture into 1- by 2-inch bars.

Makes about 4 dozen bars.

FROZEN BANANA-NUT YOGURT

Serving cups of frozen yogurt in a cloud of dry ice is sure to bring gasps of astonishment and delight from young revelers. Most ice companies can supply you with dry ice. You will need about 2½ pounds of dry ice and gloves to handle it.

- 1 quart vanilla yogurt
- 6 cups overripe bananas
- ¼ cup lime juice
- ½ cup firmly packed brown sugar
- 2 teaspoons cinnamon
- 1 cup chopped toasted walnuts
- 1 cup chocolate chips (optional)

1. In a food processor or blender, purée yogurt, bananas, lime juice, sugar, and cinnamon. Transfer to a bowl and stir in nuts and chocolate chips (if used). Cover and refrigerate 1 hour.

2. Transfer mixture to ice cream freezer and freeze according to manufacturer's directions. Serve immediately or freeze for up to 1 day.

3. To serve, wrap the outside of 12 plastic cups with plastic wrap. Spoon yogurt into cups and arrange on a serving platter. Wearing gloves, crush dry ice into ice cube–sized pieces, scatter around the platter, and mist lightly with hot water. Immediately carry into party room.

Makes about 2½ quarts.

ROASTING PUMPKIN SEEDS

When cleaned, oiled, and toasted, pumpkin seeds are a delicious snack. You can eat them unhulled, or you can hull them with a small, sharp knife. Shelled pumpkin seeds can be added to breads or muffins or sprinkled on salads.

1. *Halve pumpkin using a large knife or cleaver. Scrape seeds from pumpkin cavity with fingers. Remove as much fibrous material as possible from the seeds. Transfer seeds to a bowl. Sprinkle seeds lightly with vegetable or corn oil. Toss to coat.*

2. *Preheat oven to 350° F. Transfer seeds to a baking sheet. Salt to taste. Bake until dry and lightly browned (about 15 minutes). To hull use a small, sharp knife. Store toasted seeds in an airtight container at cool room temperature. Hulled seeds will keep for up to 1 week; unhulled for up to 6 months.*

QUICK COCKTAIL NIBBLES FOR DROP-INS

A well-stocked kitchen can mean the difference between panic and pleasure when guests arrive unexpectedly. It's a lot easier to be gracious and welcoming when you have the makings of instant hors d'oeuvres.

You won't hesitate to invite friends in for a glass of wine on the spur of the moment if your kitchen harbors a few good possibilities. Here is a suggested list of essentials for the everready host.

Anchovies Mashed with garlic and oil or worked into softened butter, anchovies can then be spread on warm toasts.

Bread Good bread for toasting should always be kept on hand. It should have an honest flavor and a relatively dense texture. Thaw aluminum foil-wrapped bread in a moderate oven, then slice, brush with olive oil or melted butter, and toast on a baking sheet. To make quick garlic bread, rub a halved clove of garlic over tops of toasts when they emerge from the oven.

Bread Sticks Commercial bread sticks freeze well and thaw quickly. To enhance them, arrange them on a baking sheet and bake in a moderate oven until thawed. Then brush them with melted butter, sprinkle with kosher salt and sesame seed, and return to the oven to crisp.

Canned Seafood Imported canned tuna in oil can be drained and puréed with softened butter and capers to make a smooth spread for crackers or toast. Similarly, canned salmon or clams can be whipped with cream cheese and capers.

Corn Tortillas Keep them in the freezer. They thaw quickly in a low oven and can then be cut into wedges, fried in hot oil, and sprinkled with salt.

Crackers Premium storebought crackers can be warmed in the oven to crisp them and to bring up their toasty aroma.

Eggs Hard-cooked eggs are a welcome addition to any hors d'oeuvre platter. Serve them with a dollop of Homemade Mayonnaise (see page 88) or mayonnaise heightened with anchovy, mustard, or capers. Or make a quick egg salad with warm chopped egg, minced parsley, and fresh mayonnaise; then spread it on lightly toasted bread (see photograph opposite, top).

Hard Cheese Cheeses present countless appetizer possibilities. Hard cheeses, such as imported Parmesan and California dry jack, are easy to have on hand because they keep well. They can be thinly sliced with a cheese plane and served with crackers or small toasts. Or, they can be grated and dusted on oiled bread rounds before baking.

Nuts Toss shelled almonds, pecans, or walnuts in melted butter, then spread on a baking sheet and bake in a 300° F oven until fragrant. Salt to taste before serving (see almonds in photograph opposite, bottom). Keep shelled nuts in the freezer to prevent rancidity.

Olives Good olives can be served as is (see photograph opposite, at right) or tossed with finely minced garlic and herbs and a little olive oil, or even warmed briefly in olive oil and finished with a squeeze of lemon.

Pita Bread Keep pita bread in the freezer. Wrap in aluminum foil and thaw in a warm oven; split the bread into two rounds and cut each round into wedges. Brush wedges with melted butter or olive oil, dust with some minced herbs or Parmesan cheese, and bake in a moderate oven until crisp and toasty.

Salami Slice a first-rate dried salami paper-thin, arrange the slices in overlapping circles on a large platter, and serve with olives or radishes, tasty bread, and softened butter.

Soft Cheese Soft cheeses are more perishable than hard ones, but they come in handy for serving to drop-in guests. Roquefort or domestic blue cheese can be whipped with butter to make a spread for crackers or toast. Cream cheese can be whipped with fresh minced herbs and green onions for a quick spread. Bread rounds topped with grated mozzarella or jack cheese and minced anchovy can be broiled to make a delicious nibble in no time.

Sun-Dried Tomatoes This new arrival on the fancy-food shelves makes a splendid hors d'oeuvre when sliced in thin strips and served atop rounds of toasted bread, perhaps with a paper-thin slice of Parmesan cheese. Also available is a purée of sun-dried tomatoes, which can be spread lightly on warm, garlic-rubbed toast.

HAM WITH HONEY MUSTARD

¼ cup plus 2 tablespoons honey mustard
12 paper-thin slices (1 oz each) smoked ham
Freshly ground pepper (optional)

Spread 1½ teaspoons of mustard on each ham slice. Roll into logs or fold in quarters and arrange on a serving tray. Grind pepper over ham, if desired.

Makes 12 ham rolls.

RADISHES WITH BASIL BUTTER

3 tablespoons unsalted butter, softened
1 tablespoon minced fresh basil
12 radishes
Coarse salt

In a small bowl combine butter and basil and mix well. Butter radishes lightly; sprinkle with coarse salt. Arrange on a serving tray.

Makes 12 radishes.

Variation Slice whole radishes thinly into fans. Spread with butter and sprinkle with salt as above.

MOZZARELLA AND SUN-DRIED TOMATO TOASTS

12 bread rounds (about 2 in. diameter and ¼ in. thick)
6 ounces whole-milk mozzarella cheese, shredded
¼ cup minced sun-dried tomatoes with oil

Preheat broiler. Arrange bread rounds on a baking sheet. Place ½-ounce cheese on each bread round; top each with 1 teaspoon tomato. Broil until browned and bubbly (about 1 minute).

Makes 12 toasts.

MUSHROOM CAPS WITH ROQUEFORT BUTTER

12 large mushroom caps, cleaned
¼ cup olive oil
½ cup unsalted butter, softened
2 ounces Roquefort cheese

Preheat broiler. Lightly brush caps with olive oil and place on a baking sheet. *To prepare in a food processor:* Place butter and Roquefort in work bowl and process until smooth. *To prepare by hand:* In a medium bowl place butter and Roquefort and blend with a wooden spoon. Place 1 tablespoon butter-cheese mixture in each cap; brush with any remaining olive oil. Broil until hot throughout (about 2 minutes).

Makes 12 mushroom caps.

SPICED NUTS

2 tablespoons butter
½ teaspoon cayenne pepper
1 teaspoon cumin
1½ cups nuts (almonds, walnuts, peanuts, or combination)
Coarse salt

Preheat oven to 325° F. Melt butter in a small saucepan; add cayenne and cumin. Add nuts to saucepan and stir to coat. Transfer nuts to baking sheet. Bake until fragrant and lightly browned (12 to 15 minutes). Sprinkle with coarse salt.

Makes 1½ cups nuts.

QUESADILLAS

6 flour tortillas (8 in. each), fresh or frozen
1 cup plus 2 tablespoons shredded Monterey jack cheese
¼ cup diced pickled jalapeño chiles
2 tablespoons vegetable oil
Hot pepper sauce, for accompaniment

Preheat oven to 450° F. Place three tortillas on a baking sheet; top each with one third of the cheese and one third of the jalapeños. Cover with remaining tortillas. Brush top tortilla with vegetable oil. Bake until hot throughout (4 to 7 minutes). Cut into quarters. Serve with hot pepper sauce (see photograph, center)

Makes 12 small quesadillas.

ALL-AMERICAN BEEF AND SPIRITS
For 6

Autumn Broccoli Salad

Three-Pepper Beef

Five-Day Beans

Frozen Whiskey Pudding

Zinfandel

A juicy steak, a green salad, and a rich and creamy dessert have special appeal with the arrival of cool autumn weather. Here, the typical steak dinner takes an imaginative turn in a meal that includes flank steak crusted with mixed peppercorns, a fresh broccoli salad, and a whiskey-spiked custard nestled in homemade chocolate cups.

Timetable

Up to 1 week ahead: Make chocolate cups.

Up to 5 days ahead: Begin bean preparation.

Up to 1 day ahead: Make salad dressing. Fill chocolate cups and freeze.

Up to 6 hours ahead: Cook and chill broccoli.

4 to 6 hours ahead: Marinate beef.

20 minutes before serving: Reheat beans.

At serving time: Dress broccoli salad. Grill beef.

Planning

What if you find you want to invite dinner guests for a day when you won't have much time to cook? With a menu that allows the major cooking to be done days ahead, the dinner can come off without a hitch.

A good part of this informal meal can be prepared in bits and snatches during the week preceding the party. On the day of the dinner, the cook needs to find only 15 minutes to trim and boil the broccoli, 15 minutes to marinate the beef, and about 10 minutes to top and reheat the beans.

What's more, the meal is easy on the cook after guests arrive. A small dinner party suffers when the host has to spend too much time in the kitchen. Here, you need to excuse yourself only for the few moments necessary to grill the steak.

To accompany cocktails or predinner wine, you might set out a bowl of eggplant and olive relish (see page 93) surrounded by sesame crackers or homemade toasts.

A California zinfandel would be an excellent choice with the meal.

Presentation

The colorful gourds and Indian corn that appear in markets in the fall are perfect materials for setting a harvest table. Design a still life of pumpkins, knobby gourds, winter squashes, dried corn, and autumn leaves, with votive candles for added sparkle.

Keep meal service simple and unfussy. The broccoli salad should be served as a first course, on a platter or on salad plates. The flank steak can be served family style from a wooden cutting board or platter, and the beans can go from oven to table. For a change of scene, move guests to the living room for dessert.

Photograph, page 79: Flank steak seasoned with green, black, and white peppercorns, creamy baked beans, and a Frozen Whiskey Pudding add up to an all-American dinner.

AUTUMN BROCCOLI SALAD

Mustard, garlic, and Parmesan cheese flavor the dressing for this simple salad. Serve the dish family style with a basket of warm crusty bread.

  1 teaspoon mustard
  2 tablespoons red wine vinegar
  2 teaspoons lemon juice
  ½ cup garlic oil (see Note) or olive oil
  ½ cup freshly grated Parmesan cheese
  Salt and freshly ground pepper, to taste
  2 pounds broccoli
  1 pint cherry tomatoes, halved
  ⅓ cup minced green onion

1. In a small bowl whisk together mustard, vinegar, and lemon juice. Add garlic oil gradually, whisking constantly. Whisk in ¼ cup of the Parmesan. Season with salt and pepper. Cover and set aside for at least 1 hour or up to 1 day.

2. Trim broccoli and cut into florets (reserve stalks for soup, if desired). Bring a large pot of salted water to a boil over high heat; add florets and cook until tender-crisp. Drain and immediately plunge into ice water. When cool, drain again and pat dry. Broccoli may be cooked up to 6 hours ahead, cooled, and stored in a plastic bag in the refrigerator.

3. Transfer broccoli to a large bowl along with tomatoes. Add dressing to vegetables and toss to coat well. Add green onion and remaining ¼ cup Parmesan and toss to blend. Taste and adjust seasoning. Transfer to a serving platter.

Serves 6.

Note To make garlic oil, add 6 whole peeled garlic cloves to 1 pint extravirgin olive oil. Marinate at least 1 week before using. Oil will keep indefinitely if covered and refrigerated.

Variation Cauliflower may be substituted for all or part of the broccoli.

PRIMER ON BEEF

Buying beef can be an expensive proposition these days. To make sure you get the most for your money, you need to know how to recognize high-quality beef and how to select the right cut for your dish. Here are some guidelines.

To select flavorful beef, look for intramuscular fat (marbling). The fat melts during cooking and acts as a natural baster. Consumer concern about dietary fat has led to a demand for lean beef, but the most flavorful beef is well marbled.

The beef's external fat should be creamy white, not yellow. The muscle should be red and firm; avoid meat that is mushy or reddish brown.

The U.S. Department of Agriculture (USDA) grading stamp can also be a guide to beef quality. However, in most of the country grading is voluntary, and only about 50 percent of American beef is graded. There are eight USDA beef quality grades, but only three that you're likely to see as a retail consumer: Prime, Choice, and Good. Most USDA Prime beef goes to restaurants and specialty retailers. Most supermarkets offer either Choice or Good beef. The major difference among grades is the degree of marbling.

The most tender cuts of beef come from muscles that are rarely used, such as those in the loin and the rib. More active muscles—such as those in the shank, shoulder, tongue, and leg (or "round")—are naturally tougher but no less delicious if properly cooked.

The more tender cuts take well to quick, dry-heat cooking methods such as roasting and broiling. The tougher cuts require slow, moist-heat cooking, such as stewing, to tenderize them. Choosing the right cut of beef for your dish, or applying the right cooking method to a given cut, is essential to a successful result.

THREE-PEPPER BEEF

Lean flank steak is marinated in papaya juice to tenderize it, then seasoned with a trio of crushed peppercorns. The thin steak, which some butchers label London Broil, cooks quickly on a grill or under a broiler; for best flavor, serve it rare or medium-rare.

    2½ pounds flank steak
     1 cup papaya juice
    1½ tablespoons each green, black,
        and white peppercorns,
        coarsely cracked
     6 tablespoons olive oil
     ¼ cup lemon juice
        Salt, to taste

1. With a small sharp knife, make ½-inch-long slits in the flank steak in several places. Put steak in a glass baking dish and pour papaya juice over; cover and refrigerate for 2 to 4 hours. Remove steak from marinade and pat dry.

2. Combine peppercorns. Press them into both sides of flank steak; put flank steak in a clean baking dish, cover, and refrigerate for 2 hours. Bring to room temperature before cooking.

3. Prepare a medium-hot charcoal fire or preheat broiler. In a small bowl whisk together olive oil and lemon juice. Salt steak lightly on both sides. Grill or broil to desired doneness, turning once and basting once with half of the oil mixture. Transfer steak to a wooden cutting board; brush with remaining oil mixture. Let stand 5 minutes to settle juices, then slice on the diagonal across the grain into wide, flat slices.

Serves 6.

FIVE-DAY BEANS

For busy cooks, it's nice to have a repertoire of dishes that can be assembled a little at a time over several days. The preparation of these beans can be stretched over five days, although it doesn't need to be. If you prefer, you can do step 1 on one day, steps 2 and 3 the next day, and step 4 on the day of the party. Refrigerating the beans for at least one day improves their flavor.

    1⅓ cups dried Great Northern
        beans or lima beans
     1 bay leaf
     1 teaspoon dried thyme
     1 teaspoon kosher salt, plus salt
        to taste
     2 tablespoons butter
     ¾ cup minced green onion
     ½ cup grated carrot
     ½ cup minced celery
     2 tablespoons minced fresh sage
        Freshly ground pepper, to taste
     ½ cup whipping cream
     ¼ cup Seasoned Bread Crumbs
        (see page 16)

1. On Day 1 cover beans with cold water and let stand 24 hours.

2. On Day 2 drain beans. Place in a medium saucepan, add bay leaf, thyme, 1 teaspoon of the salt, and water to cover. Over high heat bring to a boil, reduce heat to maintain a simmer, and cook until tender (about 1 hour). Drain beans, reserving 1 cup liquid. Transfer beans to a bowl, add reserved liquid, cover, and refrigerate.

3. On Day 3 in a large skillet over moderate heat, melt butter. Add onion, carrot, and celery and sauté 3 minutes. Add sage and cook 1 minute. Stir in beans with their liquid and simmer 5 minutes. Remove from heat, cool, cover, and refrigerate 2 days.

4. On Day 5 preheat oven to 400° F. Butter an 11- by 13-inch baking dish. Season beans with salt and pepper, then transfer to baking dish. Drizzle cream over dish and dot with bread crumbs. Bake until hot and lightly browned (15 to 20 minutes). Serve from the baking dish, if desired.

Serves 6.

FROZEN WHISKEY PUDDING

Molded chocolate cups hold a smooth frozen custard spiked with Irish whiskey. You will need 6 paper muffin cups and a pastry brush.

> 6 ounces *bittersweet chocolate*
> 1½ cups each *milk and whipping cream*
> ½ teaspoon *salt*
> 6 *egg yolks*
> ¾ cup *sugar*
> 2 tablespoons *Irish whiskey*

1. In a double boiler over barely simmering water, melt chocolate. Brush 6 paper muffin cups with melted chocolate and place in freezer 5 minutes. Repeat 5 times, forming 6 thin layers of chocolate on each cup. (Repeated layering gives cups strength.) Put muffin cups on tray in freezer until frozen (1 to 3 hours), then remove and carefully place in an airtight container and return to freezer. They may be made up to 1 week ahead.

2. In a medium saucepan over moderate heat, bring milk, cream, and salt to a simmer. With an electric mixer at medium-high speed, beat yolks 3 minutes. Add sugar gradually, beating until mixture is pale and thick (5 to 7 minutes). Remove bowl from mixer and whisk in ¾ cup of the hot-milk mixture by hand. Pour resulting mixture into the saucepan and cook over moderately low heat, stirring constantly with a wooden spoon, until mixture reaches 180° F. Do not allow custard to boil.

3. Strain custard through a fine sieve into a bowl set over ice. Stir occasionally until completely cold. Stir in whiskey.

4. Remove coated muffin cups from freezer. Peel off paper. Spoon in custard mixture. Return cups to freezer for at least 2 hours or up to 1 day. If custard seems very firm, remove cups from freezer 5 minutes before serving.

Serves 6.

---

menu

COUSCOUS FOR A CROWD
For 16

Autumn Salad With Rosewater

Vegetable Couscous

Harissa

*Almond Filo Squares
With Honeyed Oranges*

Côtes-du-Rhône or Zinfandel

A steaming mound of couscous surrounded by a spicy vegetable stew lures guests to the table with the heady aroma of cinnamon, cumin, and mace. A cool carrot salad with rosewater opens this North African feast, with a hot, honey-drenched pastry for a finale.

Timetable

Up to 3 days ahead: Marinate oranges in honey.
Up to 1 day ahead: Make vegetable stew for couscous.
Up to 5 hours ahead: Bake filo pastry. Do first steaming of couscous grains.
1½ hours ahead: Make salad.
At serving time: Reheat stew, if necessary; do second steaming of couscous grains. Make Harissa. Reheat filo pastry and oranges.

Planning

Making couscous requires some planning and effort, but a good version is a showstopper. Because it takes as much time to make a lot as a little, it's a good excuse to gather a crowd.

Packaged couscous is available in many supermarkets, and most natural-food stores offer it in bulk. To cook it properly, you will need either a *couscousière* or a Chinese bamboo steamer that fits securely over a saucepan. A traditional couscousière, available from cookware stores, resembles a double boiler: The bottom pot holds the simmering water or stew; the top part has a perforated bottom through which steam rises. You will need two couscousières or two bamboo steamers for this recipe.

Couscous is a challenge for the cook, so it should be preceded and followed by dishes that don't need attention. In this meal, both salad and dessert are made before guests arrive, although dessert will need reheating. To stand up to the spicy couscous, choose a red French Côtes-du-Rhône or a California Zinfandel.

Presentation

For a group of 16, buffet presentation is most efficient. You can give the table an exotic look with paisley fabric. Serve the couscous and salad on brass or wooden platters. For a dramatic centerpiece, fill a large, shallow brass planter with water and float tiny candles and fragrant gardenias on the surface.

In Morocco diners customarily sit on large pillows on the floor, surrounding a low table. If you suspect your guests are willing, you can scatter large pillows in the living room and enjoy the meal in traditional style. Offer tea towels for napkins, as couscous can be messy.

Photograph, page 82: A fragrant, all-vegetable couscous includes rutabagas, potatoes, yams, kidney beans, red cabbage, and red bell peppers with a mound of steaming couscous grains served in a traditional North African wooden serving dish.

AUTUMN SALAD WITH ROSEWATER

The aroma of rose petals pervades many Moroccan salads, thanks to a dash or two of bottled rosewater. In the United States, rosewater is sold at liquor stores, pharmacies, and well-stocked supermarkets. If the carrots aren't naturally sweet, you may need to add a pinch of sugar.

   2 *pounds carrot, peeled and coarsely grated*
  ½ *pound red radishes, trimmed and coarsely grated*

   1 *cup minced celery*
   1 *cup minced green bell pepper*
1½ *teaspoons cinnamon*
   3 *tablespoons lemon juice*
    Pinch sugar (optional)
   6 *tablespoons olive oil*
   1 *tablespoon rosewater*
   2 *heads butter lettuce*
    Salt and freshly ground pepper, to taste
    Lemon wedges, for garnish

1. In a large stainless steel, glass, or enamel bowl, combine carrot, radishes, celery, bell pepper, cinnamon, lemon juice, sugar (if used), oil, and rosewater. Cover; refrigerate 1 hour.

2. Remove salad from refrigerator 30 minutes before serving. Remove outer leaves of lettuce, reserving only the pale green inner hearts. Line serving platters with lettuce hearts. Just before serving, season salad with salt and pepper. Spoon salad atop lettuce; garnish with lemon wedges.

Serves 16.

VEGETABLE COUSCOUS

The tiny granules of semolina known as couscous become a soft, fluffy mound when steamed twice, the first time over water, the second time over an aromatic, bubbling stew. The stew in this case is a feast of autumn vegetables. If you are using two Chinese bamboo steamers, set over two saucepans, you will need cheesecloth, available in most supermarkets, for lining the steamers. *Couscousières* do not require cheesecloth.

> ¾ cup olive oil
> 3 cups minced red onion
> 2 tablespoons minced garlic
> 1½ teaspoons each *cinnamon, turmeric, allspice, and ginger*
> 1 teaspoon each *mace, ground coriander, and cardamom*
> 2 tablespoons ground cumin
> 3 quarts chicken stock
> 1 pound yams, peeled and cut into ½-inch cubes
> 1½ pounds potato, peeled and cut into ½-inch cubes
> 1 pound parsnips, peeled and sliced ½ inch thick
> 1 rutabaga, peeled and cut into ½-inch cubes
> 1 large red cabbage, cut into 8 wedges and cored
> 2 cups cooked kidney beans
> 1 pound yellow summer squash, coarsely chopped
> 4 red bell peppers, cut into ½-inch cubes
> 3 cups peeled, seeded, and diced tomatoes, fresh or canned
> 1 cup golden raisins
> 6 cups couscous
> ¼ cup butter
> Salt and freshly ground pepper, to taste

1. In bottom of each couscousière or saucepan, over moderate heat, warm ¼ cup of the olive oil. To each pot, add half the onion, garlic, cinnamon, turmeric, allspice, ginger, mace, coriander, cardamom, and cumin. Sauté until onion is softened and spices are fragrant (about 5 minutes). To each pot, add chicken stock, yam, potato, parsnip, rutabagas, and cabbage, dividing them equally. Bring to a simmer, reduce heat to maintain a simmer, and cook

15 minutes. To each pot, add half the kidney beans. Continue cooking 15 minutes. To each pot, stir in squash, peppers, tomato, and raisins, dividing them equally. Stew may be made up to this point, cooled, and refrigerated overnight; undercook vegetables slightly to allow for reheating.

2. In a very large bowl, place couscous and cover with cold water. Let stand 2 minutes. Drain in a fine sieve, transfer grains to a rimmed baking sheet, and let stand 15 minutes. Oil hands lightly and rub the grains gently between your palms to break up any lumps.

3. If using Chinese bamboo steamers, line them with a double thickness of dampened cheescloth. Divide grains between the steamers, and steam, uncovered, over simmering water for 20 minutes. Transfer steamed grains to 3 rimmed baking sheets, spreading them into an even layer on each sheet. Sprinkle each tray with ⅔ cup cold water. Oil hands lightly and rake grains with fingertips; cover grains with plastic wrap, and let stand at room temperature for up to 5 hours.

4. If using Chinese bamboo steamers, reline them with a double thickness of dampened cheesecloth. If you have refrigerated the stew, return the 2 pots to moderate heat and bring stew to a simmer. Return couscous to tops of couscousières or to cheesecloth-lined steamers. Set over simmering vegetables, and steam, uncovered, until grains are hot (about 10 minutes).

5. In a small saucepan over low heat, warm butter and remaining ¼ cup olive oil until butter melts. Mound hot couscous in the center of one or two warm platters. Pour butter-oil mixture over grains and toss with 2 forks to blend. Season with salt and pepper.

6. Taste vegetable stew and adjust seasoning with salt and pepper. Use a slotted spoon to arrange stewed vegetables around the couscous. Reserve 2 cups of vegetable broth for use in Harissa (see page 84); drizzle remaining broth over couscous. Serve immediately with Harissa.

Serves 16.

STEAMING COUSCOUS

The best couscous is light and fluffy, with each grain distinct. To achieve these results, couscous should be steamed twice—first over simmering water, then over a bubbling stew.

1. *Place couscous in a large bowl, cover with cold water, and let stand 2 minutes. Drain in a fine sieve. Transfer to a rimmed baking sheet; let stand 15 minutes. Oil hands lightly and rub grains gently between palms to break up any lumps.*

2. *Transfer grains to the perforated top of a* couscousière. *Set over simmering water and steam, uncovered, 20 minutes. Transfer steamed grains to a rimmed baking sheet. Sprinkle lightly with cold water. With oiled hands, rub grains gently between palms to break up any lumps. Cover and let stand up to 5 hours. Return grains to top of couscousière and set over simmering stew. Steam, uncovered, until grains are hot.*

83

HARISSA

In Tunisia, a fiery hot pepper sauce called *harissa* often accompanies a couscous, to be drizzled over the dish by each diner to taste.

> 1 tablespoon cumin seed
> 2 cups broth from Vegetable Couscous (see page 83)
> 1 tablespoon minced garlic
> 2 tablespoons hot red-pepper flakes
> 3 tablespoons lemon juice
> ¼ cup olive oil
> 1½ tablespoons minced cilantro, or more to taste

1. In a small skillet over moderately low heat, toast cumin seed until fragrant (do not allow to smoke). Grind to a powder in a mortar or spice grinder.

2. In a medium saucepan over moderate heat, combine cumin, broth, garlic, and red-pepper flakes. Bring to a simmer, then whisk in lemon juice and olive oil. Stir in cilantro to taste. Serve immediately.

Serves 16.

ALMOND FILO SQUARES WITH HONEYED ORANGES

A hot and flaky filo pastry layered with ground almonds is drenched with oranges in honey syrup to make a sensational sweet finale to this North African meal.

> 8 large navel oranges
> 1 cup honey
> 3 tablespoons orange-flower water
> 2 cups butter, melted
> 1 package (1 lb) filo dough
> 1½ pounds almonds, blanched, toasted, and ground
> Fresh mint sprigs, for garnish

1. Using a sharp knife, cut away orange rind and all white pith. Slice oranges into rounds about ¼ inch thick; place in a bowl or baking dish.

2. In a small saucepan over low heat, combine honey and flower water. Heat, stirring, until honey melts. Pour over oranges and toss to coat. Cover and refrigerate for up to 3 days.

3. Preheat oven to 375° F. Select 2 rimmed 11- by 13- by 1-inch baking sheets; brush lightly with melted butter. Put a sheet of filo in each pan. Brush lightly with melted butter and sprinkle with 2 tablespoons of the ground almonds. Continue layering filo, butter, and almonds to make 12 layers in each pan. End with a layer of filo and brush with butter. Carefully cut layered dough in each pan into 8 squares, cutting down through all the layers.

4. Bake until golden brown (20 to 25 minutes). Transfer squares to racks set over paper towels to allow excess butter to drip off and bottoms to crisp. Dessert may be made to this point up to 5 hours in advance and kept at room temperature.

5. Preheat oven to 400° F. Transfer squares to a baking sheet and reheat 5 minutes. In a saucepan over low heat, heat oranges in syrup until hot.

6. To serve, place a hot filo square on each dessert plate and spoon honeyed oranges around and over it. Garnish with a mint sprig.

Serves 16.

PREGAME TAILGATE
For 8

Roasted Eggplant Soup
Lime Chicken
Mixed Grains Salad
Clove-Scented Orange Cake
Bottled Water, Soda, and Beer

Sports fans know that a picnic rarely tastes as good as the one eaten in a stadium parking lot before the game. The tailgate of a station wagon can fold down to become the table for such filling autumn fare as smooth eggplant soup, fragrant lime-baked chicken, and a high-rising orange chiffon cake.

Timetable
Up to 5 days ahead: Make cake.
Up to 1 day ahead: Make soup. Marinate chicken.
Up to 4 hours ahead: Make grain salad.
1 hour ahead: Bake chicken.
Just before leaving: Reheat soup.

Planning

If you own a portable grill or hibachi, you may prefer to cook the chicken at the picnic site. If not, the entire meal may be prepared in advance.

For traveling, the soup is packed in an insulated container, the chicken in individual aluminum foil packets, and the cake in plastic wrap. Spoon the grain salad into a plastic container with a tight-fitting lid; you can turn the salad out into a serving bowl at the site or serve it directly from the container.

An ice chest filled with bottled water, soda, and beer provides liquid refreshment. Remember to pack a garbage bag and a radio for the pregame show.

Presentation

Your team's colors can inspire your tailgate decor, including the choice of tablecloth, napkins, and plates. Lay a blanket or oilcloth cover across the tailgate for a tablecloth; then arrange soup mugs, plates, and flatware, aluminum foil–wrapped chicken, grain salad, and cake for self-service.

Plastic mugs, paper plates, and sturdy paper napkins are fine for this tailgate picnic, but provide your guests with stainless, not plastic, cutlery. In addition to dinner plates, you'll need eight dessert plates for the cake.

Photograph, page 86: The tailgate of a station wagon is the perfect setting for a stadium pregame warm-up that includes (from top): creamy Roasted Eggplant Soup with Yogurt Topping, foil-wrapped Lime Chicken, a cool Mixed Grains Salad, and a feather-light Clove-Scented Orange Cake. A sturdy well-packed wicker hamper is an ideal carryall.

ROASTED EGGPLANT SOUP

Storebought sesame crackers or Armenian *lahvosh* (cracker bread) would complement mugs of steaming eggplant soup.

- *2 large eggplants (12 to 14 oz each), peeled*
- *¼ cup olive oil*
- *2 tablespoons butter*
- *¼ cup minced shallot*
- *½ cup minced carrot*
- *1 tablespoon minced garlic*
- *1 cup peeled, seeded, and diced tomato, fresh or canned*
- *1 teaspoon dried marjoram*
- *2 bay leaves*
- *2 quarts chicken stock Salt and freshly ground pepper, to taste*
- *1 tablespoon lemon juice*

Yogurt Topping

- *½ cup plain yogurt Grated rind of 1 lemon*
- *2 tablespoons minced chives Salt and freshly ground pepper, to taste*

1. Preheat oven to 375° F. Cut eggplants into quarters and brush cut surfaces with 2 tablespoons of the oil. In a roasting pan place eggplants and bake until soft (about 30 minutes).

2. In a large saucepan over moderate heat, warm remaining 2 tablespoons oil and butter. Add shallot, carrot, and garlic and sauté 2 minutes. Add tomato and simmer 5 minutes. Add marjoram, bay leaves, roasted eggplant, and stock. Bring to a simmer and cover; reduce heat to maintain a simmer and cook 20 minutes.

3. Remove bay leaves. Transfer soup to a blender or food processor and purée. The soup can be made 1 day ahead to this point, covered, and refrigerated. Reheat slowly; add salt, pepper, and lemon juice. Transfer to a thermos. Serve in mugs, garnishing each portion with Yogurt Topping.

Makes about 12 cups.

Yogurt Topping In a small bowl stir together yogurt, lemon rind, and chives. Season with salt and pepper. Transfer to a lidded plastic container.

Makes about ½ cup.

MIXED GRAINS SALAD

Mixing costly wild rice with inexpensive grains adds a luxurious touch to a menu at modest expense.

- *¾ cup each barley, brown rice, and wild rice*
- *⅓ cup minced red onion*
- *½ cup minced celery*
- *⅓ cup chopped toasted walnuts (optional)*
- *2 tablespoons apple cider vinegar*
- *3 tablespoons lemon juice*
- *¾ cup olive oil*
- *1 tablespoon each minced fresh dill, mint, cilantro, and parsley Salt and freshly ground pepper, to taste*

1. In a medium saucepan over high heat, bring 2 cups lightly salted water to a boil. Add barley, cover, reduce heat to low, and cook 30 minutes. Set aside 5 minutes, then uncover and transfer to a bowl to cool.

2. In a medium saucepan over high heat, bring 2½ cups lightly salted water to a boil. Add brown rice, cover, reduce heat to low, and cook for 40 minutes. Set aside 5 minutes, then uncover and transfer to a bowl to cool.

3. In a medium saucepan over high heat, bring 2 cups lightly salted water to a boil. Add wild rice, cover, reduce heat to low, and cook 40 minutes. Set aside 5 minutes, then uncover and transfer to a bowl to cool.

4. In a large bowl combine cooled barley, brown rice, wild rice, onion, celery, and walnuts (if used). In a small bowl whisk together vinegar and lemon juice; whisk in oil gradually, then add dill, mint, cilantro, and parsley. Season with salt and pepper. Pour dressing over grains and toss to coat well. Serve at room temperature.

Serves 8.

LIME CHICKEN

Individual aluminum foil packets keep the just-baked chicken warm until the convoy arrives at the stadium. When opened, the packets release a seductive aroma of sweet onions, lime, and spices.

ın *¼ cup each lemon juice, lime juice, orange juice, and olive oil*
ın *1 tablespoon hot red-pepper flakes*
ın *1 teaspoon each chili powder and cumin*
ın *1 tablespoon kosher salt*
ın *2 onions, sliced paper-thin*
ın *2 chickens, quartered*

1. In a medium bowl whisk together the juices, oil, red-pepper flakes, chili powder, cumin, and salt; then stir in sliced onions.

2. Put chicken parts in a stainless steel, glass, or ceramic bowl and pour marinade over. Cover and refrigerate for at least 12 hours or up to 1 day.

3. Preheat oven to 375° F. Transfer chicken to a roasting pan; surround with onions. Roast chicken, basting occasionally with marinade, until juices run clear (about 45 minutes). When cool enough to handle, cut quarters in half and wrap each piece loosely in aluminum foil with some of the baked onions.

Serves 8.

86

CLOVE-SCENTED ORANGE CAKE

This fluffy chiffon cake is easy to make and rises high and light in the pan. It tastes best one or two days after baking and may be made up to five days ahead, wrapped in plastic, and refrigerated. Bring to room temperature before serving.

2¼ cups cake flour, sifted
1 cup plus 2 tablespoons sugar
1 tablespoon baking powder
1 teaspoon plus 1 pinch salt
1 teaspoon ground cloves
¾ cup orange juice
2 tablespoons grated orange rind
½ cup corn oil
6 eggs, separated
1 teaspoon vanilla extract
2 egg whites

1. Preheat oven to 325° F. Sift together flour, 1 cup of the sugar, baking powder, 1 teaspoon of the salt, and cloves.

2. With an electric mixer or by hand, beat juice, rind, oil, egg yolks, and vanilla until thoroughly blended. Add dry ingredients slowly and beat until they become smooth.

3. Beat 8 egg whites with a pinch salt to soft peaks. Add remaining 2 tablespoons sugar gradually and beat to stiff peaks. Stir one fourth of the egg whites into cake batter to lighten it, then gently fold in the remaining egg whites.

4. Pour batter into an ungreased 10-inch angel food, bundt, or tube pan. Bake until tester comes out clean (40 to 50 minutes). Cake should spring back when touched. Remove cake from oven and immediately invert cake pan onto a rack; let cake cool completely upside down. Run a knife around the edge of the pan to release the cake, then turn the cake out onto a rack.

5. To serve, cut with a serrated bread knife or with two large forks.

Makes one 10-inch cake.

Variation For a denser cake, bake in a 9- by 11-inch cake pan.

---

menu

FARE FROM THE FIFTIES
For 8

Alphabet Soup

Dagwood Sandwiches

Rings 'n' Strings

Kosher Dill Pickles

Triple Chocolate Pudding

Malteds and Cherry Colas

The sounds of golden oldies fill your ears while your eyes take in stacks of fresh bread and slices of ham, turkey, cheese, and more for mile-high Dagwood Sandwiches. The sight of alphabet letters floating in soup and a whiff of Rings 'n' Strings put you right back in the era of bobby sox and T-birds. A fitting finale is a fabulous chocolate pudding.

Timetable

Up to 24 hours ahead: Prepare chocolate pudding.
Up to 12 hours ahead: Prepare soup. Prepare all sandwich ingredients.
3 hours ahead: Prepare batter for the rings and soak onions.
1 hour ahead: Prepare and soak potatoes.
30 minutes ahead: Assemble sandwiches, if desired.
At serving time: Reheat soup. Fry onion rings and potatoes. Prepare malteds and cherry colas.

Planning

Baseball cards and bubble gum can accompany your invitations to an evening saluting the fifties. Encourage guests to dress the part: in the bobby sox, ponytails, and letter sweaters that marked the era.

The soup can be served in warm mugs, either before guests are seated or along with the sandwiches. Arrange Dagwood fixings on a countertop or sideboard, and invite guests to make their own sandwiches on their way to the table. While guests are making sandwiches, you can fry the onion and potato Rings 'n' Strings and put them on the dining table along with the pickles.

Most supermarkets carry malted milk powder for adding to milk shakes to create malteds; to make cherry colas, mix equal parts (or to taste) cherry soda and cola.

Presentation

Guests know they're back in the fabulous fifties when they spot a dining table set with 78-rpm "place mats," direct from the thrift shop.

For a centerpiece, use some high-top roller skates, slip a water glass inside, and tuck in a handful of yellow and white daisies. Or, set out a collection of period items: yo-yos, baseball cards with photographs of such heros as Mickey Mantle and Willie Mays, or cutouts of such favorite Hollywood stars as Marilyn Monroe and James Dean. Deck the walls with school pennants for yet another nostalgic salute to the decade.

Photograph, page 89: An over-stuffed Dagwood Sandwich starts with stacks of fixings, including smoked turkey, ham, cheese, spinach, a thin frittata, Rémoulade Sauce, and whole-grain bread. Hot from the fryer Rings 'n' Strings and old-fashioned malteds and cherry colas add to a meal that transports guests to the fabulous fifties.

ALPHABET SOUP

The canned version may hold the memories, but this one is chock-full of homemade flavor. Check the pasta section of the supermarket for dried alphabet pasta.

> ¼ cup olive oil
> 2 medium boiling potatoes, peeled and diced
> 1 cup peeled and diced carrot
> ¾ cup minced onion
> 1½ quarts chicken stock
> 2 tablespoons minced fresh basil
> 1 teaspoon minced fresh oregano
> 3 cups diced zucchini
> 3 cups peeled, seeded, and diced tomatoes, fresh or canned
> 1½ cups dried alphabet pasta
> ½ cup cooked peas
> Salt and freshly ground pepper, to taste
> Freshly grated Parmesan cheese, for accompaniment

In a large pot over moderate heat, warm olive oil. Add potatoes, carrot, and onion and sauté 5 minutes. Add chicken stock, basil, and oregano. Bring to a boil, reduce heat to maintain a simmer, and simmer 15 minutes. Add zucchini and 1 cup of the tomatoes. Simmer 10 minutes. Add pasta, peas, and remaining 2 cups tomatoes; simmer until pasta is cooked through. Season with salt and pepper. Serve immediately and pass a bowl of Parmesan.

Makes about 16 cups.

DAGWOOD SANDWICHES

Dagwood Bumstead, of comic strip fame, is known for taking everything out of the refrigerator and piling it high between slices of bread. This sandwich is more highly designed, but it's still a double-decker construction for hearty eaters. Variations are absolutely encouraged. You will need 16 eight-inch bamboo skewers to hold the sandwiches together.

> Dijon mustard
> 1 loaf best-quality sliced whole-grain bread
> ½ cup Rémoulade Sauce (see page 67)
> 1 loaf best-quality sliced sourdough bread
> ½ pound each smoked turkey, and imported Emmenthaler or Jarlsberg cheese, sliced paper-thin
> 1 bunch fresh spinach, washed, dried, and stems removed
> 1 recipe Frittata With Herbs and Onions (see page 115)
> 1 head romaine lettuce, washed and dried
> ½ pound ham, sliced paper-thin

Homemade Mayonnaise

> 1 egg
> 1½ teaspoons Dijon mustard
> 1 tablespoon lemon juice, or more to taste
> ¼ cup olive oil
> ½ cup corn oil
> Salt, to taste

To make one sandwich, spread mustard on one side of a slice of whole-grain bread. Spread Rémoulade Sauce on one side of a second slice of whole-grain bread. Spread Basil Mayonnaise on both sides of a slice of sourdough bread. Put a slice of turkey, a slice of cheese, and two spinach leaves on one whole-grain slice. Top with sourdough bread. Stack a thin slice of frittata, a leaf of romaine, and a slice of ham on top of that. Cover with remaining slice of whole-grain bread. Secure with two bamboo skewers and slice.

Makes 8 double-decker sandwiches.

Homemade Mayonnaise In a food processor or blender, place egg, mustard, and 1 tablespoon of the lemon juice. Blend until egg is pale (about 4 seconds). With motor running, add olive oil drop by drop until mixture thickens. Gradually add remaining olive oil and corn oil in a slow, steady stream. Season with salt and add more lemon juice if desired.

Makes 1 cup.

Basil Mayonnaise Stir in 1½ tablespoons minced fresh basil.

RINGS 'N' STRINGS

French-fried onion rings and potatoes must be cooked at the last minute, but it would hardly be a fifties party without them. Line baskets with brightly colored paper napkins and pile them high with hot-from-the-fryer Rings 'n' Strings.

> 2 cups flour
> 2 cups flat beer
> 2 teaspoons salt, plus salt to taste
> 2 pounds sweet red onion, in ¼-inch-thick slices
> 2 pounds baking potatoes, peeled
> Vegetable oil, for deep-frying

1. Whisk together flour, beer, and 2 teaspoons of the salt and let stand, covered, 3 hours. Soak onion slices in ice water while beer batter rests.

2. Using a mandolin, a sharp knife, or a shoestring-potato cutter, cut potatoes into thin strips about 5 inches long and ⅛ inch thick. Transfer strips to ice water as they are cut and soak 30 minutes.

3. In a deep kettle heat at least 3 inches of oil to 375° F. Drain potato strips well and pat thoroughly dry. Fry until golden brown (about 2 to 3 minutes). Use a large wire-mesh spoon to transfer potatoes to paper towels to drain. Salt lightly.

4. Drain onions well and pat thoroughly dry. Dip in batter, letting excess drip off. Fry until golden on both sides, turning once. Drain on paper towels and salt lightly.

Serves 8.

TRIPLE CHOCOLATE PUDDING

Instant pudding from a package can't compare with this rich and creamy homemade version. Use premium-quality chocolate for best results.

    4½ cups milk
    ½   cup plus 1 teaspoon
        unsweetened cocoa
    1   cup sugar
    ¼   cup cornstarch
    3   eggs
    4   egg yolks
    5   ounces each *grated bittersweet*
        and grated semisweet
        chocolate
    1   teaspoon *vanilla extract*
    ½   teaspoon *almond extract*
    ¼   cup *unsalted butter, softened*
    1   cup *whipped cream*
    2   ounces *grated white chocolate,*
        for garnish

1. In a large saucepan combine milk, ½ cup of the cocoa, and sugar. Bring to a simmer over moderate heat, stirring constantly. Set aside.

2. In a small bowl whisk together cornstarch and ½ cup of the hot chocolate-milk mixture. In a separate bowl whisk together eggs and egg yolks. Add some of the hot chocolate-milk mixture from the saucepan to eggs to warm them, then add all of egg mixture to saucepan. Cook over moderate heat, stirring constantly, 1 minute; do not allow mixture to boil. Stir in cornstarch mixture and cook, stirring, until mixture comes to a simmer. Simmer 1 minute.

3. Strain mixture through a fine sieve into a clean saucepan. Stir in chocolates, vanilla and almond extracts, and butter. Spoon mixture into 8 dessert glasses arranged on a tray; cover glasses with plastic wrap to prevent a skin from forming on the tops of the puddings. Cool slightly, then refrigerate until thoroughly chilled (about 4 hours).

4. To serve, sift remaining 1 teaspoon cocoa over whipped cream. Fold in gently. Garnish puddings with cocoa-flavored whipped cream and white chocolate.

Serves 8.

---

menu

ANTIPASTI AND ITALIAN WINE BAR
For 16

Skewered Artichokes,
Fennel, and Peppers

Minted Scallops

Italian Baked Clams

Eggplant and Olive Relish on Toasts

Italian Wines and Apéritifs

The traditional cocktail party adopts a foreign accent with an all-Italian wine bar and a menu devoted to antipasti. While guests sip a sparkling Prosecco or a fruity Chianti, the kitchen sends forth fragrant baked clams, cool minted scallops, and colorful skewers of marinated autumn vegetables.

Timetable

Up to 1 week ahead: Prepare eggplant and olive relish.
Up to 1 day ahead: Marinate scallops. Marinate artichokes, fennel, and peppers.
Up to 12 hours ahead: Soak clams, cook, and marinate.
Up to 4 hours ahead: Skewer vegetables.
Up to 2 hours ahead: Make toasts for eggplant and olive relish.
At serving time: Assemble and bake clams.

Planning

One of the charms of this easy menu is that one person can prepare and serve it without help. Before guests arrive, both scallops and skewered vegetables can be prepared and ready to serve. When most of the guests have arrived, you can take a moment to make up a platter of eggplant toasts. If you prefer, you can spoon the eggplant into a serving bowl, surround it with toasts, and let guests help themselves. Assembling and baking the clams will take about 5 minutes and should wait until all guests have arrived.

You won't need to supply plates or utensils for this "finger fare," so cleanup is especially easy. Place some bowls or ash trays prominently around the room for guests to deposit empty skewers and clam shells.

Your self-service wine bar might feature four Italian wines—perhaps a sparkling wine, a red, and two whites. Three bottles of each should be more than sufficient. See "Italian Wines and Apéritifs" (opposite page) for more guidance. If you offer apéritifs, you'll need to add ice, lemons, and plain soda to the bar.

Presentation

The high-tech look is the rage in Italian restaurants, both in the United States and in Italy. You can imitate the look with a color scheme in silver, black, and white and with accessories in clear acrylic, black lacquer, and chrome. Mirrored trays can serve as dramatic serving pieces, for example, and sleek calla lilies in black vases add a striking note.

Two bowls of scallops, two trays of skewered vegetables, and two platters of eggplant toasts can be positioned around the room to encourage people to circulate. Put cocktail napkins alongside. Pass the baked clams when they emerge from the oven.

Photograph, page 92: Traditional Italian predinner drinks accompany an array of antipasti (clockwise from left): eggplant and olive relish; skewered vegetables; and marinated scallops and baked clams.

SKEWERED ARTICHOKES, FENNEL, AND PEPPERS

Marinated autumn vegetables threaded on 6-inch wooden skewers make colorful cocktail fare.

- 8 *large artichokes*
- 1 *cup dry white wine*
- 4 *garlic cloves, peeled and crushed*
- 1 *cup olive oil*
- ¼ *cup lemon juice*
- 3 *large red bell peppers*
- 1 *large or 2 small bulbs fennel*
- ⅓ *cup minced onion*
- 3 *tablespoons minced parsley, plus parsley for garnish*

1. Using a serrated knife, cut off the top third of each artichoke. In a large pot place artichokes along with wine, garlic, 2 tablespoons of the oil, 2 tablespoons of the lemon juice, and just enough water to cover. Bring to a boil over high heat, reduce heat to maintain a simmer, and cook until a center leaf comes out easily. Drain and cool.

2. Prepare bell peppers according to directions for Roasting Bell Peppers and Chiles (see page 62). Cut into strips ⅓ inch wide.

3. Halve fennel lengthwise. Cut out core. Slice crosswise about ½ inch thick. In a large bowl whisk together remaining oil and lemon juice, onion, and 3 tablespoons of the parsley. Add sliced fennel and peppers.

4. Peel back artichoke leaves to reveal the pale green heart. (Save outer leaves for a cold salad.) Cut enough off the top to leave hearts 1½ to 2 inches long. Quarter hearts. Use a small spoon to scrape away the fuzzy choke. Add quartered hearts to fennel-pepper mixture. Toss vegetables carefully to coat well with marinade. Cover and refrigerate for at least 2 hours or up to 1 day. Bring to room temperature before serving.

5. To serve, thread an artichoke quarter on each skewer. Follow with a pepper strip, formed into an S shape, and a slice of fennel. Mound skewers on a platter and garnish them with parsley.

Makes 32 skewers.

MINTED SCALLOPS

Most party-supply and variety stores carry festive 3-inch toothpicks to accompany cocktail fare; toothpicks with real shell tops are easy to find. You can present the scallops in two serving bowls with toothpicks alongside; or you can save and clean the extra clamshells from Italian Baked Clams (see page 93) and spoon the scallop mixture into the shells for a "walk-away" shellfish cocktail.

- 1½ *pounds fresh bay or sea scallops*
- ½ *cup loosely packed fresh mint leaves, minced*
- 2 *tablespoons minced Italian parsley*
- 2 *cups extravirgin olive oil*
- 3 *tablespoons lemon juice, plus more to taste*
- 1 *teaspoon grated lemon rind*
- 1 *cup seeded and diced tomato*
- 2 *tablespoons minced shallot*
- 1 *teaspoon salt, or more to taste*
- ¼ *teaspoon freshly ground pepper, or more to taste*

1. If using bay scallops, leave whole. If using sea scallops, trim away tough muscle and cut scallops into ½-inch dice. Transfer to a stainless steel, glass, or enamel bowl; add mint, parsley, olive oil, 3 tablespoons of the lemon juice, rind, tomato, shallot, 1 teaspoon of the salt, and ¼ teaspoon of the pepper.

2. Cover and refrigerate at least 45 minutes or up to 1 day; remove from refrigerator 30 minutes before serving. Taste and adjust seasoning; adding salt, pepper, and lemon juice. Transfer to a serving bowl or to individual clamshells.

Serves 16.

ITALIAN WINES AND APÉRITIFS

The best accompaniment to antipasti is one of Italy's delicious wines or apéritifs. To help you offer your guests a representative sampling, here is a brief guide to what's available.

Whether at home, in a café, or in a restaurant, an Italian meal is generally preceded by an *aperitivo*—a beverage designed to awaken the palate and perk up the appetite.

Among the most popular apéritifs are Campari, Fernet Branca, and Amer Picon—all Italian bitters made from the bitter and aromatic essences of plants, seeds, roots, flowers, leaves, bark, stems, and fruits dissolved in an alcohol base. Bitters are almost always mixed with soda; in fact, premixed and bottled Campari-and-soda is widely available.

Cinzano, Martini & Rossi, and Punt é Mes are all sweet Italian vermouths, each made by a slightly different formula. Serve Italian vermouth well chilled, either neat or on the rocks, or with a splash of soda and a twist of lemon.

Cynar is a wine-based apéritif flavored with artichoke. Serve it as you would vermouth.

In addition, more and more Italian producers are making dry sparkling wine by the champagne method. Look for Prosecco and Ferrari, among others. These dry sparklers make excellent apéritifs.

When selecting Italian wines for a cocktail party, choose those that are light-bodied, fresh, and young. Heavy-bodied or aged wines require a formal meal to bring out their best qualities.

Among the white wines to look for are Cortese di Gavi, Frascati, Lugana, Vernaccia di San Gimignano, Pinot Grigio, Verdicchio, and Soave.

Among the red wines to look for are Barbera d'Alba, Barbera d'Asti, Bardolino, Chianti or Chianti Classico, Dolcetto d'Alba, Grignolino, Nebbiolo d'Alba, and Valpolicella.

ITALIAN BAKED CLAMS

Clams marinated in herbs and olive oil and then baked with seasoned bread crumbs are a perfect partner to a glass of Italian white wine. Fresh clams should be tightly closed when purchased and before they are cooked. Discard any that are open. This recipe can be halved successfully to allow two clams per person instead of four.

      64 small fresh clams
       2 tablespoons cornmeal
       2 red bell peppers
       2 cups dry white wine
      ½ cup chopped onion
       3 tablespoons minced parsley
       2 tablespoons minced basil
       1 tablespoon minced garlic
      ¾ cup olive oil, plus olive oil
          for drizzling
       1 cup Seasoned Bread Crumbs
          (see page 16)

1. Scrub clams thoroughly. In a large pot place, clams and cornmeal; add water to cover. Refrigerate 4 hours.

2. Prepare bell peppers according to directions for Roasting Bell Peppers and Chiles (see page 62). Cut into long strips about ⅛ inch wide.

3. Preheat oven to 400° F. Drain clams and place in a large roasting pan with wine and onion. Cover tightly with aluminum foil and bake 10 minutes. Uncover and transfer opened clams to a large bowl. Re-cover and return roasting pan to oven for an additional 3 to 4 minutes. Uncover and transfer additional opened clams to bowl. Discard any clams that refuse to open.

4. When clams are cool enough to handle, remove from shell and return to bowl along with any juices that have accumulated. Separate shells at the hinge and discard half the shells, or save them for Minted Scallops (see page 91).

5. Add parsley, basil, garlic, and ¾ cup of the oil to clams; stir to blend. Cover and refrigerate for up to 8 hours, if desired.

6. To serve, preheat broiler. Place a clam in each half shell. Top each with a sliver of red pepper. Dust with Seasoned Bread Crumbs and drizzle lightly with oil. Broil until lightly browned (about 3 minutes). Serve immediately.

Makes 64 clams.

EGGPLANT AND OLIVE RELISH ON TOASTS

The sweet-and-sour eggplant relish called caponata is a popular anti-pasto in southern Italy. Here, it's served on toasted bread rounds for easy stand-up eating.

       1 large (about 1 lb) eggplant,
          unpeeled and cut into
          ½-inch dice
       3 tablespoons kosher salt
      ½ cup plus 3 tablespoons olive
          oil, plus olive oil for toasting
       1 cup minced red onion
     1½ cups minced celery
       1 tablespoon minced garlic
      ½ cup tomato sauce
      ½ cup each pitted and finely
          chopped imported green olives
          and black Greek olives
      ¼ cup red wine vinegar, plus
          more to taste
       2 tablespoons sugar, plus sugar
          to taste
      ¼ cup loosely packed fresh basil,
          chopped
      ½ cup minced parsley
      32 French bread rounds (about
          2 in. diameter and
          ¼ in. thick)
          Salt and freshly ground
          pepper, to taste
      ¼ cup freshly grated Parmesan
          cheese

1. Sprinkle eggplant cubes with salt and let drain in a colander 45 minutes. Rinse quickly and pat dry. Transfer eggplant to a baking dish, add ½ cup of the olive oil and toss to coat thoroughly.

2. Preheat oven to 400° F. Bake eggplant until soft but not mushy (10 to 15 minutes).

3. In a large skillet over moderate heat, warm 3 tablespoons of the oil; add onion and celery and sauté until softened (about 5 minutes). Add garlic and cook 2 minutes. Add tomato sauce, bring to a simmer, and reduce heat to maintain a simmer; cook 15 minutes. Stir in eggplant, olives, ¼ cup of the vinegar, and 2 tablespoons of the sugar. Simmer 10 minutes. Remove from heat and stir in basil and ¼ cup of the parsley. Cool, cover, and refrigerate for up to 1 week, if desired.

4. Preheat oven to 375° F. Arrange bread rounds on a baking sheet; brush one side with remaining olive oil. Bake until lightly browned (5 to 7 minutes). Remove from tray and let cool.

5. Bring eggplant mixture to room temperature. Stir in remaining ¼ cup parsley. Season with salt and pepper, and add more vinegar or sugar if desired.

6. To serve, spoon eggplant mixture onto toasts. Dust with Parmesan and arrange on platters.

Makes 32 toasts.

Mr. and Mrs. Ward Finer
18 Spruce Street
Mill Valley, California 94941

Gold lamé glamorizes a winter
table that is set with pinecones to
bring the outdoors in. For menu
zest, rely on tangy citrus and
seasonal grapes.

Winter Menus

P arty giving tends to reach a frenzy
in winter, as friends and family
assemble for the traditonal year-end
holidays. Creative cooks looking to put a
personal stamp on these parties will find
a selection of unusual ideas in this chapter.
Consider a lavish dessert buffet for Christmas
(see page 108), a wake-up New Year's Day
Buffet Brunch (see page 114), or a braised-
duck dinner for Chinese New Year (see page
120). To make all your entertaining easier,
you'll find tips on such behind-the-scenes
preparation as buying in bulk (see page 117),
and Organizing Your Kitchen (see page 105).
A Special Feature on Presenting Food for Eye
Appeal (see page 106) guides you to tantalizing
eating in every season.

WINTER ENTERTAINING

Winter entertaining gets off to a fast and furious start with the traditional round of parties for Christmas and New Year's. Buffets are an efficient way to handle holiday crowds, especially if space is at a premium. There's no need to set formal tables, provided you can offer plenty of informal seating and cocktail or corner tables for guests to place their wine or coffee.

A stand-up Champagne reception (at right) with an array of tempting finger fare is another alternative for a large holiday gathering. As long as the menu doesn't require plate and fork, you can accommodate dozens of people in a modest space.

Winter also brings with it the prospect of fireside suppers (see page 103), either at home or at a vacation ski cabin. Cozy breakfasts are another winter pleasure; on Valentine's Day, double the pleasure and present breakfast-in-bed (see page 118).

Cold weather makes spicy foods particularly appealing. An authentic Texas chili feed (see page 111) will warm guests from their toes to their ten-gallon hats.

Your creativity as a host can extend to children as well as to adults. A Children's Birthday Party (see page 100) becomes a memorable event when the fare includes Make-Your-Own Pizzas and Carrot Cake in a Cone (see page 102).

For the cook, the winter market provides such delights as crunchy snow peas and mushrooms, quince and cranberries, butter-smooth pears and persimmons, nuts in the shell, and a wealth of citrus. Winter menus can incorporate rich meats, such as duck and ham, and elaborate desserts. Most diners indulge themselves a little at holiday time, enjoying luscious chocolate creations, cookies, and fruits baked with sour cream.

To give your table a seasonal appearance, consider dressing it in such colors as holly green, cranberry, chestnut, russet, silver, gold, ice blue, or classic black and white. Deck the halls and tables with holly, pine boughs, poinsettias, and candles.

---

menu

CHAMPAGNE RECEPTION
For 50

Cocktail Crumpets
With Melted Gruyère

Peppered Crab Cakes

Spinach-Wrapped Scallops
With Lemon and Ginger

Wild Rice Pancakes
With Mixed Fruit Chutney

Skewered Honeydew Cubes
With Smithfield Ham (see Planning)

Vegetarian Grape Leaves
(see page 56)

Champagne or Other Sparkling Wine

Any special occasion sparkles when the menu includes a Champagne bar and a selection of foods that go well with it: elegant cocktail crumpets, spinach-wrapped scallops, and miniature crab cakes.

Timetable

A few weeks ahead: Make chutney.
Up to 3 days ahead: Make crumpets. Make grape leaves.
Up to 1 day ahead: Make pancake batter.
Up to 12 hours ahead: Make crab mixture.
3 hours ahead: Make scallop rolls.
2 hours ahead: Prepare crumpets for toasting.
1 hour ahead: Wrap honeydew cubes with ham, and skewer.
At serving time: Bake crab cakes. Heat crumpets. Steam scallop rolls. Make pancakes.

Planning

Nothing sets a festive mood better than sparkling wine. A good merchant can help you select a sparkling wine to fit your budget. Figure about one 4-ounce glass per hour per person; for a three-hour party for 50, two cases of Champagne should be more than sufficient. Keep it well chilled, in the refrigerator or on ice, before serving. Stocking the bar with peach nectar and raspberry and black currant liqueurs allows guests to enjoy a variety of Champagne drinks (see page 52).

Preparing food for a crowd of 50 is easy with careful planning. All the dishes in this menu can be prepared up to the final cooking before guests arrive. During the party, a kitchen helper can keep turning out crumpets, crab cakes, and scallops at an appropriate pace. Skewered honeydew melon cubes wrapped in tissue-thin slices of Smithfield ham require no cooking and can be sent forth as soon as guests arrive. To add a theatrical touch, set up a griddle station in view of the guests and cook Wild Rice Pancakes to order.

You will probably want to hire a small staff. One helper the morning of the party and two during the party should be sufficient to manage the kitchen; you'll also need a bartender and two people to serve.

Presentation

Repeat the image of sparkling wine with a decorating scheme in crystal and gold. If you have candlesticks and platters in crystal, now is the time to show them off. Shimmering gold lamé ribbon, gold balls, gold-sprayed pinecones, and holiday greens can be interwoven with candles for an elegant look on coffee tables and sideboards. Even the platters of passed hors d'oeuvres can be dressed with a votive candle in a crystal holder.

Photograph, page 98: Flutes of sparkling wine complement elegant fare (clockwise from top right): spinach-wrapped scallops, peppery crab cakes, and wild rice pancakes with sour cream and fruit chutney.

COCKTAIL CRUMPETS WITH MELTED GRUYÈRE

Crusty two-bite crumpets topped with melted Gruyère are irresistible when hot from the oven. Note that the batter must rise about 2½ hours before use.

   2 packages active dry yeast
   2 teaspoons sugar
1½ cups warm water (about 105° F)
   1 cup warm milk (about 105° F)
   ¼ cup butter, melted
2½ cups flour
   1 teaspoon salt
1½ teaspoons baking soda
   2 tablespoons hot water
   1 pound Gruyère cheese, coarsely grated
   ⅓ cup minced fresh chives

1. Dissolve yeast and sugar in the warm water. Let stand 10 minutes. In a large mixing bowl, combine milk, butter, flour, and salt. Add yeast mixture and beat 7 minutes by hand or 5 minutes with electric mixer. Cover with plastic wrap and let rise until doubled (about 1½ hours).

2. Dissolve baking soda in the hot water and add to batter. Beat well. Cover with plastic wrap and let rise again until doubled (about 1 hour).

3. Lightly butter 2-inch crumpet rings (you can use clean, empty tin cans with both ends removed). Heat a skillet, preferably nonstick, over moderate heat until very hot. Brush lightly with vegetable oil. Place rings on skillet. Put 1½ to 2 tablespoons batter in each ring. Cover skillet and cook until a light crust forms on top (about 4 minutes). Uncover, remove rings, and turn crumpets. Cook about 2 minutes more, uncovered, to brown second side. Transfer crumpets to a paper towel, then to a rack to cool.

4. Preheat oven to 350° F. Place a heaping ½-tablespoon of grated cheese on each crumpet. Transfer to a baking sheet and heat until cheese melts and bubbles (5 to 7 minutes). Arrange crumpets on a warm platter and garnish with minced chives.

Makes about 4 dozen 2-inch crumpets.

PEPPERED CRAB CAKES

Because they're baked instead of fried, these crab cakes are easy on the cook. Two kinds of pepper and a chile give the mixture a kick; you may want to add the pepper gradually and taste as you go.

   5 pounds fresh crabmeat, cartilage removed
   2 teaspoons freshly ground black pepper
   ½ teaspoon freshly ground white pepper
   1 teaspoon finely minced green chile
   1 cup whipping cream
   1 cup peeled, seeded, and diced tomato
   1 tablespoon tomato paste
   ¼ cup finely minced green onion Salt, to taste
   ¼ cup each melted butter and olive oil
   ⅓ cup freshly grated Parmesan cheese
  48 strips sun-dried tomato
   ⅓ cup minced parsley

1. In food processor or blender, combine 1 pound of the crabmeat, black pepper, white pepper, chile, and cream. Blend until well mixed but not puréed. Transfer to a large mixing bowl. Add tomato, tomato paste, onion, and remaining 4 pounds crab meat. Blend well and salt to taste.

2. Form mixture into small cakes about 1½ to 2 inches in diameter and ½ to ¾ inch thick. Place cakes on a greased baking sheet. Cover with plastic wrap and refrigerate until ready to bake, up to 12 hours in advance.

3. Preheat oven to 425° F. In a small bowl whisk together butter and oil and brush tops of cakes thoroughly. Dust with Parmesan. Bake 5 minutes. Remove from oven and garnish each cake while still on the baking sheet with a strip of sun-dried tomato and a sprinkle of parsley. Transfer to a warm serving tray and serve immediately.

Makes 4 dozen small crab cakes.

SPINACH-WRAPPED SCALLOPS WITH LEMON AND GINGER

Whole blanched spinach leaves provide a bright wrapper for lemon- and ginger-scented fresh scallops.

   3 large (at least 14 oz each) bunches fresh spinach
1½ pounds bay or sea scallops
   1 cup jicama, in ⅛-inch dice
   ¼ cup minced green onion
   2 tablespoons grated lemon rind
   ½ cup lemon juice
   2 tablespoons minced fresh ginger
      Salt and freshly ground pepper, to taste
   ¼ cup olive oil
   2 cups sake
   1 cup water

1. Trim away tough spinach stems. Wash leaves in several changes of cold water. Bring a large pot of lightly salted water to a boil. Blanch leaves 5 seconds in boiling water, then immediately plunge into cold water to stop the cooking. Lay blanched leaves on paper towels. You need about 50 perfect, untorn leaves.

2. Trim away any tough muscle from scallops. If using sea scallops, cut into ⅓-inch cubes (leave bay scallops whole). In a large mixing bowl, combine scallops, jicama, onion, 1 tablespoon of the lemon rind, ¼ cup of the lemon juice, and ginger. Let stand 5 minutes, then season with salt and pepper.

3. Arrange spinach leaves smooth side down. Put about 1½ tablespoons scallop mixture on each leaf and roll up, folding in sides like an envelope. Place rolls on a baking sheet, cover with plastic wrap, and refrigerate up to 3 hours.

4. To serve, whisk together olive oil and remaining lemon rind and lemon juice. In bottom of steamer, put sake and the water. Bring to a simmer. Place spinach rolls in steamer and steam, covered, 2 minutes. Turn off heat and uncover. Brush with oil-lemon mixture. Transfer to a warm serving platter and serve immediately.

Makes 50 scallop rolls.

WILD RICE PANCAKES WITH MIXED FRUIT CHUTNEY

These hot-off-the-griddle pancakes require some last-minute attention, but their unusual flavor well repays the effort. Wild rice gives them a rich, nutty taste that pairs perfectly with a glass of Champagne. Garnish with a teaspoon of fruit chutney or with a dab of sour cream. The Mixed Fruit Chutney yields more than you will need; reserve the rest for other uses.

- 8 eggs
- 2 cups buttermilk
- ½ cup plain yogurt
- 1½ teaspoons baking soda
- 2½ cups flour
- 1 tablespoon each baking powder and sugar
- 1 teaspoon salt
- 2 cups cooked and cooled wild rice
- ¾ cup butter, melted Vegetable oil, for brushing
- 1½ cups Mixed Fruit Chutney or 1½ cups sour cream

Mixed Fruit Chutney

- 2 cups ripe honeydew melon, diced
- 3 tablespoons kosher salt
- 1½ cups peeled, cored, and diced apple
- 1 cup peeled, cored, and diced pear
- 1 cup peeled, seeded, and diced mango or papaya
- ¼ cup each minced shallot and minced red onion
- ¾ cup currants
- 2 teaspoons each minced garlic and grated fresh ginger
- 1½ cups firmly packed brown sugar
- 1 cup cider vinegar
- 2 cinnamon sticks
- 1 tablespoon mustard seed
- 1 serrano chile, minced
- 1 teaspoon hot red-pepper flakes
- ¾ cup chopped walnuts
- 2 tablespoons grated orange rind
- ¼ cup orange liqueur

1. In a large mixing bowl, whisk together eggs, buttermilk, yogurt, and baking soda. In another bowl stir together flour, baking powder, sugar, and salt. Add dry ingredients to liquid, along with wild rice and ¼ cup of the butter. Stir just until blended. Batter may be made up to 1 day ahead, covered, and refrigerated.

2. Warm a large skillet, preferably nonstick, over moderate heat until hot. Lightly brush surface with oil.

3. Drop batter by tablespoons into 2-inch rounds. Pancakes will be thin. When small bubbles appear in the surface and the batter has set around the edges, flip and cook until colored on the second side. Brush top lightly with some of the butter while still in the skillet.

4. Transfer to a warm serving platter and top each pancake with 1 teaspoon Mixed Fruit Chutney. Serve immediately.

Makes about 4 dozen 2½-inch pancakes.

Mixed Fruit Chutney

1. Place honeydew in a bowl and add 2 tablespoons of the salt. Cover with water and refrigerate overnight. Drain melon, rinse well, and place in a large pot.

2. Add all remaining ingredients and bring to a boil. Simmer, partially covered, until mixture darkens and thickens (1½ to 2 hours). It will continue to thicken as it cools.

3. Pour while hot into sterilized jars and seal. Chutney will keep up to 1 year if unopened.

Makes 4 half-pints.

Tips

...ON PLANNING A PARTY MENU

The perfect party menu is a delicate balancing act. It should balance flavors, textures, and colors without taxing your budget, schedule, or chosen setting. Here are some tips for creating a workable and pleasurable party menu.

Set a budget and stick to it. To get as much mileage as possible out of expensive items, serve them in small but elegant portions. A half-pound of smoked salmon can be stretched to feed 50 if made into tiny two-bite quiches. Balance expensive dishes with handsome baskets of crudités or elaborate platters of marinated vegetables.

Vary textures, flavors, and colors within a menu. A creamy soup should be followed by crunchy textures (see Lunch on the Boat, page 57). A spicy, complex couscous (see page 81) might be preceded by a sweet and simple carrot salad. Visualize the whole buffet or the dinner plate, and make sure the colors are varied.

Let the season be your guide. When a produce item is least expensive, its flavor is usually at its peak. Save asparagus dishes for spring and tomato dishes for late summer. Each season has its pleasures and they are worth exploiting.

Select a menu that fits your schedule. If you won't have much time the day of the party but can prepare food in stages in the days preceding it, choose a menu that allows that kind of flexibility. If you'll have help in the kitchen, you'll be able to plan some dishes that require last-minute attention. Otherwise, it's a good idea to plan dishes that can be done before guests arrive.

Select a workable menu for the number of guests you're having. Do you have enough pots and pans to make chili for 48? Do you have enough oven space, refrigerator space, and burners for your menu?

CHILDREN'S BIRTHDAY PARTY
For 12

Apple, Lemon 'n' Lime Drink

Make-Your-Own Pizzas

Strawberry-Pineapple Pops

Carrot Cake in a Cone

At this party, the sounds of "Happy Birthday" rise over a surprising confection: scoops of scrumptious carrot-apple cake set in cones and embellished with cream cheese frosting.

Timetable

Up to 1 week ahead: Make and freeze pizza dough rounds.

Up to 4 days ahead: Prepare popsicles.

Up to 1 day ahead: Prepare carrot cake.

Up to 4 hours ahead: Prepare pizza toppings. Prepare drink base (minus seltzer). Prepare cream cheese frosting.

1 hour ahead: Assemble cones and frost. Remove dough rounds from freezer, unwrap, and place on prepared cookie sheets.

At serving time: Add seltzer to drink.

Planning

The last thing you want to do at a children's birthday party is cook. Your attention is needed elsewhere, from taking pictures to keeping the peace. This meal can be made entirely ahead, except for the final baking of the pizzas. With the children as their own chefs, you should have plenty of photo opportunities.

Presentation

Set the table with a rainbow of colors, selecting paper plates, cups, napkins, and cloth in bright and lively shades. For a centerpiece, a variety store can supply you with a child's drum; remove one end and fill the drum with popcorn and colorful suckers. Use gumdrops or jelly beans to spell out the name of each child at his or her place.

Photograph, page 101: Don't let appearances fool you: These "vanilla ice cream cones" are made of carrot-raisin cake scooped into a sugar cone, then decorated with cream cheese frosting and colored sugars. They are sure to be a hit at this Children's Birthday Party, with spaghetti-thin candles marking the guest of honor's cone.

APPLE, LEMON 'N' LIME DRINK

Better than any cola, this icy homemade soda is based on fresh fruit juices. You can make the fruit juice base several hours ahead and refrigerate, but add the seltzer just before serving to retain its sparkle.

⅔ *cup plus 2½ cups water*

⅓ *cup each sugar, lemon juice, and lime juice*

2 *quarts cold apple juice*

1 *quart cold seltzer*

1. In a small saucepan combine ⅔ cup of the water and sugar. Bring to a boil over high heat and boil 2 minutes. Set sugar syrup aside.

2. In a large pitcher combine juices, and the remaining 2½ cups water. Sweeten to taste with sugar syrup. Add seltzer just before serving.

Makes 1 gallon.

MAKE-YOUR-OWN PIZZAS

The results are sure to please when each guest gets a custom-made pizza. Set colorful toppings out in bowls and let youngsters serve themselves.

6 *cups flour*

1 *tablespoon salt*

2 *packages active dry yeast*

2 *tablespoons honey*

2 *cups warm (about 110° F) water*

¼ *cup vegetable oil*

Cornmeal

Toppings: chopped green or black olives; grated cheddar cheese; grated mozzarella cheese; grated jack cheese; diced red, green, and yellow bell peppers; thinly sliced salami; shredded ham; chopped or sliced tomatoes; tomato sauce, homemade or canned

1. Preheat oven to 475° F. In large bowl of electric mixer fitted with dough hook, combine flour and salt. In a small bowl whisk together yeast, honey, and the warm water. Let stand 10 minutes. Add oil to liquids and whisk to blend. With mixer on low speed, add liquid ingredients to dry ingredients. Knead until mixture forms a smooth and elastic ball (8 to 10 minutes). Transfer dough to an oiled bowl, turn to coat entire surface with oil, cover, and let rest until nearly doubled (about 45 minutes).

2. Divide dough into 20 pieces. On a lightly floured surface, roll each piece into a ball. Flatten each ball into a circle about ¼ inch thick and 2½ to 3 inches in diameter. Freeze for up to one week if you wish.

3. Transfer rounds to baking sheets dusted with cornmeal and thaw for 10 minutes if frozen. Let children cover rounds with any combination of toppings. Put grated cheese on top of other ingredients to keep them from burning. Bake until well browned (6 to 8 minutes). Cool slightly before serving.

Makes twenty 2½- to 3-inch pizzas.

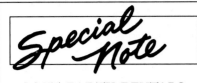
From demitasse spoons to dance floors, a rental company can offer you one-day use of supplies to make your party a hit. Among the items typically available from a party rental service are ashtrays, barbecue grills, bars and bar accessories, beverage fountains, candelabras, chafing dishes, chairs and children's chairs, china, coatracks, coffee makers (up to 100 cups), flatware, glasses, lighting fixtures, patio heaters, punch bowls, silver trays and serving pieces, tables and table linen, tents, water pitchers, and carafes.

Most party rental companies also sell disposable items: napkins, cutlery, paper tablecloths, tumblers, plastic or foam dinnerware, plastic stemware, frilled toothpicks, serving trays, and the like.

If your community is home to more than one party rental company, shop around for selection, price, and service. You may want to visit the store beforehand to view the styles and colors offered. To make sure you get the colors and styles you want, reserve your rentals at least three weeks before the party. Most services require a deposit with an order.

Discuss delivery, setup, and pickup with the service you choose. Sometimes rental personnel will set up and take down items such as tables and chairs for a fee. Ask whether dishes and silver must be washed or merely rinsed before being returned; linen is usually returned dirty. Find out whether the price includes same-day or next-day return, an important consideration if your party ends at 3:00 a.m. You'll also want to know how the company determines charges for broken items.

Have rentals delivered several hours before the party and check items off while the driver stands by. If items are missing, or if the company delivered brown napkins instead of blue, you have time to ask the driver to correct the mistake.

CARROT CAKE IN A CONE

Youngsters are fascinated by cake in a cone, especially when the cake is as good as this one. Loaded with raisins and nuts, grated carrots and apples, it's as nutritious as a cake can be. You can decorate the tops of the frosted cones with colored sugars, available at supermarkets and shops specializing in bakers' supplies. You will need a 15-inch-square piece of cardboard to hold the cones and enough aluminum foil to cover it.

    2   cups flour
    2   teaspoons each baking
        powder, baking soda, and
        cinnamon
    ½   teaspoon each nutmeg and
        allspice
    1   teaspoon salt
    1½ cups vegetable oil
    4   eggs
    1   cup granulated sugar
    1   cup firmly packed
        brown sugar
    ¾   teaspoon vanilla extract
    4   cups peeled and grated carrot
    1   apple, peeled, cored, and
        grated
    ¾   cup toasted cashews
    ½   cup golden raisins
    12 to 16 ice cream cones

Cream Cheese Frosting

    1½ pounds cream cheese, softened
    ¼   cup butter, softened
    ¼   cup honey
    2   teaspoons cinnamon
    1   tablespoon vanilla extract
    ¼   teaspoon almond extract

1. Preheat oven to 350° F. Sift together flour, baking powder, baking soda, cinnamon, nutmeg, allspice, and salt. Set aside. In a large bowl whisk together oil, eggs, sugars, and vanilla until smooth. Stir in carrot, apple, cashews, and raisins. Add dry ingredients and stir just until

blended. Pour into a greased and floured 9- by 13-inch pan. Bake until cake is firm on top and begins to pull away from sides of pan (40 to 50 minutes). Cool on a rack.

2. To assemble cones, cover the cardboard with aluminum foil. Cut out 12 to 16 well-spaced holes about 1½ inches wide. Set the foil-covered square atop four glasses to steady it. Set cones in holes. Scoop a portion of cooled cake into each cone. Place frosting in pastry bag and decorate tops of cones.

Makes 12 to 16 cones.

Cream Cheese Frosting Place all ingredients in large bowl of electric mixer. Beat until smooth. If too thin, refrigerate 30 minutes.

Makes about 4 cups.

STRAWBERRY-PINEAPPLE POPS

These homemade pops have a lively fruit flavor that isn't overridden by sugar. If you prefer, adapt the recipe to another fruit in season. Check a well-stocked variety store for the 32 wooden ice cream sticks you will need, or use thick wooden skewers. You'll also need enough plastic ice cube trays to make 32 cubes.

    24 ounces unsweetened
        pineapple juice
    3   cups strawberries
    ¼   cup honey
    ½   cup water
    2   tablespoons lemon juice

1. Place all ingredients in blender or food processor. Blend until smooth, then pour into plastic ice cube trays, and freeze.

2. Begin checking freezer after 20 minutes. When cubes just begin to harden, place a popsicle stick in each cube. Continue freezing until firm. To serve, unmold into a bowl and bring to the table immediately.

Makes 32 pops.

FIRESIDE SUPPER
For 4

Mediterranean Fish Soup

Grilled Veal Chops With Fresh Sage

Baked Orzo

Belgian Endive Salad
(see Planning)

Gratin of Winter Fruit

Red Wine

---

*After a bout with brisk
weather, skiers and others
will relish the thought of a
supper by the fire. Hot soup
and thick chops are
guaranteed to revive spirits,
especially when served at a
cozy hearthside table.*

Timetable

Up to 12 hours ahead: Make soup
through step 2.

Up to 8 hours ahead: Make marinade for chops. Make salad
dressing.

4 hours before serving dessert:
Begin marinating fruit.

1 hour ahead: Marinate veal
chops.

Up to 1 hour ahead: Prepare orzo
through step 1.

Planning

When only four friends gather for supper, the cook can afford to plan dishes that need some last-minute attention.

This meal requires the cook to make a few brief disappearances—to cook the veal, to toss endive leaves in a simple vinaigrette, and to whip up the sabayon. If all the ingredients are in place, none of these steps should take longer than 10 minutes.

To create a leisurely evening, serve the meal at a relaxed pace. Welcome guests with a glass of wine and some warm crackers or olives. After 30 minutes you can slip out to reheat the soup and put the orzo in the oven. The veal can go under the broiler or on the fire when you clear the soup. Serve the orzo with the chops, but save the salad for a separate course. Belgian endive is special enough to have the stage to itself. The fruit for dessert should not stand for more than 4 hours; finishing touches take only 5 minutes.

A dry but fruity red wine—a California Gamay, a French Beaujolais, or an Italian Chianti—would be a pleasant partner for soup and veal.

Presentation

If your dining table is too large or heavy to relocate by the fire, consider staging your fireside supper on a quilt-topped card table, or even on a large steamer trunk surrounded by pillows. Small pots of forced bulbs such as paper-white narcissus provide a cheerful and fragrant centerpiece. If there's room, add votive candles in tiny clay flowerpots.

This cozy meal calls for informal tableware and linens. You can serve the soup from a large tureen, or bring bowls or mugs in from the kitchen. The veal chops and orzo can be arranged on dinner plates in the kitchen, if there isn't room on the table for platters.

Photograph, page 104: A thick and meaty grilled veal chop rubbed with fresh sage, rice-shaped pasta called orzo, and a glass of hearty red wine warm guests at a cozy fireside supper. Paper-whites enliven the table.

MEDITERRANEAN FISH SOUP

Tomatoes, thyme, and saffron give this soup its Mediterranean flavor, with half-and-half adding a welcome enrichment. A blender makes quick work of reducing the soup to a smooth purée.

- ⅓ cup minced shallot
- 1½ cups chopped canned tomato
- ¼ cup minced celery
- ½ pound fish fillets, preferably cod, halibut, or other firm white fish
- 1 bay leaf
- ½ cup dry white wine
- ¼ teaspoon saffron threads
- 1 teaspoon minced fresh thyme
- 3 cups fish stock or clam juice
- 2 tablespoons soft bread crumbs
- ¼ pound fresh shrimp, cooked and peeled
  Salt and freshly ground pepper, to taste
- ½ cup half-and-half
- ¼ cup sour cream, for garnish
- 1 tablespoon minced chives, for garnish

1. In a large stockpot combine shallot, tomato, celery, fish, bay leaf, wine, saffron, thyme, and stock. Over high heat bring to a simmer. Reduce heat to maintain a simmer and cook until fish breaks apart very easily (about 25 minutes).

2. Remove bay leaf. Cool soup slightly, then place in blender, along with bread crumbs and shrimp. Purée mixture until smooth. Season with salt and pepper.

3. To serve, return to clean saucepan, stir in half-and-half, and reheat. Ladle into warm bowls and garnish each serving with 1 tablespoon sour cream and a sprinkle of chives.

Makes about 8 cups.

GRILLED VEAL CHOPS WITH FRESH SAGE

Delicate veal chops benefit from the flavor imparted by an olive oil and lemon marinade. Fresh rosemary or thyme could replace the sage, if desired.

> 4 large veal rib chops (about 1 in. thick)
> 1 tablespoon minced garlic
> 2 tablespoons lemon juice
> ½ cup olive oil
> ¼ cup minced parsley
> 2 teaspoons minced fresh sage
> Salt and freshly ground pepper, to taste
> Lemon wedges, for accompaniment

1. Place chops in a baking dish. Whisk together garlic, lemon juice, olive oil, parsley, and sage. Pour over chops and let marinate at room temperature 1 hour.

2. Preheat broiler or prepare a medium-hot charcoal fire. Remove chops from marinade. Season chops with salt and pepper. Broil or grill chops, turning once and basting often with marinade. Depending on heat of broiler or grill, they will need approximately 5 minutes per side. They should be firm to the touch, but still moist.

3. Transfer chops to a warm platter or to individual dinner plates. Serve with lemon wedges.

Serves 4.

BAKED ORZO

The tiny dried pasta shape known as orzo resembles an elongated grain of rice. Here it's cooked like a rice pilaf, first sautéed in butter, then steamed in hot stock.

> 2 tablespoons butter
> ¼ cup minced shallot
> 1 tablespoon minced garlic
> ¼ cup minced carrot
> 1 cup orzo
> 1¼ cups hot chicken, veal, or beef stock
> 3 tablespoons freshly grated Parmesan cheese

1. Preheat oven to 350° F. In an ovenproof skillet or casserole over low heat, melt butter. Add shallot, garlic, and carrot and cook 2 minutes, stirring. Add orzo and cook 3 minutes, stirring constantly.

2. Add stock, cover, and transfer skillet to oven. Bake 20 minutes. Uncover and stir in Parmesan with a fork. Serve immediately.

Serves 4.

GRATIN OF WINTER FRUIT

A sabayon—a froth of eggs, sugar, and wine—browns beautifully under the broiler, creating a golden mantle for wine-soaked fruit.

> 4 pitted prunes
> ½ cup Riesling or other fruity white wine
> 1 pear, peeled, cored, and sliced ⅛ inch thick
> 2 tablespoons lemon juice
> 1 large navel orange, peel and pith removed
> 3 egg yolks
> ¼ cup sugar

1. In a small bowl put prunes with ¼ cup of the wine and let stand 1 hour. Add pear slices and lemon juice. Holding orange over bowl to catch the juices, cut segments away from the membrane and add them to the bowl. This may be done up to 3 hours in advance.

2. Preheat broiler. In top of double boiler, combine remaining ¼ cup wine and egg yolks. Cook over simmering water, whisking constantly, until mixture is lukewarm. Slowly whisk in sugar, 1 tablespoon at a time. Continue whisking until mixture almost triples in volume.

3. Divide fruit and any accumulated juices among 4 ovenproof custard or soufflé cups. Spoon warm sauce over fruit. Immediately place fruit under broiler and broil until lightly browned (about 20 seconds). Watch carefully. Serve immediately.

Serves 4.

Special Note

ORGANIZING YOUR KITCHEN

Taking the time to get organized beforehand can save valuable time in the kitchen when the party starts. A well-organized kitchen prevents surprises and minimizes postparty cleanup. Here are some tips on preparing your kitchen for an onslaught of guests.

Clean and organize the refrigerator a few days before the party. Use up leftovers or throw them out. You will inevitably need all the refrigerator space you can make.

Get the kitchen as clean as you possibly can before the party. Wash and store any dirty pots and pans; empty the dishwasher and dish drainer; sweep the floor.

Countertop equipment that won't be used for the party—toaster, food processor, blender, or mixer, for example—should be transferred to another room to free up kitchen counter space.

Set up an area, preferably a large counter space, for clearing and stacking dirty dishes. Place in a separate area all clean dishes, glassware, and flatware required during the course of the party. Be sure to count dishes, glassware, and flatware one or two days before the party. You don't want to be short a soup spoon when the soup is on the stove.

Set up stations in the kitchen for the various courses. All the ingredients for a stir-fry, for example, should be measured out and waiting by the side of the stove. Trays are handy for organizing all the parts of a particular dish before assembly. Even spices and garnishes should be ready and waiting.

Party trash should never be thrown out until all silverware is cleaned and counted. Many a piece of silver has inexplicably found its way into the garbage can along with the table scraps.

PRESENTING FOOD FOR EYE APPEAL

The most delicious food in the world can fail to tempt guests if it's presented in an unbecoming way. Here are some tips for giving food special sparkle—at seated meals, on cocktail platters, and on buffet tables.

At Seated Meals

☐ Today's trend is toward less formal garnishing, forgoing the ritual sprig of parsley in favor of a more natural look. Don't be afraid to let beautiful produce or a perfect piece of fish speak for itself. A sauté of pristine green and yellow beans in a white earthenware bowl needs no decoration.

☐ Remember color when planning your menu (see page 99). Contrast colors not only within a course but also from course to course. Use a garnish of contrasting color to bring a dish to life, such as a sprinkle of minced dill on pale clam chowder, or a slice of hardcooked egg on spinach soup. Use serving pieces for color contrast, too (see photograph, opposite): Place dark foods on light dishes, pale foods on dark ones.

☐ Use symmetrical arrangements to give a plate a formal look, random arrangements to suggest a more casual meal. Generally, a platter of neatly overlapped tomato slices in concentric rings is not as inviting as a less structured arrangement.

☐ Keep your eye open for unusual serving containers. Inexpensive plastic scallop shells can be used for seviche or shrimp salad; balloon wineglasses can hold a cold soup or a fluffy mousse. Flea markets, secondhand stores, and antique shops are good sources for distinctive serving pieces.

☐ Wine looks best in clear glasses. German-style wineglasses with colored bowls, although beautiful, mask the color of the wine. When setting the table, be sure to polish glasses with a soft cloth to remove water spots.

☐ Do as professional chefs do and wipe the edges of each plate or platter with a damp cloth before serving. Drops of sauce or oil on the rim give plates and platters a messy look.

☐ Present foods best side up. Pan-fried foods are usually handsomest on the side cooked first, when the pan was hottest.

☐ Where necessary, drain foods well before arranging on plates or platters. Steamed vegetables, for example, should be lightly patted dry before being tossed with butter or oil and put on a plate. Fried foods should be drained on several thicknesses of paper towels to remove excess oil.

☐ Watercress, parsley, and hearts of lettuce add color to a plate or platter, but make sure they are fresh and unblemished. Few things look sadder than wilting parsley or lettuce with browning edges.

On Cocktail Party Platters

☐ Handsome food needs a handsome platter. If you entertain often, you'll want to invest in a varied collection of serving pieces: flat wicker baskets and trays, mirror rounds, clear and colored glass, plain and glazed earthenware, silver, and delicate porcelain. Choose a serving piece that reflects the spirit of the food and the party: gleaming silver for smoked salmon canapés, earthenware for a rustic dish of marinated eggplant relish on toast.

☐ A single striking flower can enliven a party platter, especially if it complements the color of the food. A florist can provide you with small plastic water tubes for keeping blossoms bright.

☐ Use garnishes of a contrasting color to give hors d'oeuvres eye appeal: a tiny spoonful of bright avocado sauce on pale salmon (see page 56), a fine dusting of minced chives on *tapénade*-topped beef (see page 54), lemon wedges alongside dark green stuffed grape leaves (see page 56).

☐ Passed finger food should be easy to pick up and eat. Guests will be deterred by canapés dripping with butter or toasts so heavily topped that they threaten to break. And always remember to offer cocktail napkins with each passed tray.

On Buffet Tables

☐ When planning a menu, remember that buffet food often has to look good on a platter or in a chafing dish for more than an hour. Vary colors and textures as you would for a sit-down dinner menu. Because most of the buffet items end up sharing a plate, you'll want to avoid dishes with runny sauces or colors and tastes that clash. If possible, provide a separate plate for dessert so that sweet and savory dishes aren't forced to mingle.

☐ Get out all your serving pieces and design the buffet at least a day or two ahead, making a written diagram of what goes where. The diagram will save you time on the day of the party and will spare you the chagrin of discovering all your wonderful potato salad in the back of the refrigerator after the party is over.

☐ A buffet can be spread over several stations, especially for large parties. You might set up four separate buffets in opposite corners of the room—one for appetizers, one for main course and accompaniments, one for desserts, and one for beverages. Different stations minimize potential traffic tie-ups and give guests an excuse to circulate and mingle.

☐ For large parties, give some thought to devising a buffet traffic pattern that moves swiftly. Moving the buffet table away from the wall allows traffic to circulate on all sides. Using a long rectangular table allows two lines of people to serve themselves simultaneously— just be sure to provide each dish with two sets of utensils. To operate four lines at once, set up a large centerpiece in the middle of a long rectangular table to divide the table in half. Arrange platters and chafing dishes in a mirror-image setup on each half of the table to create two separate but identical buffets, and have guests circulate on both sides.

☐ Aim for varied heights when organizing a buffet table; a flat buffet is visually boring. Stand baguettes on end in a tall basket, or use an overturned broad-bottomed cloth-covered bowl as a perch for a platter. Footed platters, candles, and flowers can also help you achieve different heights. To minimize accidents, keep items that are easily overturned out of the way of reaching arms.

☐ Unusual and varied serving pieces can give a buffet originality. Hollowed-out fruits and vegetables can hold complementary salads, relishes, or dips. Large seashells can hold sauces or pats of butter. Biscuits or cookies can be piled in napkin-lined flowerpots.

☐ Arrange food for the guests' maximum convenience and minimum confusion. The chutney should be next to the ham, the butter next to the corn bread. Remember that guests will have a plate in one hand and can't be expected to carve or slice; lasagne, turkey, tarts, and similar items should be presliced. If you'd like to add the drama of a whole turkey, ham, or standing rib roast, station an experienced carver alongside.

☐ If the buffet table is small, stack plates, napkins, and silverware on a nearby sideboard or table.

☐ Keep a close watch on the table for dishes that look ravaged or depleted. Be prepared to remove the offending dish and either replace it immediately with a ready-and-waiting backup platter of the same dish, or refill and reorganize it in the kitchen. Never do the refilling at the buffet table.

☐ Buffet food is more appealing when it looks bountiful. Muffins mounded in a small basket are more tempting than the same number of muffins in a single layer on a platter.

CHRISTMAS DESSERT BUFFET
For 24

*Sweet Zucchini-Walnut Bread
With Soft Cheeses*

*Christmas Cinnamon-Buttermilk
Cookies*

Colette's Chocolate Splurge

Brandied Chestnut Pound Cake

Seckel Pears and Mandarin Oranges

Glacéed Apricots and Dried Dates

Mixed Nut Cornucopia

*Brandied Coffee, Hot Cider and/or
Eggnog (see page 53)*

*Christmas cheer comes in all
sorts of holiday packages:
sweet breads, brandied
cakes, chocolate loaves, and
sugar cookies, to name a
few. In a season devoted
to feasting, no mortal
can resist the delights of
a table laden with these
festive sweets.*

Timetable

Up to 1 month ahead: Make
cookie dough and freeze, or
bake cookies and freeze.

Up to 1 week ahead: Make zucchini-walnut bread.

Up to 4 days ahead: Make cookie
dough and bake cookies, if
not freezing.

Up to 3 days ahead: Make splurge.

Up to 2 days ahead: Make pound
cake and topping.

Planning

Christmas entertaining ought to be easy on the cook, because the season makes so many other demands. This menu can be entirely prepared two days before the party; if time allows, however, it's nice to fill the house with the smell of cookies baking when guests arrive.

Baked goods from your kitchen can be rounded out with seasonal specialties, from fresh, dried, and candied fruits to nuts.

Keep guests' hands warm with mugs of steaming hot cider or freshly brewed coffee and tea. With a bottle of brandy and a bowl of whipped cream on the table, guests can make their own brandied coffee.

The cinnamon cookies can be individually wrapped in brightly colored aluminum foil, or they can be hung on a miniature Christmas tree for a buffet centerpiece.

Presentation

This holiday party can be scheduled as a late-afternoon tea, but it is perhaps more elegant as an after-dinner gathering. The buffet table should be away from the wall, so that it can be reached from all sides. Drape it in white and dress it up with holly and holly berries, fat red candles of different heights, and a collection with a holiday theme: perhaps a variety of cookie cutters, Christmas cards from around the world, or a miniature Santa and reindeer.

Check department and variety stores for sturdy paper goods in holiday designs. Festive holiday tins or boxes can be used for the cookies. Arrange the dried apricots and dates in footed candy dishes, the pears and mandarin oranges in baskets, and the mixed nuts in a wicker cornucopia. For departing guests, set a tray by the door with tiny loaves of Sweet Zucchini-Walnut Bread wrapped in red cellophane and tied with a green ribbon with a fresh holly sprig.

Photograph, page 109: A dazzling dessert buffet (clockwise, from top): zucchini-walnut bread with ricotta cheese, Colette's Chocolate Splurge, whimsical cutout cookies, and a magnificent chestnut pound cake.

SWEET ZUCCHINI-WALNUT BREAD WITH SOFT CHEESES

Fresh, spreadable cheeses such as cream cheese, ricotta, or Italian mascarpone are delicious with this fruit-nut bread. The bread can be frozen for up to one month or refrigerated for up to one week.

> *2 cups vegetable oil, plus oil
> for greasing pans*
> *6 eggs*
> *3 cups sugar*
> *2 tablespoons vanilla extract*
> *4 cups grated zucchini*
> *1 can (16 oz) pineapple,
> crushed and drained*
> *6 cups flour*
> *1 tablespoon plus 1 teaspoon
> baking soda*
> *2 teaspoons salt*
> *1 teaspoon baking powder*
> *1 tablespoon cinnamon*
> *1½ teaspoons freshly ground
> nutmeg*
> *2 cups toasted walnuts*
> *½ cup currants*
> *A selection (about 2½ lb) of
> soft cheeses (cream cheese,
> ricotta, or mascarpone)*

1. Preheat oven to 350° F. Lightly oil four 9-inch loaf pans or eight 5-inch pans. In a large mixing bowl whisk eggs well. Add oil, sugar, and vanilla. Beat until thick. Stir in zucchini and pineapple.

2. In a large bowl stir together flour, baking soda, salt, baking powder, cinnamon, and nutmeg. Add to egg mixture and beat just to blend. Stir in walnuts and currants.

3. Pour into prepared pans and bake until a tester inserted in the center comes out clean (about 1 hour). Cool 10 minutes in pans, then remove bread from pans and finish cooling on a rack.

4. To serve, slice bread and arrange on a platter with soft cheeses.

Makes four 9-inch loaves or eight 5-inch loaves.

May this Christmastime
be filled with joy
and the New Year —
Health and Happiness!

CHRISTMAS CINNAMON-BUTTERMILK COOKIES

For youngsters, stage a design-your-own-cookie contest, with spreadable confectioners' sugar frosting in several colors and a rainbow of colored sugars, sprinkles, and balls. To prepare cookies for hanging, pierce them with a plastic straw before baking them.

    3 cups sifted flour
    ¼ teaspoon baking powder
    ¾ teaspoon baking soda
    1 teaspoon each *cinnamon*
        and salt
    ½ cup butter, room temperature
    ½ cup shortening
    1 cup sugar
    1 egg
    1 teaspoon vanilla extract
    ¼ cup buttermilk

1. Sift together flour, baking powder, baking soda, cinnamon, and salt; set aside ½ cup of the mixture. With electric mixer cream butter and shortening. Add sugar gradually and beat well. Beat in egg and vanilla. Add buttermilk alternately with the 2½ cups sifted dry ingredients.

2. Transfer dough to a clean surface and sprinkle with just enough of the reserved dry ingredients to make a dough that can be patted into a rectangle. Wrap in waxed paper; chill 2 hours, or freeze for up to 1 month. Thaw in refrigerator before rolling.

3. Preheat oven to 400° F. On a lightly floured surface, roll dough ⅛ inch thick. Cut with floured cookie cutters. Place on ungreased baking sheets; decorate as desired. Bake until lightly browned (8 to 10 minutes). Cool completely on racks before icing. (See Note.)

Makes 4 to 6 dozen 2½- to 4-inch cookies.

Note Cookies may be stored in an airtight container for up to 1 week or frozen either before or after baking. To freeze before baking: Cut out and arrange on trays. Place trays in freezer until cookies are frozen, then stack cookies in freezer containers. To bake, arrange separated frozen cookies on baking sheets, thaw at room temperature a few minutes, then bake as directed. Baked cookies may be frozen for up to 1 month.

COLETTE'S CHOCOLATE SPLURGE

Dessert doesn't get much richer than this frozen chocolate loaf, studded with brandied apricots and scented with coffee.

    ¾ pound dried apricots, chopped
    ⅔ cup brandy
    2 pounds bittersweet chocolate,
        in small pieces
    1 cup strong brewed coffee
    2½ cups unsalted butter, cut
        into small pieces
    12 egg yolks
    16 egg whites
    ½ teaspoon salt
        Lightly whipped cream, for
        accompaniment

1. Soak apricots in brandy at least 6 hours, or overnight. They will absorb all the liquor. Line two 4- by 11-inch loaf pans with plastic wrap; let plastic hang over edges of pans.

2. Combine chocolate, coffee, and butter in top of double boiler. Heat over barely simmering water until melted. Remove from heat and stir in apricots. Transfer mixture to a very large bowl.

3. In a large bowl beat egg yolks until pale and thick. Fold into chocolate mixture. Chill 1 hour.

4. In a large bowl beat egg whites with salt to soft peaks. Fold into chocolate mixture. Pour into prepared pans, cover tops with plastic, and freeze for at least 4 hours or up to 3 days.

5. To serve, place a serving platter in freezer until well chilled. Unmold one loaf onto platter. Use a knife dipped in hot water and wiped dry to cut loaf into ½-inch-thick slices, preferably to order. Unmold second loaf when needed. Accompany with unsweetened, lightly whipped cream.

Makes two 4- by 11-inch loaves.

BRANDIED CHESTNUT POUND CAKE

This easy batter requires no sifting or creaming and can be ready for the oven in five minutes.

        Butter, for greasing pans
    5 *cups all-purpose flour*
    ¼ *cup ground almonds*
    2 *cups sugar*
    1½ *tablespoons baking soda*
    ½ *teaspoon salt*
    6 *eggs*
    1 *cup vegetable oil*
    2 *cans (17 oz each) sweetened*
        chestnut purée
    1 *teaspoon almond extract*
    1 *cup brandy*
        Confectioners' sugar, for
        dusting (optional)

Sour Cream Topping
    2 *cups sour cream*
    ½ *cup ground almonds*
    ½ *teaspoon almond extract*

1. Preheat oven to 350° F. Grease two 9-inch loaf pans or two 8-inch springform pans. In a large bowl stir together flour, almonds, sugar, baking soda, and salt. Add eggs and oil and beat well. Add chestnut purée and almond extract; beat until blended. Pour batter into pans and bake until tester inserted in center comes out clean (about 1½ hours for loaf pans, 1¼ hours for springform pans).

2. Remove cakes from oven and slowly pour ½ cup brandy over top of each. Cool in pan 45 minutes, then unmold loaf pans or release sides of springform pans. Cakes will be very moist. Cool completely, then wrap in plastic. Cakes may be stored at room temperature for up to 2 days.

3. To serve, sift confectioners' sugar over cakes, if desired. Slice cakes and arrange overlapping slices on a serving platter. Accompany with a sauceboat of Sour Cream Topping.

Makes two 9-inch loaves or two 8-inch rounds.

Sour Cream Topping Combine all ingredients. Stir until smooth. Topping may be made up to 2 days in advance, covered, and refrigerated.

Makes 2½ cups.

TEXAS CHILI FEED AND FIXIN'S
For 12

Soft Tacos With Beans and Salsa

All-Beef Texas Chili

Pickled Relish Platter

Soft Lemon Pudding Cake

Cold Beer and Iced Tea

You don't have to be a Texan to cook a mean bowl of red or greet guests with a "Howdy, y'all!" Even without the greeting, transplanted Texans will feel right at home in the presence of chili, pinto beans, and pickles. Country music and cold beer are the other authentic essentials.

Timetable

Up to 1 week ahead: Make relish.
Up to 2 days ahead: Make beans.
Up to 1 day ahead: Make chili.
Up to 8 hours ahead: Make pudding cake.
Up to 2 hours ahead: Make salsa.

Planning

This menu is especially easy on the cook, because everything but the salsa can be made ahead. Indeed, both chili and beans improve with reheating.

You might want to set out baskets of warm tortilla chips and bowls of salsa for guests to munch on until dinner is served. If so, make a double batch of salsa, one for the tacos and one for the chips.

Stock your refrigerator with iced tea and an assortment of beers to serve both before and with dinner.

Presentation

Salute the land of the Rio Grande with a buffet table draped in red and dressed with yellow roses. Colorful plates and earthenware, if you have them, would suit the mood. Wrap the cutlery in yellow bandannas from a variety store (they're cheaper than napkins), and set out an assortment of chilled beers from Texas and Mexico. Line a cowboy hat or two with red and yellow bandannas and fill with warm tortilla chips.

Photograph, page 112: A "mean bowl of red"—an authentic Texas chili—is surrounded by a fresh tomato salsa, a piquant Pickled Relish Platter, well-seasoned pinto beans, and corn tortillas.

SOFT TACOS WITH BEANS AND SALSA

Soft fat beans and salsa spooned into a warm tortilla make a quick and delicious accompaniment for the chili. For a variation, spoon some chili into the tacos, too.

1½ pounds dried pinto beans
¼ cup corn oil
2 cups chopped green onion
1 cup chopped yellow onion
1 tablespoon minced garlic
2 teaspoons each *ground cumin and dried oregano*
   Salt, to taste
24 corn tortillas

Fresh Tomato Salsa

10 small tomatoes, diced
1 cup fresh lime juice
2 serrano chiles, or any small hot chiles, minced
⅓ cup minced cilantro
½ cup minced green onion
   Salt, to taste

1. Soak beans overnight in cold water to cover. Drain and place beans in large pot. In a large skillet over moderately low heat, warm oil. Add onions and garlic and sauté until fragrant (about 3 minutes). Add to beans. Add cumin and oregano and enough cold water to cover. Over high heat bring to a simmer, then reduce heat to maintain a simmer. Cook until beans are just tender (about 1½ hours). Season with salt. Cool, cover, and refrigerate for up to 2 days, if desired.

2. *To steam tortillas:* Wrap tortillas in a damp tea towel and heat over simmering water. *To fry tortillas:* Fry on both sides on a griddle or in a lightly oiled skillet, then stack and wrap in napkins.

3. To serve, reheat beans; taste and reseason if necessary. Place a scoop of hot beans on each tortilla and top with 2 tablespoons Fresh Tomato Salsa. Either roll tortillas or serve open-faced with the chili on the side. Or, serve beans and tortillas family style, allowing guests to make their own soft tacos.

Serves 12.

Fresh Tomato Salsa In a large bowl, combine tomatoes, lime juice, chiles, cilantro, onion, and salt. Set aside. Do not make more than 2 hours in advance.

Makes 3¾ cups.

ALL-BEEF TEXAS CHILI

No Texan worth his ten-gallon hat would put beans in his chili. This one's all beef, calling on beer and freshly ground cumin to give it distinction. *Masa harina*, the finely ground corn flour used for corn tortillas, is often used to thicken soups or chili. It is available in Latin markets and some supermarkets.

⅓ cup (approximately) corn oil
6 pounds beef chuck, cut into ½-inch cubes
4 cups minced onion
⅓ cup minced garlic
3 cups (approximately) beef broth
3 cups flat beer
1½ cups water
¼ cup high-quality chili powder, or more, to taste
3 cans (2 lb each) tomato, drained and chopped
⅓ cup tomato paste
1½ tablespoons minced fresh oregano
3 tablespoons cumin seed
Salt, to taste
Cayenne pepper, to taste
Masa harina or cornmeal, if needed

1. In a large heavy skillet over moderately high heat, warm 3 tablespoons of the oil. Brown beef in batches, adding more oil as necessary and transferring meat with a slotted spoon to a large stockpot when well browned. Do not crowd skillet.

2. Reduce heat to moderately low. Add onion and garlic and sauté until softened (about 10 minutes). Add to stockpot along with broth, beer, the water, chili powder, tomato, tomato paste, and oregano.

3. In a small skillet over low heat, toast cumin seed until fragrant; do not allow to burn. Grind in an electric minichopper or with a mortar and pestle. Add to stockpot.

4. Over high heat bring mixture to a simmer. Add salt, cayenne, and more chili powder to taste. Reduce heat to maintain a simmer and cook, partially covered, until beef is tender (about 1½ hours). Check occasionally and add more broth if mixture seems dry. If chili is too thin when meat is tender, stir in up to 2 tablespoons masa harina. Cook an additional 5 minutes to thicken. Serve chili hot.

Serves 12.

PICKLED RELISH PLATTER

This quick sweet relish is ready to eat in one day, although the flavor continues to improve for at least one week. Mushrooms, yellow squash, or Jerusalem artichoke could substitute for any vegetable listed.

2 pounds zucchini, sliced thin
1½ cups onion, sliced ¼ inch thick
2 cups carrot, cut into ¼- by ¼- by 3-inch strips
3 cups celery, cut into ¼- by ¼- by 3-inch strips
12 radishes
¼ cup kosher salt
3 cups white vinegar
1½ cups sugar
1 tablespoon each celery seed and fennel seed
2 tablespoons ground mustard
3 dried hot red-pepper pods

1. In a large bowl combine zucchini, onion, carrot, celery, radishes, and salt. Cover with cold water and let stand 45 minutes. Drain thoroughly.

2. In a large pot combine vinegar, sugar, celery seed, fennel seed, mustard, and pepper pods. Bring to a simmer. Remove from heat and pour over vegetables. Let cool, then refrigerate at least 1 day. To serve, lift vegetables out of their brine with a slotted spoon. Transfer to relish trays or bowls. Vegetables may be stored, in their brine and refrigerated, for up to 1 month.

Serves 12.

SOFT LEMON PUDDING CAKE

Not quite a pudding and not quite a cake, this luscious dessert is a little of both. It's soft on the bottom and firm on top, with a lively lemon kick.

Butter, for greasing dishes
½ cup finely ground almonds or walnuts
4 eggs, separated
1⅓ cups buttermilk
½ cup lemon juice
2 teaspoons vanilla extract
½ cup flour
1½ cups sugar
½ teaspoon each salt and baking powder
1 tablespoon grated lemon rind, plus 1 teaspoon grated lemon rind, for accompaniment (optional)
¼ teaspoon cream of tartar
2 cups whipping cream, lightly whipped but not sweetened, for accompaniment (optional)

1. Preheat oven to 375° F. Lightly butter two 4-cup soufflé dishes or baking dishes. Dust sides and bottom with nuts.

2. In a medium bowl whisk together egg yolks, buttermilk, lemon juice, and vanilla. Sift together flour, sugar, salt, and baking powder. Add to egg yolk mixture, along with 1 tablespoon lemon rind. Beat egg whites with cream of tartar until stiff but not dry. Fold into egg yolk mixture. Pour batter into prepared dishes and place dishes in a large roasting pan. Place pan in oven. Add boiling water to pan to come halfway up sides of baking dishes. Bake 20 minutes, then reduce heat to 350° F and bake until well browned and firm to the touch (20 to 25 minutes longer).

3. Serve at room temperature or chilled. Fold 1 teaspoon lemon rind into whipped cream (if used) and serve alongside.

Serves 12.

NEW YEAR'S DAY BUFFET BRUNCH
For 24

Deviled Crab

Frittata With Herbs and Onions

*Baked Ham With Peach Jam Glaze
(see page 16)*

*Watercress and Avocado Salad
(see Planning)*

*Corn Bread With Honey-Pear Butter
(see page 72)*

Chunky Applesauce

Pear and Sour Cream Kuchen

*Champagne, Juices,
Coffee, Cocoa, and Tea*

---

*A bubbling dish of deviled
crab and a platter piled
high with corn bread call up
images of bountiful southern
country breakfasts. The first
meal of the New Year should
be generous and soothing,
with an array of familiar
"comfort foods."*

Timetable

Up to 1 day ahead: Assemble crab casserole. Make applesauce. Make Kuchen Crumb Crust, line tart tins, and refrigerate. Make Honey-Pear Butter.

Up to 12 hours ahead: Make Herbed Bread Crumbs.

Up to 4 hours ahead: Bake kuchen. Glaze and bake ham.

Up to 2 hours ahead: Make frittatas.

30 minutes ahead: Bake corn bread. Bake crab.

Planning

You'll want to schedule your New Year's Day fête for noon or later, allowing the guests and the cook to rise at a reasonable hour.

Everything that can be done the day before should be, including cleaning the house, setting out china and serving pieces, and arranging flowers. The morning food preparation will take about three hours.

The buffet table can be set with linen, china, and flowers the day before the party, but you won't want to put out the food until all guests have arrived. Deviled Crab should be set on a warming tray, if possible. Watercress and sliced avocado can be tossed with a walnut oil vinaigrette just before serving. Corn bread from your favorite recipe should be timed to come out of the oven as guests arrive, and served along with Honey-Pear Butter.

Greet your guests with a choice of hot and cold beverages: pitchers of tomato juice and fresh orange juice; carafes of hot coffee, cocoa, and tea; and a sparkling wine. Drinkers can enjoy their Champagne straight or as a Bellini (see page 53).

Presentation

Create a winter wonderland on your New Year's brunch table using mirrors, glass, and "snow." Choose a long mirror for the center of the table and top it with glass vials holding snow-covered branches. These iridescent branches are available at wholesale flower markets, but you can make your own with birch branches, glue, and silver glitter or crystal beads. If the day is dark and snowy, add long white tapers in glass candle holders. Dust the mirror with display snow. White plates and white napkins tied with silvery bows add to the wintery look.

Photograph, page 116: A bountiful buffet brunch includes (from top): Chunky Applesauce, Pear and Sour Cream Kuchen, an herb-laced frittata, and spicy Deviled Crab amid a cool winter backdrop of spray-painted birch branches and glass ice cubes.

DEVILED CRAB

Creamed crab bubbling under a coat of buttered crumbs is certain to be enjoyed to the last bite. It's a luxurious dish, worthy of your best serving pieces and silver spoons.

    4 *cups minced celery*
    2 *cups each minced yellow
        onion and minced
        green onion*
    1 *cup each red and green bell
        peppers, in ¼-inch dice*
    5 *pounds fresh crabmeat,
        cartilage removed*
    4 *eggs, lightly beaten*
    4 *cups Herbed Bread Crumbs*
    3 *tablespoons Dijon mustard*
    1 *cup sour cream*
        *Hot pepper sauce, to taste
        (optional)*
    2 *cups butter, melted, plus but-
        ter for greasing baking dishes*
    ½ *cup minced chives*

Herbed Bread Crumbs

    4 *cups soft bread crumbs*
    1 *tablespoon salt*
    2 *teaspoons freshly ground
        black pepper*
    ½ *teaspoon cayenne pepper*
    1 *teaspoon each dried oregano
        and dried thyme*
    ½ *teaspoon ground bay leaf*

1. Preheat oven to 350° F. In a large bowl combine celery, onions, peppers, and crabmeat. Add eggs and stir to blend. Stir in 2 cups of the Herbed Bread Crumbs, mustard, sour cream, hot pepper sauce, if using, and 1 cup of the melted butter.

2. Generously butter several gratin dishes or three 8-cup soufflé dishes. Divide mixture among dishes and top with remaining 2 cups Herbed Bread Crumbs. The dish may be assembled up to this point 1 day ahead, covered, and refrigerated. Drizzle with remaining butter and bake until bubbly and golden brown (about 35 minutes). Top with minced chives and serve hot from the pan.

Serves 24.

Herbed Bread Crumbs Combine all ingredients in a medium bowl.

Makes 4 cups.

FRITTATA WITH HERBS AND ONIONS

One of the few egg dishes that doesn't have to be made to order, a frittata tastes best when barely warm. This version is flavored with mixed herbs, onions, and greens, then cooked in a large skillet like a thick pancake. It can be made in a 12-inch skillet or several smaller ones.

> 4 cups parsley, stems removed
> 6 green onions, white and pale green parts only, root ends trimmed
> 2 large leeks, white and pale green parts only, well washed, root ends trimmed
> 1 cup fresh spinach leaves, stems removed
> ½ cup fresh dill
> ¾ cup fresh mint leaves
> 30 eggs
> 1½ teaspoons freshly ground pepper, plus more to taste
> ½ cup butter, melted
> ¼ cup olive oil
> Salt, to taste
> 6 tablespoons freshly grated Parmesan cheese, for garnish

1. *To prepare in a food processor:* Combine parsley, onions, leeks, spinach, dill, and mint in a work bowl. Pulse to mince; do not purée. *To prepare by hand:* Mince parsley, onions, leeks, spinach, dill, and mint finely.

2. Break eggs into a large bowl. Add minced greens and pepper, to taste, and whisk to blend. In a small bowl, whisk together butter and oil.

3. In a 12-inch skillet over moderately high heat, warm ¼ cup butter-oil mixture. When mixture foams, pour in one third of the beaten egg mixture. Cover, reduce heat to moderately low, and cook until egg is firm but moist (7 to 10 minutes). Season top with salt and pepper, then slide frittata onto a serving platter. Continue with remaining butter-oil and egg mixtures, making 2 more frittatas. Slide each onto a clean platter as it is done.

4. Serve frittata slightly warm or at room temperature. Just before serving, garnish with Parmesan and slice each into 8 wedges.

Serves 24.

CHUNKY APPLESAUCE

The best applesauce is made with fragrant, flavorful apples. Choose Gravenstein, McIntosh, or other aromatic varieties, then cook with honey, cider, lemon, and spices.

> 6 pounds tart apples, peeled, cored, and cut in 1½-inch cubes
> 1 vanilla bean, split
> ⅓ cup honey
> 1 cup apple cider
> ¼ cup lemon juice, or more to taste
> 2 cinnamon sticks or 1 tablespoon ground cinnamon
> 1 teaspoon ground allspice
> ½ cup brandy or apple brandy (optional)
> Brown sugar, to taste
> ¼ cup minced fresh mint, or more to taste (optional)
> Whipping cream, for accompaniment (optional)

1. Place apples in a large pot. Use a knife to scrape vanilla seeds into pot, then add whole bean. Add honey, cider, lemon juice, cinnamon, allspice, and brandy, if desired. Over moderate heat cook, covered, until apples are soft but not mushy (about 10 minutes). Cool.

2. Remove cinnamon sticks, if used. Taste and adjust sweetness. If mixture is not sweet enough, add brown sugar, not more honey. If it is too sweet, add more lemon juice. Place applesauce in batches in food processor and pulse briefly; mixture should remain chunky. Transfer to a serving bowl and stir in mint, if used. Serve warm or chilled. Offer a pitcher of whipping cream alongside, if desired.

Serves 24.

Tips

...ON BUYING AT A RESTAURANT SUPPLY STORE

A good restaurant supply store stocks a broad range of professional equipment, from stoves and giant stockpots to swizzle sticks. Most stores are happy to deal with the public, although you should call ahead to make sure.

Even if you're not planning a party, a restaurant supply store is a good source for small items such as spatulas, whisks, sieves, ladles, tart tins, and cake pans. You can often buy less expensive versions of these items in housewares or hardware stores, but equipment intended for restaurant use is generally of exceptional design and durability.

For baking, especially, the heavy-weight professional equipment yields superior results. Professional cake pans, baking sheets, muffin pans, and tart tins distribute heat evenly and are worth some added expense.

Among the other useful items available at a restaurant supply store are large cutting boards in wood or plastic, bar supplies such as cocktail shakers and strainers, and chef's bib aprons or half-aprons. Extrawide rolls of plastic wrap and heavy-duty aluminum foil are useful for covering large trays and baking dishes, and are of higher quality than the wraps available in grocery stores.

For large-scale entertaining, you will spare yourself headaches if you invest in a few extralarge stainless steel bowls, storage containers, and sheet pans (heavy-duty baking sheets). Plastic bus tubs (deep rectangular bins with handles) and hotel pans (rectangular stainless steel baking pans) are also invaluable for quantity cooking. Be sure any large items you buy will fit in your refrigerator or oven, as needed.

PEAR AND SOUR CREAM KUCHEN

Sweet ripe pears and sour cream in a tender cinnamon crust make a fitting finale for a midwinter meal. A Riesling would be a delicious companion.

> 5 *pounds ripe pears, peeled, cored, and roughly chopped*
> 3 *eggs*
> 9 *egg yolks*
> 1 *cup sour cream or Crème Fraîche (see page 38)*
> 2 *cups sugar*
> ⅔ *cup flour*
> 1 *teaspoon salt*
> 2 *teaspoons cinnamon*
> 1½ *teaspoons nutmeg*
> 1 *cup finely chopped toasted almonds*
> *Confectioners' sugar (optional)*

Kuchen Crumb Crust

> 5 *cups unbleached flour*
> ⅓ *cups sugar*
> 2 *teaspoons salt*
> 1 *teaspoon each baking powder and cinnamon*
> 2 *cups butter, softened*

1. Prepare Kuchen Crumb Crust.

2. Preheat oven to 350° F. Fill 3 prepared Kuchen Crumb Crusts with equal amounts of cubed pear. In a large bowl whisk together eggs, egg yolks, sour cream, sugar, flour, salt, cinnamon, and nutmeg. Pour mixture over pears. Sprinkle each kuchen with ⅓ cup almonds and bake until filling is set and lightly browned (30 to 40 minutes). Remove from oven and set on racks to cool. Serve warm or at room temperature. Sift confectioners' sugar over tops of kuchen before serving, if desired.

Makes three 9-inch kuchen.

Kuchen Crumb Crust In a large bowl, combine flour, sugar, salt, baking powder, and cinnamon; stir to blend. Cut in butter quickly with two knives, a pastry blender, or fingertips until mixture resembles coarse crumbs. Divide dough in thirds and press firmly into three 9-inch tart tins. Lined tart tins may be refrigerated for up to 1 day.

Makes three 9-inch crusts.

... ON BUYING IN BULK

For large-scale entertaining, you may want to explore the options for buying party supplies in bulk.

A farmers' market is an excellent source for high-quality produce in bulk. Although many farmers are prepared to sell a single apple, they will usually make a deal if you want a case. Visiting a major farmers' market early in the morning can be a delightful experience. Find out when the market is in full swing; at some markets, farmers begin packing up to go home by 9:00 a.m. Be sure to bring your own bags or boxes for hauling produce.

If you don't live near a farmers' market, talk to produce managers at local supermarkets. They may be willing to sell produce by the case at modest savings.

Many major cities have a wholesale flower terminal where florists buy their wares. If possible, visit the market at least a few days before your party to see what will be available and which merchants will be willing to sell to you. In many cases the savings can be significant. Do the wholesale vendor the courtesy of knowing exactly what you want, and do not expect the service typical of a retail store.

Health-food and natural-food stores are good sources for grains, dried pasta, spices, nuts, dried fruits, and flours in bulk. Do check the prices, however. Bulk prices at specialty stores can be higher than supermarket prices.

Savings are minimal on eggs and dairy products purchased in bulk. However, when cooking in quantity, it is far more convenient to have the cream in quarts and the butter in 1-pound blocks. If these items aren't available at a supermarket, check with a local dairy.

Buying meat and fish wholesale is also possible, depending on the policy of local suppliers. Many are willing to sell to you at or near the wholesale price if you know just what you want and do not need special service. Most fish wholesalers will happily sell you a whole salmon, but do not expect them to clean and fillet it for you. Always call ahead to determine the wholesaler's policy and the best time to stop by.

If you live in or near an agricultural area, consider buying food supplies direct from the farm. Some state agriculture departments publish directories of farmers who are willing to sell to the public. A trip to the country for a bushel of apples or a spring lamb can be a family excursion.

Party supply stores generally have good prices on bulk paper and plastic products, from napkins and colored streamers to serving trays. These stores are always fun to visit and can prompt some good decorating ideas for your home and table.

Many wine merchants offer discounts on wines purchased by the case, generally in the range of 10 percent to 15 percent. The merchant may not mention it, but you should not hesitate to ask. Better yet, call the local wine shops and ask about their discount policy before deciding where to buy. Even if you don't think you can use a whole case, the savings may persuade you to keep a couple of bottles for yourself.

If you plan to serve beer at the party, consider renting a keg. Many liquor stores can supply several brands of beer in kegs at significant savings over bottled beer. Kegs add a festive note to outdoor parties, and they eliminate the need for disposing of or returning cans or bottles. In addition to the price of the beer, the merchant will expect a deposit, refunded when you return the keg.

**VALENTINE'S DAY
BREAKFAST IN BED
For 2**

Apple and Dried-Apricot Compote

Egg Crêpes With Preserves

Homemade Brioches

Coffee

The aroma of brewing coffee and warm buttery brioches should make the recipient of this special breakfast wake with a smile. A tray filled with morning favorites takes only minutes to assemble: After a brief stint in the kitchen, the chef can crawl back into bed for breakfast, too.

Timetable

1 day ahead: Make brioches. Soak apricots.

At serving time: Reheat brioches. Finish compote. Prepare crêpes.

Planning

The only drawback to breakfast in bed is having to get up to make it. Fortunately, the chef has only about 15 minutes' work to do in the morning: brewing coffee, warming brioches, completing the fruit compote, and quickly frying the eggs.

Make a large pot of coffee and transfer it to an insulated container, so that no one has to get out of bed for refills. With fresh flowers and the morning paper, this valentine breakfast may well become a tradition.

Presentation

When breakfast is in bed, a sturdy wicker tray becomes the table. Dress this one with dainty china and formal silver, a propped-up Valentine's Day card, and a small present wrapped in gold metallic paper.

The fruit can be spooned into Champagne goblets for an elegant presentation. If there's room on the tray, a single orchid spray in a crystal vase adds a touch of luxury.

Photograph, page 119: Wake your sweetheart on Valentine's Day or any lazy weekend morning with crunchy Apple and Dried-Apricot Compote, rolled egg crêpes with raspberry preserves, and tender, golden brioches. You can serve butter cradled in rose petals and carve a couple of small hearts from red apples.

APPLE AND DRIED-APRICOT COMPOTE

A compote of fresh and dried fruits and walnuts makes an appealing winter wake-up. The raspberries may be expensive, but the flavor and fragrance of good ones are worth the splurge.

¾ cup dried apricot
1 cup hot tea, preferably spice tea
1 crisp green or red apple, quartered, cored, and diced
2 tablespoons chopped, toasted walnuts
1 tablespoon orange liqueur or cinnamon sugar (optional)
½ pint raspberries (optional)

Soak dried apricots in hot tea overnight. Drain, slice in half, and place in a medium bowl. Add apple and walnuts and toss to blend. Sprinkle with liqueur or cinnamon sugar (if used) and toss to blend. Divide fruit between two small plates. Spoon raspberries (if used) onto each plate. Serve immediately.

Serves 2.

EGG CRÊPES WITH PRESERVES

They're not technically crêpes, of course, but rather thin egg "pancakes" spread with preserves and folded or rolled. Because the eggs should be eaten as soon as they're made, you may want to work with two skillets at once.

3 eggs
   Pinch salt
2 tablespoons butter
4 tablespoons best-quality preserves
   Sugar, to taste (optional)

1. In a small bowl lightly whisk together eggs and salt. Heat an 8-inch nonstick skillet over moderate heat. Add 1½ teaspoons of the butter and swirl to coat pan. Place 2 tablespoons of the egg mixture in skillet and swirl to coat pan; do not scramble. When egg is firm on the bottom, slide onto a warm plate and quickly cook remaining egg mixture. Keep cooked crêpes warm in a low oven.

2. To serve, spread each crêpe with 1 tablespoon preserves and fold in quarters or roll into cylinders. Sprinkle tops lightly with sugar, if desired. Serve immediately on warm dinner plates.

Makes 4 pancakes.

HOMEMADE BRIOCHES

The tender buttery brioches found in almost every bakery in France are actually easy to make at home. To have them ready when you are in the morning, bake them a day ahead and wrap in plastic when cool. Reheat at 350° F and they'll taste fresh from the oven. Leftovers can be frozen, tightly wrapped, for up to one month.

   2 tablespoons sugar
   ½ cup plus 1 tablespoon butter
   1 cup milk
   1 package active dry yeast
   2 teaspoons salt
   2 eggs, lightly beaten
   3½ to 4 cups flour
      Vegetable oil, for pans
   1 egg yolk
   ½ tablespoon whipping cream

1. In a small saucepan combine sugar, ½ cup of the butter, and the milk. Cook over low heat until butter just melts. Remove from heat, transfer to a large bowl, and cool to luke-warm. Sprinkle yeast over mixture and whisk with a fork to blend. Let stand 10 minutes.

2. Add salt and eggs to yeast mixture and whisk to blend. Add flour, ½ cup at a time, stirring with a wooden spoon. When mixture becomes too stiff to stir, turn out onto a lightly floured surface. Knead dough until it loses most of its stickiness and will hold a shape, adding more flour as necessary.

3. Transfer dough to a buttered bowl, using part of the remaining 1 table-spoon butter, and turn to coat all sides. Cover bowl with buttered plastic wrap, using remaining butter, then cover with a warm, moist towel. Set bowl in a warm place until dough is doubled in bulk (about 2½ hours). Punch dough down and knead briefly in the bowl to force out air. Cover again with buttered plastic wrap and a warm, moist towel and let dough rise again until doubled.

4. Preheat oven to 400° F. Shape dough into a loaf and place in a lightly oiled 9-inch pan. Or, to make individual brioches, divide dough into two unequal portions, one third and two thirds. Then divide each portion into 12 balls. Place larger balls in 12 lightly buttered 3-inch brioche tins. With a floured thumb, make an indentation in each larger ball. Nestle a small ball in each indentation.

5. Let dough rise again until doubled (about 30 minutes). Whisk together egg yolk and cream. Brush glaze on top of brioche loaf or on individual brioches. Bake at 400° F for 7 min-utes. Reduce heat to 375° F and cook until bread is golden brown and sounds hollow when tapped (25 to 30 more minutes for loaf, 15 to 20 minutes for individual brioches). Cool 5 minutes in pan, then remove to a rack to finish cooling.

Makes 1 loaf or 12 individual 3-inch brioches.

Dilled Brioche Add 1 tablespoon minced fresh dill to the yeast mixture along with eggs.

Menu

CHINESE NEW YEAR'S SUPPER
For 8

Stir-fried Bass in Lettuce Cups

*Braised Duck
With Shanghai Cabbage*

*Stir-fried Snow Peas and
Black Mushrooms*

Steamed Rice

*Steamed Rice-Wine Custard
With Mixed Fruit*

Fortune Cookies

*Sparkling Wine, Pinot Noir,
and Hot Tea*

Chopsticks will dance when your guests sit down to this festive banquet of Chinese dishes. Spicy stir-fried fish and tender braised duck bring in the Chinese New Year in style.

Timetable

1 day ahead: Marinate fish. Braise duck and cabbage. Bake and chill custard.

Up to 12 hours ahead: Prepare lettuce cups. Wash and trim vegetables to be stir-fried.

Up to 4 hours ahead: Marinate fruit.

30 minutes ahead: Soak black mushrooms.

At serving time: Stir-fry fish. Reheat duck. Steam rice. Stir-fry vegetables.

Planning

Entertaining with a Chinese menu requires careful planning to avoid burdening the cook with too many last-minute dishes to stir-fry. Here, both the dessert and the main dish are made ahead. The stir-fried bass is a first course, requiring less than three minutes' attention. The second stir-fry—the peas and mushrooms—doesn't get under way until the first course is cleared. Steamed rice can be started when guests arrive and held for up to 30 minutes in a low oven.

Ideally, you'll want to seat guests at one large round table. A party rental service (see page 102) can supply you with a lazy Susan to give guests easy access to the food. Serve the fish course first, then follow with duck, vegetables, and rice all at once.

A glass of sparkling wine would be delightful with the stir-fried bass, and a California Pinot Noir should flatter the duck. With fortune cookies from a Chinese bakery or nearby restaurant, bring out a pot or two of hot tea.

Presentation

Oranges, tangerines, and other members of the orange family are a symbol of prosperity in China, a good reason to make them a centerpiece for a New Year's table. For a formal occasion, use a red or gold tablecloth and black lacquer trays instead of plates. For an informal setting, use a blue and white scheme, beginning with a white table covering in paper or fabric and inexpensive, patterned oriental china, available in import stores. Sheets of a Chinese newspaper can be folded for place mats. If possible, ask someone who can write in Chinese to approximate the name of each guest on each place mat alongside the English spelling. Unless you know that all your guests are adept with chopsticks, set Western utensils to the left and right of each place, chopsticks across the top.

Photograph, page 123: A festive Chinese New Year's banquet includes (clockwise from left) Stir-fried Bass in Lettuce Cups, snow peas with black mushrooms, and a rich Braised Duck With Shanghai Cabbage.

STIR-FRIED BASS IN LETTUCE CUPS

A dark and complex sauce of hot, sweet, and tangy flavors lightly coats the stir-fried bass in this elegant dish. Guests wrap the warm fish in cool lettuce leaves to make neat, edible packages.

- 2 pounds bass fillets, skinned and boned
- 2 egg whites
- 2 tablespoons each Chinese rice wine and cornstarch
- 1 tablespoon soy sauce
- ½ teaspoon freshly ground pepper
- 1 teaspoon turmeric
- 3 tablespoons corn oil or peanut oil
- ¼ cup each minced fresh ginger and minced green onion
- 2 tablespoons minced garlic
- 1 serrano or jalapeño chile, minced
- ¼ cup each plum sauce and hoisin sauce
- 1 tablespoon balsamic vinegar
- 1 tablespoon clam juice or water
- 1 teaspoon sesame oil
- 1 cup each minced jicama and minced red bell pepper
- 3 tablespoons chopped cilantro
- 16 unblemished leaves from the hearts of butter lettuce
- 1 tablespoon toasted white sesame seed, for garnish

1. Cut bass into strips about ¼ inch thick and 2 inches long. In a large bowl whisk together egg whites, rice wine, cornstarch, soy sauce, pepper, and turmeric. Place fish in bowl, toss to coat well with marinade, and refrigerate overnight.

2. Heat a large skillet or wok over moderate heat until very hot. Add corn oil and swirl pan to coat all surfaces. Add ginger, onion, garlic, and chile and stir-fry 30 seconds. Add fish and stir-fry another 30 seconds. Add sauces, vinegar, clam juice, and sesame oil. Reduce heat to low. Add jicama and bell pepper and let simmer 1 minute. Remove from heat and stir in 2 tablespoons of the cilantro.

3. To serve, arrange lettuce leaves on a large platter or on individual plates. Spoon a little of the hot fish mixture onto each leaf and garnish with remaining cilantro and sesame seed. Or put the hot fish mixture into a warm serving bowl and serve it alongside the platter of lettuce wrappers. Serve immediately.

Serves 8.

STIR-FRIED SNOW PEAS AND BLACK MUSHROOMS

Chinese dried black mushrooms are available in Chinese markets and in some Japanese markets, where they are known as *shiitake*. They add a woodsy flavor and a pleasing texture.

- 16 dried black Chinese mushrooms of uniform size
- 1 cup warm water
- 2½ tablespoons peanut oil
- ½ teaspoon hot red-pepper flakes, or more to taste
- ½ cup minced green onion
- 1 tablespoon minced garlic
- 2 teaspoons minced fresh ginger
- ¾ pound snow peas, strings removed
- 1 tablespoon each soy sauce, rice wine, and chicken stock
- 2 teaspoons sesame oil
  Salt and freshly ground pepper, to taste
- 1 teaspoon sugar (optional)

1. Soak mushrooms in the water at least 30 minutes or up to 1 day. Drain, reserving liquid for use in Braised Duck With Shanghai Cabbage (see page 122), if desired. Cut away and discard tough stems. If caps are large, slice about ¼ inch wide; if small, leave whole.

2. In a large wok or skillet over moderately high heat, warm peanut oil until almost smoking. Add ½ teaspoon of the hot red-pepper flakes, onion, garlic, and ginger; reduce heat to moderately low and stir-fry 20 seconds. Add mushrooms; stir-fry 20 seconds. Add peas, soy sauce, wine, and stock. Cover and steam until peas are tender (about 2 minutes). Add oil and toss to coat. Season with salt, pepper, and sugar (if used).

Serves 8.

BRAISED DUCK WITH SHANGHAI CABBAGE

The braising method used here results in chopstick-tender duck, with cabbage that virtually melts into the stew. For a more dramatic presentation, serve with storebought mandarin pancakes or homemade crêpes for wrapping up duck and vegetables. Black soy sauce, which contains molasses, adds richness and depth to the sauce without thinning it. It is readily available in Chinese markets.

  2 *ducks (5 lb each), cut into serving pieces*
  2 *tablespoons peanut oil*
  4 *slices fresh ginger, about ⅛ inch thick, lightly smashed*
  ½ *cup dry sherry*
  3 *cups chicken stock (see Note)*
  ½ *cup plus 2 tablespoons black soy sauce*
  ¾ *cup firmly packed brown sugar*
  1 *head Napa cabbage, quartered lengthwise, cored, then cut in half crosswise*
 24 *pearl onions, peeled*
  2 *tablespoons chopped cilantro, for garnish*

1. Wash and dry ducks and remove excess fat from neck and tail areas. In a large skillet over moderately low heat, warm oil. Add duck and brown slowly on all sides (about 15 minutes). Duck will exude excess fat as it browns; do not drain off fat until browning is completed.

2. Transfer duck to a clean skillet or wok set over moderately low heat. Add ginger and sherry and simmer 10 minutes. Add chicken stock, soy sauce, and sugar. Cover and simmer 30 minutes. Add cabbage and pearl onions; cover and continue to cook until duck is very tender (about 45 minutes). Remove from heat, cool to room temperature, then cover and refrigerate overnight.

3. With a slotted spoon, lift off any congealed fat on the surface of the stew. In a skillet or wok over moderately low heat, slowly reheat duck. Transfer duck and vegetables to a large platter. Raise heat to high; reduce sauce to 1¾ cups and spoon over duck. Garnish with cilantro. Serve with crêpes, if desired.

Serves 8.

<u>Note</u> You may substitute water and/or mushroom soaking liquid from Stir-Fried Snow Peas and Black Mushrooms (see page 121) for all or part of the chicken stock.

STEAMED RICE-WINE CUSTARD WITH MIXED FRUIT

A rich and complex meal calls for a light and refreshing dessert, such as this delicate custard with its ring of tart fruit. The fruit can be cut up and marinated up to 4 hours ahead; refrigerate, but remove from refrigerator 30 minutes before serving.

 1½ *cups evaporated milk*
  ¾ *cup each half-and-half and water*
  6 *egg yolks*
  3 *egg whites*
  ¼ *cup each firmly packed brown sugar and granulated sugar*
  ½ *teaspoon salt*
  3 *tablespoons rice wine*
  1 *tablespoon orange liqueur or brandy plus 1 teaspoon orange liqueur, or more to taste*
  1 *teaspoon vanilla extract Pinch nutmeg*
  2 *large navel oranges and 2 tangerines, peeled, all membrane removed, and sectioned*
  ½ *pound green grapes, stemmed*
  2 *tablespoons lemon juice*
  1 *teaspoon grated orange rind*
  1 *tablespoon brown sugar or honey (optional)*

1. In a medium saucepan combine evaporated milk, half-and-half, and the water. Over high heat bring to a simmer. In a large bowl whisk together egg yolks, egg whites, sugars, salt, wine, 1 tablespoon of the liqueur, vanilla, and nutmeg. Add hot-milk mixture gradually, whisking constantly.

2. Butter 8 individual custard cups or one 6- to 8-cup mold and pour in custard. *To prepare in a steamer:* Set custard over simmering water in a large steamer, cover, and steam until a knife inserted in center comes out clean (about 35 minutes for individual custards, 60 minutes for a large mold). *To prepare in an oven:* Preheat oven to 325° F. Set molds in a large baking dish, cover them tightly with aluminum foil, and add boiling water to come halfway up the sides of the molds.

3. Bake approximately 30 minutes for individual custards, 60 minutes for large ones.

4. Remove from heat and cool to room temperature, then refrigerate for at least 4 hours or up to 1 day.

5. In a large bowl combine oranges, tangerines, and grapes. Add juice, rind, and remaining 1 teaspoon liqueur. Taste and add more liqueur, if desired. If the fruit lacks natural sweetness, add brown sugar or honey to sweeten it; however, to complement the custard, the fruit should be slightly tart.

6. To serve, unmold custard onto a large platter or individual plates. Surround with fruit compote and some of the accumulated juice.

Serves 8.

INDEX

Note: Page numbers in italics refer to photographs separated from recipe text.

A

Anchovy
  quick hors d'oeuvres of, 76
  in salad, 33
  sauce of, 54
Antipasti and Italian Wine Bar, menu for, 90–93
Aperitifs, Italian wines and, 91
Apple
  in chutney, 99
  in compote, 118
  green, in crêpe filling, 72
  in wassail bowl, 67
Applesauce, chunky, 115, *116*
  as crêpe filling, 72
Apricot, dried
  in chocolate loaf, 110
  compote of, 118
Artichoke
  green
    in antipasto sandwich, 59
    in salad, 22
    skewered, 91
  Jerusalem, in relish, 113
Asparagus, salad of, 22
Avocado
  salsa of, 57
  in sandwich, 45
  sauce of, for shrimp *burro,* 60

B

Baba, pecan, 11
Baby Shower, menu for, 11–19
Banana, in frozen yogurt, 75
Bar, guide for a party, 52
Barbecue, July Fourth, menu for, 36–39
Barley
  salad of, 85
  in stuffed grape leaves, 56
Bars
  candy, 75
  Hallie's High-Energy, *44,* 45
Basil
  butter, with radishes, 76
  mayonnaise, 88
  in pesto, 59
Bass, stir-fried, 121, *123*
Bean
  baked, 16, *79,* 80
  cannellini, in salad, 18, *19*
  Great Northern
    baked, 80
    in salad, 18, *19*
  green
    in cracked wheat salad, 42
    in salad, 33, 56
    soup of, 59
  kidney, in couscous, 83

Bean *(continued)*
  lima, baked, 80
  pinto
    baked, 16
    for tacos, 111
Beef
  burgers. *See* Handburger
  chuck, in chili, 113
  fillet, cold, 54, *55*
  flank steak, peppercorn, *79,* 80
  ground, in Handburgers, 73
  tips on buying, 80
Beer
  buying by the keg, 117
  dark, in wassail bowl, 67
  in Irish fruitcake, 69
Beet
  in cold borscht, 21
  in salad, 26, 33
Beverages
  cherry cola, 87
  cocktail party, rules for mixing, 52
  soda, apple-citrus, 100
  wassail bowl, 67, *68*
Birthday Party, Children's, menu for, 100–102
Bitters, Italian, 91
Blueberries, in madeleines, 14
Boat, lunch on board, menu for, 57–59
Borscht, cold, 21, *23*
Branches, snow-covered, 114
Bread
  pita, *41*
    for quick hors d'oeuvres, 76
    sandwich of, 45
  quick garlic, 76
  sticks
    green onion, 21, *23*
    quick hors d'oeuvres of, 76
    rye salt, 14–15
    zucchini-walnut, 108, *109*
Bread crumbs
  herbed, 114
  seasoned, 16, 80, 93
Breakfast in Bed, on Valentine's Day, menu for, 118–120
Brioche, *119,* 120
  dill-flavored, 28, 120
Brittany Brunch, menu for, 70–72
Broccoli, salad of, 78
Brunch, menus for
  Brittany, 70–72
  New Year's Day buffet, 114–117
Buffet, food presentation, 106–107
Buffet, menus for
  Christmas Dessert, 108–110
  New Year's Day brunch, 114–117
Bulk, buying supplies in, 117

Burro, shrimp, 60, *61*
Butter
  basil, 76
  to clarify, 14
  pear, with honey, 72
  Roquefort, 77
Buttermilk
  in bread sticks, 14–15
  in cinnamon cookies, 110
  in cold borscht, 21
  in pudding cake, 113
  in wild rice pancakes, 99

C

Cabbage
  green
    in cracked wheat salad, 42
    in slaw, 16
  Napa, with braised duck, 122
  red
    in couscous, 83
    in slaw, 16
Cake
  carrot, *101,* 102
  chiffon, orange, 87
  clove and orange, *86,* 87
  fruit, 69
  pound, chestnut, *108,* 110
  pudding, lemon-flavored, 113
Carrot
  in salad, 16, 82
  sautéed, 71
Catfish, cornmeal-fried, 49
Cats' Tongues, 46–47
Cauliflower
  salad of, 78
  in vegetable chowder, 43
Celery
  in pickled relish, 113
  in salad, 82
Celery root, salad of, 67
Champagne
  cocktails, 52, 53
  reception, menu for, 96–99
Chard
  with ham hocks and corn, 51
  in sauté, 10
Cheese
  Bel Paese, with fruit salad, 22
  blue, quick spread of, 76
  cream
    with figs, 42
    frosting of, 102
    with fruit salad, 22
    quick spread of, 76
    in Stilton tart, 69
    with zucchini bread, 108
  Danbo, with bread sticks, 21
  Emmenthaler
    with bread sticks, 21
    in sandwich, 88
    in tart dough, 17

Cheese *(continued)*
  feta, 41
  fontina, in sandwich, 59
  goat, with fruit salad, 22
  Gorgonzola, with figs, 42
  Gruyère
    in cheese puffs, 13
    on cocktail crumpets, 97
    in tart dough, 17
  hors d'oeuvres, quick, 76, *77*
  Jarlsberg, in sandwich, 88
  mascarpone
    with fruit salad, 22
    with zucchini bread, 108
  Monterey jack, 72
    with fruit salad, 22
    for quesadillas, 77
    for quick hors d'oeuvres, 76
  mozzarella, 72
    for Handburgers, 73
    quick hors d'oeuvres of, 76
    in sandwich, 45
    toasts of, 77
  Parmesan
    for quick hors d'oeuvres, 76
    in *tian,* 33
  ricotta
    in bread sticks, 14–15
    with fruit salad, 22
    with zucchini bread, 108
  Roquefort
    butter, 77
    quick spread of, 76
  Stilton, tart of, 69
  St. André, and fruit salad, 22
  teleme, with fruit salad, 22
Chestnut pound cake, 110
Chicken
  fryer, in paella, 26
  legs, stuffed, *44,* 45
  roast, with lime, 86
  smoked, 28, *29*
Chile
  to roast, 62
  stuffed Anaheim, *61,* 62–63
Chili, beef, *112,* 113
Chinese-style menu, 120–123
Chocolate
  cookie crust, 48
  cups of molded, 81
  in macaroons, 59
  Splurge, Colette's, *108,* 110
Chowder, vegetable, 43, *44*
Christmas dessert buffet, menu for, 108–110
Chutney, fruit, *98,* 99
  with ham, 16
Cinnamon sugar, 28, 72
Clam
  baked Italian, *92, 93*

U.S. MEASURE AND METRIC MEASURE CONVERSION CHART

		Formulas for Exact Measures			Rounded Measures for Quick Reference		
	Symbol	When you know:	Multiply by:	To find:			
Mass (Weight)	oz	ounces	28.35	grams	1 oz		= 30 g
	lb	pounds	0.45	kilograms	4 oz		= 115 g
	g	grams	0.035	ounces	8 oz		= 225 g
	kg	kilograms	2.2	pounds	16 oz	= 1 lb	= 450 g
					32 oz	= 2 lb	= 900 g
					36 oz	= 2¼ lb	= 1,000g (1 kg)
Volume	tsp	teaspoons	5.0	milliliters	¼ tsp	= ⅟₂₄ oz	= 1 ml
	tbsp	tablespoons	15.0	milliliters	½ tsp	= ⅟₁₂ oz	= 2 ml
	fl oz	fluid ounces	29.57	milliliters	1 tsp	= ⅙ oz	= 5 ml
	c	cups	0.24	liters	1 tbsp	= ½ oz	= 15 ml
	pt	pints	0.47	liters	1 c	= 8 oz	= 250 ml
	qt	quarts	0.95	liters	2 c (1 pt)	= 16 oz	= 500 ml
	gal	gallons	3.785	liters	4 c (1 qt)	= 32 oz	= 1 liter
	ml	milliliters	0.034	fluid ounces	4 qt (1 gal)	= 128 oz	= 3¾ liter
Length	in.	inches	2.54	centimeters	⅜ in.	= 1 cm	
	ft	feet	30.48	centimeters	1 in.	= 2.5 cm	
	yd	yards	0.9144	meters	2 in.	= 5 cm	
	mi	miles	1.609	kilometers	2½ in.	= 6.5 cm	
	km	kilometers	0.621	miles	12 in. (1 ft)	= 30 cm	
	m	meters	1.094	yards	1 yd	= 90 cm	
	cm	centimeters	0.39	inches	100 ft	= 30 m	
					1 mi	= 1.6 km	
Temperature	°F	Fahrenheit	5/9 (after subtracting 32)	Celsius	32°F	= 0°C	
	°C	Celsius	9/5 (then add 32)	Fahrenheit	68°F	= 20°C	
					212°F	= 100°C	
Area	in.²	square inches	6.452	square centimeters	1 in.²	= 6.5 cm²	
	ft²	square feet	929.0	square centimeters	1 ft²	= 930 cm²	
	yd²	square yards	8361.0	square centimeters	1 yd²	= 8360 cm²	
	a.	acres	0.4047	hectares	1 a.	= 4050 m²	